D0829268

PRAISE FOR *TEAR DOWN THIS MYTH*

"[Bunch's] book capably puts into perspective an imperfect but fascinating administration."

—*Publishers Weekly*

"The Ronald Reagan who won the cold war, cut taxes, shrank the government, saved the economy, and was the most beloved president since FDR is a myth, Bunch says. . . . The truculent jingoist of the myth was concocted after Alzheimer's silenced the man and the would-be juggernaut launched by the GOP's 1994 election triumph crashed and burned before a Democratic president who shrank government and the deficit, balanced the budget, and even racked up surpluses. Bunch names the leading, venal mythmakers and shames the myth exploiters, too. Anyone interested in America's immediate future should read this book."

—*Booklist* (starred review)

"With help from a loving Beltway press corps, Republicans sold Reagan as the iconic American leader. From promotions like the Ronald Reagan Legacy Project and Operation Serenade, the GOP marketing machine worked to perfection. Will Bunch's long overdue book, *Tear Down This Myth*, pulls back the curtain and looks at Reagan, minus the branding. It's a sobering sight."

—Eric Boehlert, author of *Lapdogs: How the Press Rolled Over for Bush*

"Will Bunch's book couldn't come at a better time. Following an election that saw America reject Reaganism, *Tear Down This Myth* explores how that conservative ideology came to power and what was so destructive about it."

—David Sirota, author of *The Uprising: An Unauthorized Tour of the Populist Revolt Scaring Wall Street and Washington*

TEAR DOWN THIS MYTH

The Right-Wing Distortion
of the Reagan Legacy

Will Bunch

FREE PRESS

NEW YORK · LONDON · TORONTO · SYDNEY

ƒP

FREE PRESS
A Division of Simon & Schuster, Inc.
1230 Avenue of the Americas
New York, NY 10020

Copyright © 2009 by Will Bunch

All rights reserved, including the right to reproduce this book or portions
thereof in any form whatsoever. For information address Free Press Subsidiary
Rights Department, 1230 Avenue of the Americas, New York, NY 10020

First Free Press trade paperback edition February 2010

FREE PRESS and colophon are
trademarks of Simon & Schuster, Inc.

For information about special discounts for bulk purchases,
please contact Simon & Schuster Special Sales at
1-866-506-1949 or business@simonandschuster.com.

The Simon & Schuster Speakers Bureau can bring authors
to your live event. For more information or to book an event
contact the Simon & Schuster Speakers Bureau at
1-866-248-3049 or visit our website at www.simonspeakers.com.

Designed by Paul Dippolito

Manufactured in the United States of America

1   3   5   7   9   10   8   6   4   2

ISBN 978-1-4165-9762-9
ISBN 978-1-4165-9763-6 (pbk)
ISBN 978-1-4165-9772-8 (ebook)

For my family, especially Julia and Jesse, who never stop me from thinking about America's tomorrow.

Facts are stubborn things; and whatever may be our wishes, our inclinations, or the dictates of our passion, they cannot alter the state of facts and evidence.

—John Adams, "Argument in Defense of the Soldiers in the Boston Massacre Trials," December 1770

Facts are stupid things—stubborn things, I should say.

—Ronald Reagan, addressing the Republican National Convention in 1988

CONTENTS

INTRODUCTION TO THE
NEW EDITION

I t was December 2008, just weeks after a watershed event in U.S. political history, the election of the first African American president. Little more than a generation after Ronald Reagan had launched a successful bid for the White House by speaking of "states' rights"—a coded appeal to white Southerners—in the Mississippi town where three civil rights workers had been murdered, Barack Obama had been elected the forty-fourth president of the United States.

Many wondered in that postelection glow—as they still do now—how to view Obama's presidency through the prism of Reagan and the lingering myths about Reagan's accomplishments. Oddly enough, you could make the case that Obama won by recasting in a center-left mold some of the broad qualities that once endeared the Gipper to a majority of voters—confidence, self-deprecating humor, and the most important feature: optimism.

But that wide-angle view clashed with a clear new direction in underlying political philosophy. Unlike Reagan, Obama believed that Republican-ignored problems like climate change and a health care crisis were real—and the government had a major role in fixing them. And while both men believed in Reagan's famous phrase that "America's best days are yet to come," for the fortieth president that statement was rooted deeply in his hazy backward glance toward a small-town utopia that never really was.

Obama's optimism, on the other hand, was more reality-based. It sought to build upon the here and now—and the election of a biracial child of the American rainbow state known as Hawaii—and looked toward a very different kind of "morning in America" that would be more inclusive, more welcoming to millions of recently arrived Latinos and other ethnic minorities, as well as others seeking their proper place at the nation's table, more tolerant of the nonreligious or of gays, more rooted in science and rational thought.

So did that mean that, in electing Barack Obama, Americans had demolished the myth of Ronald Reagan? Why not ask Obama himself? That is exactly what two reporters for the *Washington Post,* Dan Balz and erstwhile Reagan chronicler Haynes Johnson, did in December 2008 as they prepared a book about the Democratic upstart's remarkable victory over GOP senator John McCain. Here is what Obama told them:

> What Reagan ushered in was a skepticism toward government solutions to every problem, a suspicion of command-and-control, top-down social engineering. I don't think that has changed. I think that's a lasting legacy of the Reagan era and the conservative movement, starting with Goldwater. But I do think [what we're seeing] is an end to the knee-jerk reaction toward the New Deal and big government.

The then-president-elect also told the *Post* scribes that he wanted to bring to the Oval Office "a new, more pragmatic approach that is less interested in whether we have big government or small government, [but is] more interested in whether we have a smart, effective government." In other words, Obama's plan seemed not to smash at the Reagan myth with a sledgehammer but to seek to carefully wean the nation off Reaganism, away from its core tenets of magical thinking about everything from the geology of petroleum to the economics of bottomless credit. But his early months in office proved that even that very modest goal was difficult to achieve.

The challenges Obama faced on January 20, 2009, were every bit as daunting as those Reagan had confronted in 1981: The shock of astronomical gasoline prices had eased, but the housing crisis and the fall of Wall Street's massive house of cards had brought rising unemployment and home foreclosures as well as economic anxiety greater than at any time since the Great Depression; the aftershocks of George W. Bush and Dick Cheney's eight bungled years in the White House were everywhere, from America's diminished standing in the eyes of the world to the festering problems of energy conservation and reducing greenhouse gases as evidence mounted that the planet faced a climate-change crisis. They were serious problems that required radical solutions, but one of the things that hampered the new president's room to maneuver was the lingering power of Reaganism, especially among Republicans and a few conservative Democrats with just enough votes to muck up change.

So when President Obama needed a handful of GOP votes to pass his first major initiative, a $787 billion stimulus package aiming to jolt the economy out of the recession, he was forced to modify the idea into what you might call an Obama-Reagan hybrid, scaled back and more weighted toward GOP-friendly tax cuts than to the kind of infrastructure projects that created the most jobs. And when Obama declared it was high time to stop believing the folly that tax cuts are the only solution to the nation's woes, this is how South Carolina senator Jim DeMint responded: "It's incredible that he said that. It's clear that whether it's John Kennedy or Ronald Reagan or when Bush did this in 2001 and 2003, the economy came out of recession." Indeed, Republicans sought to rally massive resistance to the idea that health care for all Americans—including the roughly 47 million who did not have health insurance when Obama took office— could be financed by raising taxes on the wealthiest sliver of Americans. Never mind that the rich would still pay much less to the federal government than during most of the Reagan presidency, when the top marginal tax rate was still 50 percent. The conservative foes of change were aided by the Beltway media, now composed largely of journalists who came of age during the Reagan years and fervently believed that America was still a center-right nation—despite poll after poll establishing that it is not— and that rural Republican-red hamlets in the Deep South are "the real America" in some mystical way that places like East L.A. or West Philadelphia are not.

As the American electorate grew not only younger but more non-white and more nonreligious than ever before, the early years of Obama's presidency would have been an ideal time for the Republican Party to reinvent itself, to promote a center-right path to the American dream that would be inclusive for Latinos, African Americans, or other growing blocs of voters, one rooted in economic freedom while moving away from xenophobia and religious intolerance. Instead, the GOP retreated within itself, retreated within the myth of Ronald Reagan. When six candidates competed in a public forum to become the new chairman of the

Republican National Committee, they were asked to name their favorite Republican president; each one, including the eventual winner, Michael Steele, blurted out the name of Ronald Reagan without even a second's pause to consider the option of Abraham Lincoln, who seemed to hold little appeal to the party's rabid and increasingly Southern base, or even the hero of D-Day, Dwight Eisenhower, who presided over a remarkable era of American might.

And so it was that Barack Obama—the man who entered politics in the early 1980s as a community organizer in the shadows of Chicago's shuttered steel mills, fighting what he saw as the ravages of Reagan's trickle-down economics and a society that was ignoring its citizens most in need—found himself a quarter-century later standing in the Diplomatic Room of the White House with the then-87-year-old Nancy Reagan, who looked seemingly lost in the 1980s in her bright red pants suit, leaning heavily on Obama's right arm.

It was June 2, 2009, almost five years to the day after the Gipper had passed away in Los Angeles, and on this date Obama was doing what any good politician must do: He was playing the hand that was dealt him. Today, this hand was a seemingly inconsequential one: a bill sent to him from Congress to create an eleven-member commission to plan activities for the centennial of Reagan's birth in February 2011. But now with Reagan's widow at his side, Obama played it to the hilt. He declared: "President Reagan helped as much as any president to restore a sense of optimism in our country, a spirit that transcended politics—that transcended even the most heated arguments of the day."

Indeed, taking on the Reagan myth was an argument that President Obama was clearly not eager to have. As a new era unfolded in Washington, it would be still be left to a minority of journalists and political progressives with long memories to take a sledgehammer to Reagan's distorted legacy, even as that legacy was further enshrined with a new Reagan statue in the Capitol Rotunda. Obama's approach to the toxic residue of rampant Reaganism would instead require a scalpel. Under the surface, a Democratic president was working to cut away at the entrenched legacy of the Reagan era: the reluctance to regulate Wall Street or to take seriously environmental issues, the lack of a national dialogue on race, the notion that any role for government in improving health care was, in the words of Reagan's famous and unsuccessful 1960s diatribe against the impending Medicare, "socialized medicine." But Obama would do so while embracing the ideals of bipartisanship and speaking of America's hopes and its place in the world with a kind of romanticism that might have made the Gipper tear up.

There is a deep irony here. Even as he told America that government was not the solution to the nation's problems, Reagan had been especially fond of invoking the words and the lessons of Democrat Franklin Roosevelt, the father of Social Security, the Tennessee Valley Authority, and a host of large-scale government programs. Now, Obama was signaling that he would try to marshal voter nostalgia for the Gipper even as he looked to restore government as a partner in solving national problems, the role that it relinquished during the Reagan years.

Still, it will be fascinating for me, as both a student of the fortieth president and an ongoing chronicler of current events, to watch exactly how and in what style President Obama will honor the Great Communicator when the hundredth birthday finally arrives on February 6, 2011. There seems to be enormous potential for both political risk and reward, but in particular I will be looking to see if Obama reaches for the most relevant common ground that the two presidents share—and that is their shared vision of a world without nuclear weapons.

It was in 1983 that President Ronald Reagan privately screened the antinuclear movie *The Day After* at Camp David and wrote in his diary of his resolve "to see there is never a nuclear war"—the ambition that fueled his remarkable series of summits with Soviet leader Mikhail Gorbachev. That very same year, Barack Obama was just an undergraduate in his senior year at New York's Columbia University, still very uncertain of his place in the world, when he publicly voiced the idea that Reagan shared but kept secret, an ambition of eliminating all nuclear warheads. As reported by the *New York Times,* the young Obama wrote an article for a campus magazine entitled "Breaking the War Mentality." In it, he railed against "billion-dollar erector sets" and what he called "the twisted logic" of a winnable nuclear war. Little did the then-22-year-old Obama imagine that it would be Reagan who would start the job of reducing the world's nuclear stockpiles or that he himself would be the president in a position to carry that mission forward in the twenty-first century.

On Reagan's one hundredth birthday, Obama will finally have the power to make some serious headway in taking down the Reagan myth before the American people—not by trashing the worst that the 1980s presidency had to offer but by embracing the best, which was Reagan's powerful imagination of a nuclear weapon–free planet. Imagine a major televised speech in which Obama celebrates Reagan's most liberal tic. The Great Communicator himself would have chuckled at the irony.

TEAR DOWN THIS MYTH

CHAPTER ONE

RONALD REAGAN BOULEVARD

"Who controls the past" ran the Party slogan, "controls the future: who controls the present controls the past."

—George Orwell, *1984*

The present was January 30, 2008, when four powerful men walked onto a freshly built debate stage in Simi Valley, California, seeking to control the past—most ironically, the American past that was at its peak in that very "Morning in America" year of 1984. They knew that whoever controlled the past on this night would have a real shot at controlling the future of the United States of America.

Lest there be any doubt of that, the large block letters UNITED STATES OF AMERICA hovered for ninety minutes over the heads of these men—the last four Republican candidates for president in 2008—who had made the pilgrimage to the cavernous main hall inside Simi Valley's Ronald Reagan Presidential Library. This was the final debate of a primary campaign that had basically started in this very room nine months ago and now was about to essentially end here—in what was becoming a kind of National Cathedral to Ronald Reagan, even complete with his burial vault. The block letters were stenciled across the hulking blue and white frame of a modified Boeing 707 jetliner that officially carried the bland bureaucratic title of SAM (Special Air Mission) 27000, but bore the title of Air Force One from 1972 through 1990—a remarkable era of highs and lows for the American presidency.

1

To many baby boomers, this jet's place in history was burnished on August 9, 1974, when it carried the disgraced Richard Nixon home to California on his first day as a private citizen. But that was before SAM 27000 was passed down to Ronald Reagan and now to the Ronald Reagan legacy factory, which flew it back here to the Golden State, power-washed it clean, and reassembled it as the visual centerpiece of Reagan's presidential library. It was now part American aviation icon and part political reliquary, suspended all deus ex machina from the roof in its new final resting place, with Reagan's notepads and even his beloved jelly beans as its holy artifacts.

And for much of this winter night, the men seeking to become GOP nominee—and hopefully win the presidency, as the Republican candidate had done in seven out of the ten previous presidential elections—looked and felt like tiny profiles on a sprawling American tarmac under the shadow of the jetliner, and of Reagan himself. Fittingly, each chose his words carefully, as if he were running not to replace the hugely unpopular George W. Bush in the Oval Office—at an inauguration 356 days hence—but to become the spiritual heir to 1980s icon Reagan himself, as if the winner would be whisked up a boarding staircase and into the cabin of SAM 27000 at the end of the night and be flown from here to a conservative eternity.

As was so often the case, news people were equal co-conspirators with the politicians in creating a political allegory around Reagan. The debate producer was CNN's David Bohrman, who'd once staged a TV show atop Mount Everest and now said the Air Force One backdrop was "my crazy idea" and that he had lobbied officials at the library to make it happen. He told the local *Ventura County Star* that the candidates were "here to get the keys to that plane."

By picking Reagan's Air Force One and the artifacts of his life as props for a Republican presidential debate that would be watched by an estimated 4 million Americans, CNN shunned what would have been a more obvious motif: the news of 2008. If you had been watching CNN or MSNBC or Fox or the other ever-throbbing arteries of America's 24-hour news world, or sat tethered to the ever-bouncing electrons of political cyberspace in the hours leading up to the debate, you'd have seen a vivid snapshot of a world superpower seeking a new leader in the throes of overlapping crises—economic, military, and in overall U.S. confidence.

On this Wednesday in January, the drumbeat of bad news from America's nearly five-year-old war in Iraq—fairly muted for a few weeks—resumed loudly as five American towns learned they had lost young men to a roadside bomb during heavy fighting two days earlier. Most citizens were by now so numb to such grim Iraq reports that the casualties barely made the national news. The same was true of a heated exchange at a Senate hearing involving new attorney general Michael Mukasey. He was trying to defend U.S. tactics for interrogation of terrorism suspects, tactics that most of the world had come to regard as torture—seriously harming America's moral standing in the world. Meanwhile, it was a particularly bad day for the American mortgage industry, which had a major presence in Simi Valley through a large back office for troubled lender Countrywide Financial. That afternoon, the Wall Street rating agency Standard & Poor's threatened to downgrade a whopping $500 billion of investments tied to bad home loans, while the largest bank in Europe, UBS AG, posted a quarterly loss of $14 billion because of its exposure to U.S. subprime mortgages. Such loans had fueled an exurban housing bubble in once-desolate places like the brown hillsides on the fringe of Ventura County around Simi Valley, and had been packaged and sold as high-risk securities.

That same day, nearly three thousand miles to the east, Jim Cramer—the popular, wild-eyed TV stock guru, and hardly a flaming liberal—was giving a speech at Bucknell University in which he traced the roots of the current mortgage crisis all the way back to the pro-business policies initiated nearly three decades earlier by America's still popular—even beloved by some—fortieth president, the late Ronald Wilson Reagan. "Ever since the Reagan era," Cramer told the students, "our nation has been regressing and repealing years and years' worth of safety net and equal economic justice in the name of discrediting and dismantling the federal government's missions to help solve our nation's collective domestic woes."

But there would be no questions about economic justice or the shrinking safety net at the Ronald Reagan Presidential Library, the epicenter of America's political universe, what with California's presidential primary—the crown jewel of the delegate bonanza known as Super Tuesday—less than a week away. The GOP's Final Four evoked the parable about the blind man. Each seemed to represent a different appendage of the Republican elephant—the slicked-back businessman-turned-pol Mitt Romney, the good-humored former Baptist minister Mike Huckabee, the fiery fringe libertarian Ron Paul, and Vietnam War hero and POW John McCain, a self-described "straight talker" on a meandering political odyssey. Despite their unique and compelling stories and their considerable differences—both in background and in appeal to rival GOP voting blocs—each was apparently determined to stake out the same contrived identity. It was like an old black-and-white rerun of *To Tell the Truth* with four contestants all declaring: "My name is Ronald Reagan."

CNN's moderator, Anderson Cooper, followed a script for the night that was clearly inspired by this massive effort—including the construction of a special floor underneath the plane—to make Reagan's Air Force One and thus the spirit of Reagan himself the stars of this slick TV production in the guise of a debate. The opening shot featured widow Nancy Reagan, eighty-six years old then, in a trademark red dress, greeting Cooper and then welcoming the candidates to Simi Valley. Cooper talked up the Boeing 707—the "stirring backdrop for our debate tonight"—and a camera toured the cabin, ending up at the jelly bean tray.

The whole ninety minutes was drenched in Reagan idolatry. It peaked later when Cooper asked the candidates about abortion and quoted from an entry in Reagan's diary about the 1981 appointment of Sandra Day O'Connor to the Supreme Court. "And the Reagan Library has graciously allowed us to actually have the original Reagan diary right here on the desk," he said. "I'm a little too nervous to actually even touch it, but that is Ronald Reagan's original diary."

It was this kind of 1980s hero worship that carried the debate and framed the discussion, rather than frank talk about the grim headlines of war and economic uncertainty that dominated the world of the present. It almost didn't even seem bizarre that Cooper worked into the abortion issue by asking not about their stances in 2008 but about what they thought of Reagan's nomination of the abortion-rights-friendly O'Connor some twenty-seven years earlier. The CNN host reminded the candidates of Reagan's so-called eleventh commandment against speaking ill of fellow Republicans—adding gratuitously that "no one was tougher and more formidable in debates than Ronald Reagan"—and Cooper's first question was an update of Reagan's famous 1980 debate line "Are you better off now than you were four years ago?"

The candidates were asked several different ways whether they were conservative enough, or about the state of the modern Republican Party, matters that would be of little concern to the average voter. Meanwhile, the list of things that Cooper didn't ask them about that night is mind-boggling: the high cost of gasoline, and energy policy. Health care. The increasingly powerful role that China, India, and other emerging countries are playing on the world stage. Iran, Afghanistan, or Israel. America's image in the world in the face of outrage over torture and the detentions at Guantanamo Bay.

None of the candidates even seemed to notice what was left out, since they were too busy trying to hit the Reagan stage marks laid out in front of them. McCain, under conservative fire for opposing a GOP-backed tax cut in 2001, insisted he did so because it violated Reagan's principles by not cutting government spending enough. "I was part of the Reagan revolution," boasted McCain. "I was there with Jack Kemp and Phil Gramm and Warren Rudman and all these other fighters that wanted to change a terrible economic situation in America with ten percent unemployment and twenty percent interest rates. I was proud to be a foot soldier, support those tax cuts, and they had spending restraints associated with it."

Later, asked his thoughts about then–Russian president Vladimir Putin, who had been an unknown KGB "foot soldier" in the Reagan era, Huckabee quickly migrated to a seemingly disconnected riff about U.S. military spending, adding: "And I do believe that President Reagan was right, you have peace through strength, not vulnerability."

Paul, the one Republican who opposed the war in Iraq and some of the constitutional abuses of the George W. Bush presidency, was a little more circumspect about Reagan until Cooper asked the candidates explicitly about whether the late president would have endorsed any of them. "I supported Ronald Reagan in 1976, and there were only four members of Congress that did [against GOP incumbent president Gerald Ford]. And also in 1980. Ronald Reagan came and campaigned for me in 1978."

But, for reasons that seemed obvious to his critics, no one was more eager to grab the Reagan mantle than Mitt Romney, so desperately anxious to calm wary conservatives because he had been governor of one of the nation's most liberal states, Massachusetts. Asked the same question about whether Reagan would endorse him, he leapt in: "Absolutely."

Ronald Reagan would look at the issues that are being debated right here and say, "One, we're going to win in Iraq, and I'm not going to walk out of Iraq until we win in Iraq." Ronald Reagan would say lower taxes. Ronald Reagan would say lower spending. Ronald Reagan would—is pro-life. He would also say "I want to have an amendment to protect marriage." Ronald Reagan would say, as I do, that Washington is broken. And like Ronald Reagan, I'd go to Washington as an outsider—not owing favors, not lobbyists on every elbow. I would be able to be the independent outsider that Ronald Reagan was, and he brought change to Washington. Ronald Reagan would say, yes, let's drill in ANWR. Ronald Reagan would say, no way are we going to have amnesty again. Ronald Reagan saw it, it didn't work. Let's not do it again. Ronald Reagan would say no to a fifty-cent-per-gallon charge on Americans for energy that the rest of the world doesn't have to pay. Ronald Reagan would have said absolutely no way to McCain-Feingold. I would be with Ronald Reagan. And this party, it has a choice, what the heart and soul of this party is going to be, and it's going to have to be in the house that Ronald Reagan built.

Spurred on in part by Cooper's questions and the Reagan-inspired "stirring backdrop," the candidates uttered the name "Reagan" some thirty-eight separate times over the course of the debate. Ironically, that was a sharp increase from the first time that the Republican presidential hopefuls had gathered in this very same hall in Simi Valley, on May 3, 2007, when a field of ten candidates drew a lot of media scrutiny and some ridicule from places like Jon Stewart's *The Daily Show* for invoking Reagan nineteen times.

That first 2007 debate, nearly nine months earlier, saw almost comically desperate attempts by the candidates to link themselves to Reagan. Even the soon-to-flame-out front-runner, Rudy Giuliani, was so eager to free-associate Reagan that he ascribed the 1980s president with quasi-magical powers that could seemingly be harnessed to resolve the crises of the present.

Asked about Iran's reported push to develop nuclear weapons in the late 2000s under its radical president, Mahmoud Ahmadinejad, Giuliani said that the current Iranian president "has to look at an American president and he has to see Ronald Reagan. Remember, they looked in Ronald Reagan's eyes, and in two minutes, they released the hostages." He made it sound like a standoff scene from an old Western, the kind that was in vogue when Reagan himself had arrived in Hollywood in the 1930s. And just like in the movies, the scene that Giuliani imagined with Reagan and the Iranians had never really happened. But increasingly, that didn't seem to matter. One historian wrote around the time of the CNN debate that discussions of Reagan in the 2000s increasingly reminded him of one of the last great Westerns, 1962's *The Man Who Shot Liberty Valance*, in which a journalist famously notes that "when the facts become legend, print the legend."

The legend of Ronald Reagan is one that few can resist, in politics and especially in the media. It has not only survived but flourished and grown quite separate from Reagan himself, who left the White House some two decades ago now, in 1989, who disappeared completely from the public eye with his poignant 1994 announcement that he was suffering from Alzheimer's disease, and who finally died in 2004, touching off a week-long festival of nationally televised, advertiser-supported grief that not only interrupted the reelection bid of George W. Bush but probably helped make it successful. Four years later, with the Republican Party at low ebb because of voter unrest over the war and economic woes that had festered the longer that Bush remained in the Oval Office, a posse of flawed candidates was hoping that lightning would strike again.

In the end, only one of the many candidates grasping for the Reagan mantle would be able to pull it down. That candidate, of course, was McCain, who would win a majority of the delegates in California and elsewhere on Super Tuesday and stake his claim to the nomination in a matter of days. In the winter blitzkrieg that carried the Arizona senator to the nomination, the McCain camp produced a TV ad called "True Conservatives," which made a claim (called fantastic by some) that the younger Reagan had inspired him when he was a POW at the notorious Hanoi Hilton from 1967 to 1973, and repeated that McCain was a "foot soldier in the Reagan revolution." What's more, McCain ran ads attacking 2008-Reagan-worshipping Romney for 1994 remarks on Reagan that were highly critical. McCain's tag line: "If we can't trust Mitt Romney on Ronald Reagan, how can we trust him to lead America?" The push was the key to McCain's victory against long odds—his campaign had nearly run out of money in 2007, and he faced withering assaults from right-wing opinion makers, such as radio's Rush Limbaugh, who claimed McCain was a phony conservative. The Reagan comparisons had undercut the notion that McCain was too liberal or too old for the job. Now McCain hoped he would write the epilogue to the legend of Reagan, which had been printed so many times and was deeply ingrained with the electorate.

The legend of Ronald Reagan has a story line that would have surely wowed any studio executive hearing a pitch: Small-town lifeguard and varsity football player with a loving, churchgoing mother and a roguish, hard-drinking dad heads for Hollywood and becomes a movie star—and when that dream stalls out, comes up with a second act that is bigger and more audacious than the first. The hero undergoes a 180-degree political conversion and becomes a fiery, reactionary public speaker, then a governor, and then, finally, improbably, the president of the world's greatest superpower. And not just any president, but the noblest commander in chief of the postwar era, a man who won an ideological war at home—reversing a half century of growing government and rising taxes—and then won a cold war abroad, the global conflict between freedom and totalitarian communism, before riding off into the Pacific sunset. And like *It's a Wonderful Life,* the story line became more iconic in the frequent rebroadcasts than when it was actually in the theaters. The postpresidency Reagan became not just the most revered figure in modern American history but so much more—a kind of homespun public intellectual, as expressed through handwritten diaries and radio commentaries, a humanitarian who exchanged letters with everyday Americans, someone who was as much a man of God as a man of politics.

It was this powerful and increasingly ingrained story that was both celebrated and retold in Simi Valley and on CNN on this particular night—and given the powerful narrative, who could blame presidential candidates and TV producers for embracing it? Visitors to the debate at the Reagan Library filed past a larger-than-life bronze statue called *After the Ride,* which depicts Reagan not as a political leader or even as a movie star but as a figure of popular imagination—a cowboy in blue jeans, Stetson hat in hand. Simi Valley might be the capitol of the Ronald Reagan legend, but by the winter of 2008 it was hardly the only place where candidates could go to stake their case as true heir to the political legacy of the man many still call "the Gipper," after his most famous Hollywood role from 1940, as dying Notre Dame football star George Gipp.

Indeed, even though it's been just a few short years since Reagan joined Gipp and departed this world, it seems as if one could drive from coast to coast on one long Ronald Reagan Boulevard, sometimes literally, sometimes metaphorically, especially across the hot asphalt of the Sunbelt, where Reagan and his acolytes worked so hard to build up a permanent GOP majority. You could start your tour down the Ronald Reagan Freeway, the main highway leading out of Simi Valley. The first stops could be a couple of Ronald Reagan Elementary Schools, one down in the Central Valley in Bakersfield—billed as home of "The Patriots"—and one in the Valley town of Chowchilla, where the new structure with a bust of the fortieth president was dedicated in September 2007, with the necessary fanfare of a military helicopter bearing an American flag that had been flown over the U.S. Capitol. Be sure to stop in the small town of Temecula, where a sports park that Reagan mentioned in a speech to raise money for the 1984 Olympics is now named for the late president, or at Ronald Reagan Park in Diamond Bar in Orange County, the heart of his political base. Another small shrine erected at the time of his passing is the Ronald Reagan Community Center in El Cajon, California, a small community near San Diego that Reagan apparently never visited, even in eight years as the state's governor. The local newspaper did note a connection, however: Nancy Reagan showed up once to select an Olaf Wieghorst painting for her husband's birthday. Said a glib archivist from the Reagan Library at the time of the 2004 renaming: "I don't know if he's ever been to El Cajon, but I do know he set policies as governor that affected El Cajon and its citizens."

Of course, given Reagan's long history with the state he governed, perhaps it's not surprising that so many places in California are named for him—the Ronald Reagan Federal Building and Courthouse in Santa Ana; the Ronald Reagan State Office Building in Los Angeles; the headquarters of the state GOP, of course, in Burbank, now known as the Ronald Reagan California Republican Center. Then there is the Ronald Reagan UCLA Medical Center, a name change that was announced in 2000 when friends of the ex-president, then deep in the throes of Alzheimer's disease, said they would raise $150 million for a new facility. The irony was not lost on some of the staff, who recalled that as president, Reagan sought to cut federal funding for medical research and that he also had become governor in 1966 largely by crusading against the hospital's parent, the University of California, by calling its main campus in Berkeley "a hotbed of communism and homosexuality." At the time of the announcement, one staffer compared it to "renaming the Federal Reserve for Herbert Hoover," while the man who Reagan had fired as the university's president in the late 1960s, Clark Kerr, mused that "I didn't know Reagan was interested in UCLA's medical center."

The discordant notes from UCLA are a jarring reminder that, well, maybe Reagan's greatness wasn't absorbed by every citizen of his home state, which in fact has voted for the Democratic candidate in every presidential election since Reagan himself appeared on the ballot in 1984, the year that the state basked in the afterglow of those Olympics. Indeed, increasingly the long list of honors named for Ronald Reagan is stretching out beyond the Golden State and into the so-called Republican red states of the Sunbelt, especially in the Deep South. It is getting harder and harder to traverse America south of the Mason-Dixon Line without crossing roads like the Ronald Reagan Turnpike in Florida (known as the Florida Turnpike before 1998), or the Ronald Reagan Parkway in Tampa, or the Ronald Reagan Parkway in Gwinnett County, Georgia, or the Ronald Reagan Parkway in Polk County, Florida, or one of several Ronald Reagan Streets or Boulevards or Highways. Even up north one finds Indiana's I-469 Ronald Reagan Expressway and, in his native Illinois, a Ronald Reagan Memorial Tollway. Increasingly, small newspapers feature headlines like this one in a small community near Austin, Texas: CITY COUNCIL REJECTS DEVELOPMENT ALONG RONALD REAGAN. This one appeared around the same time: CARJACKING VICTIM SHOT, DUMPED ON RONALD REAGAN HIGHWAY.

Not far from the stretch of Interstate 65 in Alabama now known as the Ronald Reagan Memorial Highway, there is the Ronald Reagan Spirit of America Field in Decatur, where the reelection-seeking president spoke at a July 4 picnic event in 1984 and praised "the good sense" of southerners in the overwhelmingly white area of that state. A contemporaneous story in the *New York Times* said Reagan agreed to speak there because his aides were worried about offsetting registration gains by black supporters of the Reverend Jesse Jackson earlier that campaign season. That fact probably isn't mentioned on any plaques inside the park.

Actually, Reagan could have spoken at the Ronald Reagan Fundamental School in Yuma, Arizona, during that reelection campaign, since the back-to-basics school—with an emphasis on discipline, patriotism, and old-fashioned teaching techniques—was named for him in March 1984. It is said to feature Reagan's picture in every classroom. Ten years later, in 1994, San Antonio, Texas, grabbed the honor of first city to name a high school after Reagan; today all freshmen at the school file down a Hall of Honor with pictures and quotes of the fortieth president. Some of the students could be on their way to an introductory course on Reagan.

In Covington, Louisiana, another community not necessarily associated in any way with the late president, civic officials in the summer of 2008 unveiled the world's largest Ronald Reagan statue, fifteen feet high and made from bronze. It greets visitors at the trailhead of a city park. City officials were quick to boast that the pricey tribute was a gift from a foundation founded by the late oil magnate Patrick F. Taylor. Taylor had founded Taylor Energy in 1979, two years before Reagan began his successful mission to eliminate oil taxes and slash tax rates for the affluent; Taylor's widow is said to be the wealthiest woman in Louisiana.

In New Hampshire in June 2003, state lawmakers voted to rename Mount Clay—named for nineteenth-century lawmaker Henry Clay, who was known as the Great Pacifier because of his efforts to prevent the Civil War. Apparently, pacifiers were out in 2003, and the Great Communicator was in. The proposed renaming as Mount Reagan was opposed by some as too early; the federal Board of Geographical Names told New Hampshire it could not rename a mountain until at least five years after that person had died, and Reagan was still living. A state senator successfully urged lawmakers to ignore that technicality "so that he would know how much he is loved by the public"—even though at that point Reagan hadn't been seen in public in nine years because of his Alzheimer's disease.

Even some Democratic-voting "blue states" where Reagan wasn't quite as popular have joined the rush to honor the late president. That list includes the Ronald Reagan Academy School No. 30 in Elizabeth, New Jersey, where the academic curriculum is based on the popular book *The*

7 Habits of Highly Effective People. Elizabeth's school board president said in 2006 that the school was named for Reagan because "we are proud to have a school named after a great leader who demonstrated his beliefs in world peace and diversity through his actions"—a rather odd remark considering that Reagan is well-known for his large military buildup and for largely pushing back on civil rights issues. Less successful was an effort in the late 1990s to name a "Ronald Reagan Esplanade" on the waterfront in Brooklyn. A Republican city councilman leading the effort credited Reagan with ending the Cold War and balancing the federal budget, ignoring the fact that he did neither.

Other Reagan tributes seem odd, too. When county commissioners renamed a park as the Ronald Reagan Voice of Freedom Park in southern Ohio's Butler County—they were inspired by the Voice of America radio towers once located there at the popular sledding hill—they also made plans for a live bait shop and a boat rental office. Others made more sense. In the northwestern suburbs of Chicago, heavily populated in the era of "white flight" from cities, some suburbanites still want to break away from heavily Democratic Cook County to form a Reagan County. The Ronald Reagan Missile Defense Site at California's Vandenberg Air Force Base was dedicated in 2008 and celebrates Reagan's push—obsession, some would argue—with a high-tech missile defense system that sought to render a nuclear attack against the United States as useless. It joins a larger site on the Marshall Islands, the Ronald Reagan Ballistic Missile Defense Test Site. And that's not the only Reagan tribute outside the continental United States. There's Ronald Reagan Square in the heart of Krakow, Poland. That Eastern European nation seems to compete against the island of Grenada for the most Reagan tributes. Grenada has a Ronald Reagan Scholarship Fund and a commemorative stamp for the man who sent seven thousand U.S. troops to occupy the country in a 1983 mission called Operation Urgent Fury, credited with restoring American pride even though Grenada did not even have an army, navy, or air force worth mentioning and was lightly defended by Cubans.

To some dreamers back here at home, these parks and middle schools—and missile sites—are just baby steps along the road not just to memorializing Reagan in towns and counties across America, but to elevating the 1980s president to a level that puts him on a par with Washington, Jefferson, and Lincoln. These more ambitious tributes would include renaming the Pentagon for Reagan, or replacing Alexander Hamilton's image on the ten-dollar bill, or perhaps alternating Reagan with Franklin Roosevelt on new dimes, thus simultaneously honoring the founder of the New Deal safety net and the man who once threatened to roll it back.

Since 1999, some Republican members of Congress have pushed to add Reagan's face to Mount Rushmore—appropriately to the far right side of the South Dakota monument. Park rangers have warned that a Reagan addition could damage the fragile granite, and so for now advocates have to be content with ordering an artist's conception of Reagan as a kind of "fifth Beatle" etched into Rushmore from a website, Reagan-Rushmore.com.

Increasingly, these discussions heat up around Reagan Day, February 6, the late president's birthday in 1911. When lawmakers in Utah, arguably the most conservative state in the union, declared Reagan Day in February 2008, four of them acknowledged that they had named children for Reagan and one, Republican state representative Chris Herrod of Provo, said he would not have met his Russian wife were it not for Reagan's presidency and the subsequent collapse of the Iron Curtain. When Reagan died in 2004, an Associated Press story declared that Reagan "had a special relationship" with Utah—"He loved Utah," declared Republican senator Orrin Hatch—but noted lower down that he had only visited the state twice.

Politicians—mostly Republicans but even some Democrats—routinely run for office claiming they will be another Reagan, often by promising things that were the exact opposite of what the 1980s president accomplished, or didn't. In 2008, New Hampshire Republican congressional candidate John Stephen held a fund-raiser around a showing of the film *Ronald Reagan: A Retrospective*. "With two trillion dollars in deficit spending in Washington over the last three years and overall growth in government, that has the potential for bankrupting our children and grandchildren, John thinks it is important to get back to those basic values of limiting government that Ronald Reagan brought to the party," the candidate's spokesman said. Never mind that—coincidentally—the debt increased by about $2 trillion in 1980s dollars under Reagan, while federal spending, in real dollars, and the federal payroll also rose.

In the 1990s, the serial plagiarist Stephen Glass made up—and successfully published in the *New Republic*—the fantastical story of the First Church of George Herbert Walker Christ, whose members shunned broccoli while worshipping Reagan's 1989–93 successor and viewing Saddam Hussein as the Antichrist. In hindsight, Glass might have had even more luck selling the story had his phony church bowed down to Reagan, given the increasing tendency of followers to attribute to the late president ideas he likely did not possess, things he did not accomplish, and powers he could not have had. It won't be surprising if we see more places like a Markleville, Indiana, facility for children with disabilities named the Ronald Reagan Miracle Ranch. But unlike the wandering nomads of Glass's phony Bush 41 congregation, the increasingly mythologized Gospel of Ronald Reagan is a Living Word, spread quickly and electronically, advanced by our most powerful political leaders and pundits.

The Simi Valley location for the 2008 presidential debate might have been an even more appropriate venue than its promoters had realized, since the arid yellow hills with their long-distance view of the Pacific Ocean had never been a location actually associated with the long and complicated life of Ronald Wilson Reagan, but with Hollywood's penchant for mythmaking, centered on the Old West. Near the site where the Spanish mission–style Reagan shrine rose up in the 1990s was the two-thousand-acre ranch of well-known movie stunt man Ray Corrigan, used for the filming of hundreds of Western films and TV shows. That fictional backdrop had seemed oddly appropriate for the Reagan Library, especially when the first choice, reality-based Stanford University, rejected it for a host of reasons that included anathema toward the then incumbent president's politics. Now this movie paradise near the Pacific was the setting for a Ronald Reagan who was inspired by actual events, but not a straight documentary.

Remember Rudy Giuliani's statement about the Iran hostages in the first May 2007 debate? He was referring, of course, to the very first day of the Reagan presidency, January 20, 1981, the same day that the Islamic fundamentalist revolutionaries released the fifty-two American hostages they had been holding for the last 444 days of the presidency of Reagan's predecessor, Jimmy Carter. Of course, it would have been hard for the Iranian hostage takers to look Reagan in the eye, since the brand-new president was gazing out over the west front lawn of the U.S. Capitol in Washington. In fact, the Iranians had looked into the eyes of a Carter administration official, Warren Christopher, who had negotiated the Algiers Accords, which were completed on January 19, 1981, the day before the Reagan inauguration.

What's more, when Reagan did become president, representatives of his administration would talk to Iran frequently—not to talk tough but to sell weapons in a desperate bid to free new American hostages that had been taken in the Middle East. The effort was lamely unsuccessful and flat-out embarrassing, with more U.S. citizens in captivity at the end of the deals than there had been before. It was not as if Reagan's aides' inept negotiations with terrorists had been some obscure chapter of long-ago history—it is the cornerstone of the so-called Iran-Contra affair, which dominated headlines in the last third of the Reagan presidency, and greatly weakened his power and popularity at the time—even if it's barely mentioned in the Reagan Library. It is highly doubtful that Rudy Giuliani could have forgotten this—in 1986 and 1987, while the scandal raged, he had been the U.S. attorney for Manhattan, appointed to the job by Ronald Reagan.

And so just as CNN's Anderson Cooper failed to challenge Giuliani's claim that Reagan had ended the hostage crisis, he also did not interrupt when Mitt Romney of Massachusetts claimed that Reagan saw that amnesty for illegal immigrants "didn't work." Cooper could have noted that the reason Reagan saw that amnesty didn't work was that *he championed it*. Reagan signed into law the Immigration Reform and Control Act of 1986, which legalized an estimated 2.7 million undocumented workers in the United States—an action he never renounced in the ensuing years.

Likewise, Reagan might "say lower spending," as Romney noted, but the stubborn fact is that federal spending grew 2.5 percent per year in real dollars under Reagan. There's no way of knowing for sure, of course, whether Reagan would have said "I'm not going to walk out of Iraq," but when confronted with a similar situation after one deadly large-scale bombing in Lebanon in 1983, he acted in just a few months to redeploy the U.S. Marines far from harm's way.

Of course, in their eagerness to channel Reagan's spirit, the candidates made some remarkable claims about themselves as well—such as

McCain saying he "was there" for Reagan's economic plan, when much of the major tax-cutting action took place before he arrived as a freshman House member from Arizona in January 1983. In fact, strikingly, the three most prominent GOP contenders in the 2008 race had all tried to distance themselves in some way from Reagan during the 1980s and early 1990s, before the Ronald Reagan myth machine had cranked into full gear.

As for Giuliani, he had spent much of his first campaign—for New York City mayor in 1989, with the co-endorsement of the Liberal Party— seeking to distance himself from the just-departed president who had appointed him U.S. attorney. In an October 1989 interview with the *New York Times* he "maintained that he never embraced Mr. Reagan's broad conservative agenda."

Romney, who offered the most effusive praise of Reagan, had declared back in 1994, when he was running for a U.S. Senate seat in Massachusetts, that "I was an independent during the time of Reagan-Bush. I'm not trying to return to Reagan-Bush."

As for the eventual nominee McCain, he certainly could claim a close association with the Reagans, since he and his first wife, Carol, had become close to the then–California governor and his wife, Nancy, in the 1970s, when McCain was a newly returned former Vietnam POW. But then he left Carol—who was seriously injured in a car wreck and became a personal aide to Nancy Reagan after she became First Lady in 1981—for his second wife, the younger and blonder and richer Phoenix beer heiress Cindy Hensley. And if McCain returned to D.C. from Arizona as a "foot soldier in the Reagan revolution" in 1983, there were times when he could have been tried for mutiny. Two months after he was sworn in that year, the freshman GOP congressman sounded at times like a Democrat when he told the *National Journal* that the administration was wasting money on defense, expressed alarm about soaring deficits, and said the GOP needed to reach out to minorities and women, as he urged Reagan to name a commission on equal rights for women. Two years later, he was voting against legislation supported by the Reagan White House nearly one-third of the time.

Those aren't myths, but facts. Ironically, it was Reagan himself who, as the spotlight faded on his presidency in 1988, tried to highlight his eight-year record by reviving a quote from John Adams, that "facts are stubborn things." The moment became quite famous because the seventy-seven-year-old president had botched it, and said that "facts are stupid things." The tragedy of American politics was that just two decades later, facts were neither stubborn nor even stupid—but largely irrelevant. Any information about Iran-Contra or how the 1979–81 hostages were released that didn't fit the new official story line was being metaphorically clipped out of the newspaper and tossed down the "memory hole"—the fate of any information that would have undercut Reagan's image as an all-benevolent Big Brother still guiding the conservative movement from above.

A more factual synopsis of the Reagan presidency might read like this: That Reagan was a transformative figure in American history, but his real revolution was one of public-relations-meets-politics and not one of policy. He combined his small-town heartland upbringing with a skill for storytelling that was honed on the back lots of Hollywood into a personal narrative that resonated with a majority of voters, but only after it tapped into something darker, which was white middle-class resentment of 1960s unrest. His story arc did become more optimistic and peaked at just the right moment, when Americans were tired of the "malaise" of the Jimmy Carter years and wanted someone who promised to make the nation feel good about itself again. But his positive legacy as president today hangs on events that most historians say were to some great measure out of his control: an economic recovery that was inevitable, especially when world oil prices returned to normal levels, and an end to the Cold War that was more driven by internal events in the Soviet Union and in Eastern Europe than Americans want to acknowledge. His 1981 tax cut was followed quickly by tax hikes that you rarely hear about, and Reagan's real lasting achievement on that front was slashing marginal rates for the wealthy—even as rising payroll taxes socked the working class. His promise to shrink government was uttered so often that many acolytes believe it really happened, but in fact Reagan expanded the federal payroll, added a new cabinet post, and created a huge debt that ultimately tripped up his handpicked successor, George H. W. Bush. What he did shrink was government regulation and oversight, which critics have linked to a series of unfortunate events from the savings-and-loan crisis of the late 1980s to the subprime mortgage crisis of the late 2000s. The fall of the Berlin Wall in 1989 helped paper over some less noble moments in foreign policy, from trading arms for Middle East hostages to an embarrassing retreat from his muddled engagement in Lebanon to unpopular adventurism in Central America. The Iran-Contra scandal that stemmed from those policies not only weakened Reagan's presidency when it happened, but it arguably undermined the respect of future presidents for the Constitution because he essentially got away with it. Over the course of eight years, the president that some want to enshrine on Mount Rushmore rated just barely above average for modern presidents in public popularity. He left on a high note—but only after two years of shifting his policy back to the center, seeking peace with the Soviets rather than confrontation, reaching a balanced new tax deal with Democrats, and naming a moderate justice to the Supreme Court. It was not the Reaganism invoked by today's conservatives.

Yet Ronald Reagan hovers over not just our politics but our policy debates, almost as vividly as his Air Force One jetliner loomed over his would-be successors. This is no accident or historical curiosity. There has always been a place for mythology in American democracy—the hulking granite edifices of the National Mall in Washington are a powerful testament to that—but this nation has arguably never seen the kind of bold, crudely calculated, and ideologically driven legend-manufacturing that has taken place with Ronald Reagan. It is a myth machine that has been spectacularly successful, launched in the mid-1990s when the conservative brand was at a low ebb. It has operated not in secrecy but at a low enough frequency that its central premise has infiltrated our current politics to the extent that few bothered to protest at the bizarre framing or misstatements of events like the Simi Valley debates. The docudrama version of the Gipper's life story, successfully sold to the American public, helped to keep united and refuel a right-wing movement that consolidated power while citing Reaganism—as separate and apart from the flesh-and-blood Reagan—for misguided policies from lowering taxes in the time of war in Iraq to maintaining that unpopular conflict in a time of increasing bloodshed and questionable gains. Despite what viewers saw and heard in the 2008 campaign, the modern conservative agenda is not based on the once-sentient Ronald Reagan who ruled America a generation ago. Instead, a brand-new Ronald Reagan was cast out of bronze—

just like the cowboy model with the Stetson hat at the Simi Valley library entrance—in order to fit the modern conservative agenda and cover up its flaws.

"The Reagan Cult of Personality is what happens when a political ideology becomes exhausted, when they have nothing to sell the voters and they recourse to a cult of personality for somebody's who's dead," said Rick Perlstein, the author of *Nixonland*. Reagan's legend took on greater significance when conservatives ran out of new ideas and inspiring leaders at the same time: "That's a canary in a coal mine for the movement. It's what the Democrats did in the '70s and '80s with John F. Kennedy, when every year a younger and more charismatic candidate was going to lead the Democrats out of the wilderness."

Many would argue that Kennedy's presidency has been mythologized, too, as an idyllic Camelot cut down by a hail of bullets in an act that seemed to trigger the violence of the 1960s, the very mayhem that would give rise to the age of Reagan. It is very much like the Reagan myth that we make movies about the Cuban Missile Crisis but don't talk so much about the Bay of Pigs or Kennedy's stumbling 1961 summit with Nikita Khrushchev. However, the legend of JFK is largely attached to his youthful charm—as so famously and disastrously cited by the GOP's Dan Quayle in a 1988 vice presidential debate—and his astute handling of a crisis in Cuba graver than anything ever faced by the Gipper, and not by Kennedy's forgotten and probably obsolete center-left policies.

That's quite different from the Reagan story line that was launched by a new aggressive breed of conservatives while he was still very much alive, as a tool not just to win elections but to sell a specific ideology—to hold the line on new taxes even as the federal deficit soared and stay the course in Iraq even as the American presence seemed to create even more senseless violence. Just like the facts of the Reagan presidency, the fallacies of the Reagan myth are too complicated to sum up in a glib sound bite. Instead, it's a kind of political three-step tango.

Step one involves simply eliminating references to any negative things that took place in America from 1981 to 1989, especially in the White House. That's why you must look hard to find references to the Iran-Contra scandal, which came so close to destroying Reagan's presidency, in the many Reagan hagiographies that have been published in the 2000s

and even at the Reagan Library. (Can you imagine Anderson Cooper asking the GOP candidates in that 2008 debate: "President Reagan delivered
aid to Nicaraguan rebels even though Congress passed an amendment
barring the White House from doing that—under what circumstances
would you violate the Constitution?") More than twenty years after Reagan's presidency, one must dig hard to learn of his failure to connect with
black voters or other minority groups, or that he failed to address issues
such as AIDS or homelessness in any meaningful way, or the sense that
many had in the late 1980s that America had been overrun by greed.

Step two is to award Reagan more credit than he deserves for good
things that happened during his presidency, or, in even more extreme
mode, to remember things as taking place when they actually did not.
This is certainly true of the two subjects that dominate the Reagan legacy:
the economy and the Cold War. As for economic issues, the Reagan mythmakers give credit for the financial turnaround of the 1980s and beyond
almost exclusively to his one major tax cut, in 1981; ignore the impact of
the long-term business cycle, which was due for a 1980s rebound, and the
steep global drop in oil prices; and bypass the fact that the economy actually performed better during the 1990s and the quite unmythologized
presidency of Bill Clinton. On the Cold War, most historians believe that
the Soviet Union and the Iron Curtain collapsed more from their own
dead weight than from any pressure applied by the United States. As for
reducing the size of government, Reagan said it so many times that many
of today's acolytes believe he actually did it.

But step three of the Reagan legacy tango is the trickiest of all. It involves conservatives whitewashing not so much Reagan's bad qualities
but some of his better ones—because they don't fit the modern agenda of
the right wing. That largely involves Reagan's penchant for pragmatism,
even on those matters that were most important to him, which stands in
sharp contrast to the portrait of a man with the unyielding views that
have been attributed to him. As California governor and then as president, Reagan was willing to make sharp turns to get things done—whether
it was signing the bill on legalized abortion in the Golden State or approving, as president in 1982, what was at the time the largest tax increase in
American history, just a year after his much better-known rate cut, or his
aggressive negotiations with the same Soviets that he had branded an

"evil empire." It's hard to imagine that Reagan would have cut taxes steeply going into wars on terrorism and in Iraq, as his self-proclaimed disciple George W. Bush did, in part because it is hard to imagine Reagan invading Iraq in the first place—since Reagan said he believed that military attacks that killed civilians were not a proper response to terrorism.

"Reagan's devotion to certain principles was genuine, but it was coupled with an equally genuine belief in the importance of compromise and an understanding that you had to get the best deal you could under the circumstances," notes Stephen Knott, an associate professor of political science at the U.S. Naval War College, and who previously ran the Reagan Oral History Project at the University of Virginia. "I'm not sure this part of Reagan's legacy is appreciated by George W. Bush and those Republicans looking for 'another Reagan.' "

But the Reagan myth isn't just a political problem for the GOP. Increasingly, as the idealized Reagan took hold in the American imagination, Democrats seemed to struggle even harder with the question of just who Ronald Reagan was—and whether political success going forward depended upon undercutting Reagan's legend, simply ignoring it, or embracing all or part of it. That's why it was a political bombshell when Senator Barack Obama made it clear in early 2008 that Reaganism was playing some role in his thinking as he mapped out his own more progressive route to the White House—but the specifics of what Obama was getting at were open to debate.

"Ronald Reagan changed the trajectory of America in a way that Richard Nixon did not, and a way that Bill Clinton did not," Obama told the editorial board of the *Reno Gazette-Journal* in January 2008. Seeking to elaborate, the Democratic senator said that "we want clarity, we want optimism, we want a return to that sense of dynamism and entrepreneurship that had been missing." Obama's comments caused a scramble among the Democrats: Was the presidential front-runner simply praising the political style of the twice-elected Republican, or was his comment also intended to voice support for some of Reagan's policy ideas? Obama advisors stressed the former—that he was merely seeking to remind voters of Reagan's "hope and optimism."

Obama's statements seemed to flummox the Democrats in 2008 almost as much as Reagan himself did circa 1984. John Edwards, the former North Carolina senator who was appealing to the party's more progressive wing in those early primaries, said Reagan "openly did extraordinary damage to the middle class and working people, created a tax structure that favored the very wealthiest Americans and caused the middle class and working people to struggle every single day . . . I can promise you this: this president will never use Ronald Reagan as an example for change."

And yet just a couple of weeks later, it was Edwards who was gone from the presidential race, and Obama who was soldiering on—leaving the unanswered questions of whether even a progressive Democrat in the White House could tackle not just the immediate problems of Iraq, record-high gasoline prices, and a skyrocketing federal debt but also the more ominous issues of world energy supply and climate change, without doing so under the deepening shadow of the legacy of Ronald Reagan.

How did we get to this point in American politics? It would be easy to give all the credit to the Ronald Reagan myth machine, to the neoconservatives and tax-warriors-turned-lobbyists, for trying to create one long Ronald Reagan Boulevard from sea to shining sea. But no myth would be possible without the man. And if there was ever a man who instinctively knew how to write that screenplay—who rode in from Hollywood to create a new kind of presidency that would focus on strong words and cinematic images that would last long after people forgot the policies sometimes loosely attached to them—it was Ronald Wilson Reagan.

CHAPTER TWO

A MAN BEFORE MYTH

I got a tremendous reception—interrupted 28 times by cheers. Then it was back to the airport.

—Ronald Reagan, writing in his diary on June 12, 1987, the day he spoke near Berlin's Brandenburg Gate and declared, "Mr. Gorbachev, tear down this wall."

The most famous moment of Ronald Reagan's presidency wasn't front-page news on the day it happened. The *New York Times'* coverage the next day, headlined RAZE BERLIN WALL, REAGAN URGES SOVIET, ran on page 3 and was fairly concise. The president had just wrapped up an economic summit meeting in Venice and had traveled to Berlin to celebrate the city's 750th birthday. He used the occasion to deliver strident anticommunist remarks that were somewhat newsworthy because they harked back to Reagan's early presidency, when he branded the Soviets "an evil empire," but seemed a little jarring in the context of 1987, when new president Mikhail Gorbachev was beginning to liberalize society through the policy known as *glasnost,* and when Reagan himself was engaged in a series of summit talks with Gorbachev that included some ideas for radically reducing the numbers of nuclear weapons.

That day in Berlin, Reagan said: "There is one sign the Soviets can make that would be unmistakable, that would advance dramatically the cause of freedom and peace. Secretary General Gorbachev, if you seek peace—if you seek prosperity for the Soviet Union and Eastern Europe—if you seek liberalization: come here, to this gate. Mr. Gorbachev, open this gate. Mr. Gorbachev, tear down this wall." In its article, the *Times* noted that "Administration officials had portrayed the speech as a major policy statement. But the main new initiative was a call to the Soviet Union to assist in helping Berlin become an aviation hub of Central Europe by agreeing to make commercial air service more convenient." A generation later, reading the *Times* article is a stark reminder of how the world had moved on to *perestroika* and peace talks by 1987. The paper called the president's words "reminiscent of the cold war"—and its treatment was hardly unique. One journalist who reviewed the original newspaper coverage on the twentieth anniversary of the speech in 2007 seemed surprised to find it "muted." Arguably, the anniversary drew far more attention than the actual speech had.

But newspaper coverage, of course, isn't the best way to gauge Reagan's Berlin speech—nor was it ever intended to be. The event—like so many of the Reagan presidency, some well remembered but many long forgotten—was artfully crafted for the tele-vision cameras. In planning for the address, aides pushed aggressively with the West German authorities to use the 196-year-old Brandenburg Gate, whose powerful Doric columns were the best-known symbol of the then-divided city of Berlin, as the backdrop. According to Richard Reeves, author of *President Reagan*, local authorities thought the proposed location for the address was "just too gimmicky, too provocative and perhaps too dangerous," but the American aides called in their political chits with West German chancellor Helmut Kohl, who still owed Reagan for one of the most disastrous public relations moments of this presidency, his May 1985 visit to the German military cemetery at Bitburg, where some members of the Nazi's elite SS corps are buried. The image of the towering gate behind Reagan as he spoke—shielded by two panes of bulletproof glass—put some muscle into Reagan's words, as did the seeming anger in his voice, which he later told biographer Lou Cannon was not really aimed at the supposed target Gorbachev but at East German authorities who kept citizens of the communist nation far from the loudspeakers pointed at them.

The black-and-white newspaper headlines from June 13, 1987, have faded to gray, as have the complexities of U.S.-Soviet relations that served as the real-world stage. But the color images of that event have grown more vivid over time—especially after the Berlin Wall did come down, overwhelmed in November 1989 by the rapid liberalization of Eastern Europe and finally dismantled by the time East and West Germany were reunified a year later. Since then, the seconds-long Reagan sound bite has become American TV's down-and-dirty shorthand to describe the complicated fall of communism. What casual viewer on his living room couch could fail to make the connection? Reagan told the Soviets to tear down the wall—and suddenly it's gone. A classic case of cause and effect.

In 2007, for example, viewers of CNN were treated to a fifty-year retrospective of its popular evening host, Larry King, hosted by (yes again) Anderson Cooper:

COOPER (voice-over): *The eighties—Michael moonwalked, Reagan ruled.*
RONALD REAGAN: *Mr. Gorbachev, tear down this wall.*
COOPER: *And the Cold War cooled.*

An American decade in three taut sentences. Three years earlier, CBS's Harry Smith introduced a segment on *The Early Show,* an interview with speechwriter Peter Robinson, who actually crafted the words uttered in Berlin that day. "There's no question that words can change the world, and there is no better proof of that than the famous phrase spoken by former President Ronald Reagan at the Berlin Wall in 1987," Smith said, introducing the famous video clip. "Two years later, the wall, which many considered a symbol of the Cold War, did, in fact, come down."

But did Ronald Reagan cause the wall to come down, the Soviet Union itself to crumble, and the Cold War to end? That's a broad question that will be analyzed in greater detail later in this book. But the growing consensus among historians is that Reagan's contributions, while positive, weren't the definitive factor that America-centric commentators make them out to be. Madeleine Albright, the secretary of state under Bill Clinton, has insisted that attributing the end of the Cold War to Ronald Reagan is like attributing the sunrise to the rooster's cackle.

Indeed, some experts believe the 1987 speech wasn't even aimed so much at people trapped behind the Iron Curtain as at his own critics at home—critics on the far right who believed that Reagan had grown conciliatory in his willingness to meet with Gorbachev and to consider significant arms reductions. In fact, when Reagan began his series of summits with Gorbachev in 1985, one American icon of the far right, future House Speaker Newt Gingrich, went so far as to say their initial meeting could be "the most dangerous summit for the West since Adolf Hitler met with Chamberlain in 1938 at Munich"—and similar sentiments were voiced by conservatives throughout Reagan's second term.

Conversely, moderates were beginning to see the youthful Gorbachev, with his unprecedented and unexpected reforms, as seizing center stage from the initially more confrontational Reagan in U.S.-Soviet relations. Gorbachev himself told an interviewer at the time of Reagan's death that as the Cold War was winding down, both he and Reagan decided they wanted to be known as "peacemakers," that Reagan's military buildup had little impact in Moscow and that Soviet intelligence reports showed that in 1987 the Reagan administration was concerned that reformer Gorbachev's "growing credibility and prestige did not serve the interests of the United States."

James Mann, author in residence at Johns Hopkins University's School of Advanced International Studies, wrote in a *New York Times* op-ed in June 2007 that the real intent of the "tear down this wall" speech was to provide a kind of political cover for Reagan while he was successfully negotiating a move toward the intermediate-range nuclear force, or INF, treaty with the Soviets. Mann was amazed at the interpretations of the speech by conservatives like Reagan speechwriter turned California congressman Dana Rohrabacher, who claims—without any corroboration—that Gorbachev began looking for ways to take down the wall the day after the speech. Mann called this "a triumphal storyline" that "runs counter to Mr. Reagan's actual policies." He noted that even George W. Bush's future secretary of state, Condoleezza Rice, in a 1990s paper co-authored with another GOP foreign policy expert, said the Berlin Wall speech is overrated, that there was no policy follow-up and "American diplomats did not consider the matter part of the real policy agenda."

But the legacy of Reagan's Berlin speech endures, burned into the nation's consciousness in a way that dramatizes his impact on the presidency—and the future myths of White House leadership—more than any other episode. A generation spent in Hollywood before entering politics taught Reagan the power of dialogue, of narrative, of anecdotes, and of scene setting, and he brought those skills to bear in the White House in ways that confounded critics determined to grade his presidency on more traditional standards—such as his actual policies. Reagan and his savvier aides, especially Michael Deaver, his image maker, understood the ways that a seemingly perfect turn of phrase, delivered against postcard-perfect scenery, such as the white cliffs of Normandy, where Reagan memorably commemorated the fortieth anniversary of D-Day in June 1984, or the Brandenburg Gate, could drive perceptions.

Essentially one-minute dramas packaged for the nightly news in an era when longer-form live cable news coverage was not yet a factor, a Reagan event often not only papered over the underlying complexities of the issue at hand but produced more stunning contradictions—as when Reagan spoke in July 1984 from the deck of an oyster skipjack amid the picturesque crabbing grounds of Chesapeake Bay, touting environmental programs that had largely rolled back key protections enacted during the 1970s. When reporters tried to shout questions about some of his more unpopular environmental policies, the president smiled and said, "My guardian says I can't talk," adding, "If I answer that question, none of you will say anything about what we're here for today, and I'm not going to give you a different lead"—an unscripted plot twist toward an unhappy ending.

Reagan may have earned his nickname of Great Communicator, but his preferred form of communication was one-way, a carefully scripted monologue. He used television more often and better than any president who came before him and delivered more prime-time speeches—yet held far fewer formal press conferences than other chief executives, at least until George W. Bush aggressively mimicked the Reagan model. His radical new approach to leading the nation was clear from the early days of his administration; just nineteen months after Reagan took office, *Time* magazine fretted about his "TV presidency" and noted "our agreeable and anecdotal president is well suited for [the] medium," while old-school senator J. William Fulbright mourned the fact that in making policy through TV appearances "your reasons are usually left out because they're not flamboyant."

"He's an actor," an unnamed Reagan aide told journalist Mark Hertsgaard for his seminal 1988 book on the Reagan presidency and the press, *On Bended Knee*. "He's used to being directed and produced. He stands where he is supposed to and delivers his lines, he reads beautifully, he knows how to wait for the applause line. You know how some guys are good salesmen but can't ask the customers to give them the order? This guy is good for asking for the order, and getting it."

Just as in Berlin, where he was interrupted by applause those twenty-eight times, before it was on to the airport—and the next performance.

The success of the Reagan presidency in using narrative and imagery to manipulate the media and appeal to the American public achieved the short-term goals of winning national elections in 1980 and 1984 and, by the second term, boosting Reagan for the history books. But there were harmful unintended consequences, a kind of political "blowback." The indelible sound bites that Reagan left behind are what helped make it possible for a second generation of acolytes to argue falsely that the fortieth president only cut taxes, that he shrunk government when he grew it, or that we should not leave Iraq because he declared that the Berlin Wall must come down, and it did. We have it on film. Even in the 1980s, the rhetoric was divorced from reality. Today these images are used to motivate those who were not even born in the era of *perestroika*—or Iran-Contra.

The legend that's been built up for Ronald Reagan in death, by others, wouldn't be possible were it not for the legend that the Gipper himself constructed—often aided and abetted by an adoring press corps—during his lifetime. "The mythologizing of him that occurred during his presidency has helped to spread the power of his ideas," such as smaller government and American military might, says media critic Hertsgaard. And that was no accident. It took being in the right place at the right time, but it also required the right man.

Ronald Wilson Reagan was a product of the twentieth century and its long evolution away from the small-town America that he would later depict in slick 30-second television spots. When Reagan was born on February 6, 1911, in an apartment above the bank in Tampico, Illinois, the president of the United States was William Howard Taft; the airplane and the World Series were less than a decade old; and Nestor, the first motion picture studio in Hollywood, would not open for another eight months. When Reagan died on June 5, 2004, it was during George W. Bush's re-election campaign, facing John Kerry in the fall; his remains were flown from coast to coast aboard the massive 747 that serves as the current Air Force One (dipping low over Tampico and setting off flares), and the week of mourning and his funeral were beamed live into living rooms from 24-hour news channels.

Presidential historian Robert Dallek, who wrote one of the earliest analyses of the Reagan presidency and Reagan's use of the mass media, has argued that the true significance of Reagan was his being able to straddle two eras in American life, from the 1920s and its emphasis on small-town virtues and Horatio Alger stories, to the more outwardly directed era that started with the rise of large newspapers, film, radio, and finally TV. Many Reagan biographies stress the first half of that equation—his official biographer, Edmund Morris, embraced the clichés about rural swimming holes and trapping muskrats, calling the 1920s "the last days of American innocence." Reagan himself encouraged that view, writing in his autobiography of "swimming and picnics in summer . . . the long thoughts of spring, the pain with the coloring of the falling leaves in the autumn. It was a good life. I have never asked for anything more, then or now."

However, he was actually a lot more excited about the direction that America was headed in, the world of heroes like Illinois football legend Red Grange. Dallek wrote in *Ronald Reagan: The Politics of Symbolism* that "the new ethos of entertainment and pleasure had the greatest impact on his life."

"What he was able to do was knot together two separate traditions," Dalleck says today. "One was the traditional nineteenth-century small-town beliefs—frugality, productivity, and modesty, or what they called 'character.' At the same time, he was a product of the consumer culture of the twentieth century, with an emphasis on radio and film, and his personality played on all of these things."

The outline of Reagan's biography, including his upbringing as the son of John Reagan, known to all as "Jack," and Nelle Wilson Reagan, is well-known. Jack Reagan was a shoe salesman who moved the family around frequently during the future president's youth—and a lifelong alcoholic. Nelle was the bedrock of the family and a stark contrast—a deeply religious member of a teetotaling fundamentalist sect, the Disciples of Christ. Both left their imprint. From his mother, who purchased play scripts and performed them in small productions for townspeople, the future star of Hollywood B movies inherited a love of acting. But Ronald Reagan was arguably more influenced, consciously and subconsciously, by the alcoholism of Jack Reagan, whose son would later write candidly about his "week-long drinking bouts" and the time at age eleven he found his dad passed out on their snowbound front porch, looking as if he had been "crucified."

His father's hard drinking and the family's frequent moves led Ronald Reagan to become strangely withdrawn, with big dreams and a rich imagination that he learned to keep to himself. If there is a consensus among those who have tried to serve as amateur psychoanalysts, it is that his upbringing—especially his lifelong disappointments with his father— provoked the strange mix of ambition and distance that made Ronald Reagan what he was, a driven yet genial man whom most voters wanted to have a beer with, yet was a mystery oftentimes even to his own family members and to close aides who felt they never really got to know him. As a boy in rural Illinois, he shunned playing with other kids in order to play with toy soldiers or tend to his growing collection of birds' eggs and butterflies. On the person-to-person level, Reagan struggled to keep his inner life to himself.

Martin Anderson, a former Reagan aide turned biographer, has said he discovered a movie magazine from the late 1930s in which newly minted film star Reagan said "he had discovered when he was a kid that he had many dreams and ideas and things that he loved to talk about, and people made fun of him. And he said, 'I just stopped talking about that stuff.' I think that Reagan had a very private life, I think he had very private thoughts, things that he felt strongly about. He was highly intelligent, he didn't argue, and he did not share that with people."

But this new outward and media-oriented America that Dallek described would provide Reagan with the new kind of canvases that made it—bizarre as it sounds—easier for him to perform and share his thoughts with thousands than to talk to one person sitting next to him. These platforms would be first Hollywood and then politics. Reagan's rich imagination propelled him forward in ways that were profound and ultimately changed history. This would be especially true as president, when he fretted in public about his nightmares of Armageddon or his dreams of a sci-fi-movie–style shield against such a nuclear attack—and even spoke to the United Nations about how the Americans and the Soviets would surely act together if the earth were ever invaded by extraterrestrial beings.

The source of his sense of optimism—which would become his most appealing political trait—was also likely the result of his father's drinking. Haynes Johnson noted in his book on the American politics of the 1980s, *Sleepwalking Through History*, that child-of-an-alcoholic Reagan "exhibited character traits resembling those associated with what psychiatrists sometimes call the indestructible child, the child who becomes capable of sustaining and surmounting any amount of misfortune." And despite his reserve and distance, he was also drawn to the center of attention, even in his favorite summer job of lifeguard, which Reagan himself once explained "was like a stage. Everyone had to look at me." His favorite narratives were heroic ones about how one man could make a difference—which is clearly how he came to imagine himself. Children of alcoholics are also said to crave approval . . . and applause.

From early in his life, he saw the power in words as a way to achieve that. Throughout his rise, Reagan marveled at the ability of public figures like the pope to move millions with spoken words, and clearly craved that talent and power for himself. Over the course of a lifetime, his Hollywood-trained voice and inflection became a remarkable tool for delivering those words—but he also cared deeply about the content and narrative. In high school and college, he wrote short stories that were heroic in nature, later scrutinized closely by the woman who had become his best-known speechwriter, Peggy Noonan.

"When you read Reagan's youthful writing," Noonan states in her book *When Character Was King*, "you get a sense that he is not only betraying his preoccupations but suggesting the future. He is not only writing about life as he knows it but life as he imagines it—as if he were a hero, as if he were a gentleman in the woodified walls of a gentleman's club, taking brandy by the fire, as if he had been born to go to Yale, to be a pennant-waving son of the American aristocracy. In his writing, you see the style and assumptions of his time, but also a yearning, a wistfulness."

These opposing forces, private distance and a yearning for public adulation, that pulled on Reagan—keeping a barrier from the people intimately around him even as he sought the public's adulation—may help to explain the seeming contradiction that made the man a puzzle to many who desperately tried to figure him out. (That includes Morris, who put himself and other made-up characters into fictional encounters in his 1999 book, *Dutch*, from apparent frustration in understanding Reagan even after having considerable access to him.) As an amiable politician, Reagan practically invented the concept of the candidate that voters would like to have a beer with, even though his own family found him distant to the point that he famously didn't recognize his adopted son Michael at his graduation. The leader who, along with his supporters, helped to introduce the phrase "family values" into the American political lexicon was also the nation's first divorced president, abandoned by his movie star wife Jane Wyman, who found him too consumed by politics and a tad boring. The GOP icon who forged the party's historic alliance with Christian fundamentalists hardly ever attended church during his White House years, remarried an astrology-obsessed nonbeliever in Nancy Davis, and spoke of his own religion in only the vaguest terms. Gerald Ford, of all people, seemed to nail the Reagan persona when he called him "one of the few political leaders I've met whose public speeches revealed more than his private conversations."

The contradictions seem to trouble those who write about Reagan a lot more than they bothered Reagan himself. His strange blend of optimism and reserve helped keep him moving—upward, as well as westward to the Pacific, and past the disappointments of divorce or career setbacks or political defeats (such as his 1968 and 1976 White House bids) that would surely slow up a different type of person.

"Life is just one grand sweet song, so start the music," Reagan wrote next to his yearbook picture when he graduated from Dixon (Illinois) High School in 1928, and the melody carried him to nearby Eureka College, the small Disciples of Christ–run school where he was elected student body president and even led a strike against faculty cuts, writing later in his autobiography that "for the first time in my life, I felt my words reach out and grab an audience, and it was exhilarating." The clapping pushed him west to Des Moines, where a stint broadcasting Chicago Cubs baseball games over WHO, a newly amped-up 50,000-watt clear channel radio station, using telegraphed play-by-plays, called upon his remarkable skill in imagination and made Reagan a regional star. But he wanted more, and he got that opportunity after a 1937 screen test at Warner Bros. on a trip to California. His arrival in Hollywood altered his life trajectory upward again—though ultimately not in a way that either he or anyone else could have imagined.

Ironically, Reagan's actual film career—dominated by the forgettable B movies that were a staple of the Saturday double-feature era—is increasingly a footnote. His role as famed Notre Dame athlete George Gipp in *Knute Rockne: All-American* gave Reagan the "Gipper" nickname that stuck with him long after the celluloid faded; the line "Where's the rest of me" from the amputee drama *King's Row* gave him a title for his 1965 autobiography; and his chimpanzee comedy *Bedtime for Bonzo* ultimately gave America a great running joke, as well as a lyric for an awesome 1980s punk rock song by the Ramones ("Bonzo goes to Bitburg . . ."). But movie acting also provided Reagan with two wives—Wyman followed by Davis, also an actress—and an unorthodox path into politics, beginning with his election as president of the Screen Actors Guild in 1947, a post that he would hold through 1952. Reagan's stint as leader of the main actors' union in Hollywood coincided with growing public concern over communist influence in the movie industry, peaking with the so-called blacklist of some prominent actors, writers, and directors in the heyday of McCarthyism. As guild president, Reagan learned to become a strident anticommunist, telling the notorious House Un-American Activities Committee in 1947 that "I happen to be very proud of the way in which we conducted the fight [against communism]. I do not believe the communists have ever at any time been able to use the motion picture screen as a sounding board for their philosophy or ideology." He also shared what he found out about communists as an informant for the FBI.

The zealousness with which Reagan turned to anticommunism was part of a lifelong habit of basing his broad policy ideas on life experiences, part of his preference for the anecdotal over the ideological, for the personal over the polemical. That may explain why Reagan spent his early adulthood as a New Deal Democrat; he saw firsthand the impact that FDR's policies had on his dad—who actually worked for a time as the local functionary dispensing public works jobs in Dixon for one of the key agencies of the New Deal, the Works Progress Administration—and the role that Roosevelt's policies had played in slowly bringing depressed central Illinois back to life. But Reagan's lifelong war against income taxes—and especially against the high marginal rates paid by the wealthiest Americans—seems to have been inspired by his later experiences in Hollywood, especially when he received a lucrative $1 million contract in 1941 for his next seven films but marginal tax rates exceeded 90 percent. Despite the big payday, as biographer Lou Cannon noted, Reagan felt he was giving way too much of his check to the government and still felt financially insecure, especially after his divorce from Wyman. Reagan himself wrote in his 1990 biography, *American Life:* "I think my own experience with our tax laws in Hollywood probably taught me more about practical economic theory than I ever learned in a classroom or from an economist . . ." That experience, it seems, can be boiled down to the idea that the rich pay too much in taxes—and it was a personal lesson that would change the course of American society.

Meanwhile, the nexus of Hollywood and politics—so established now in the twenty-first century—was essentially a new script that Reagan helped to write and then memorized as he went along. He was even assigned to help America win World War II through movies. In 1937, not long after arriving in Hollywood, Reagan had enlisted in the Army National Guard and was commissioned a second lieutenant in the cavalry, in a time when cavalry members still rode horses. In the aftermath of Pearl Harbor, Reagan, then thirty-one, joined the Army Air Forces but because of his lifelong nearsightedness was not eligible for front-line duty. Instead he joined what was a cutting-edge effort for its day—using the storytelling wiles and technology of the movie industry to rally Americans behind the war.

It was army officials, particularly the head of the Army Air Forces, General Hap Arnold, who saw the potential of the Hollywood movies as a tool for recruiting soldiers and boosting the morale of civilians. In creating the First Motion Picture Unit and eventually locating it at the Hal Roach Studios in Culver City, California, Arnold reached out to Jack Warner and the Warner Bros. studios, where Reagan was under contract. The unit went on to produce four hundred films, including several that Reagan narrated or even acted in. The list includes *Stilwell Road,* which celebrated not only the brutal construction of the nearly 500-mile road on the

China-Burma border but also the multinational crews that built it, and *The Fight for the Skies.*

Years later, this critical three-year period in Reagan's life received little attention—with one exception. In 1984, when President Reagan was seeking reelection, reports would surface of two conversations—one with then Israeli prime minister Yitzhak Shamir and another with famed Nazi hunter Simon Wiesenthal—in which Reagan claimed that he personally had filmed the liberation of Nazi death camps during World War II and even saved the footage that he shot as proof that the Holocaust occurred. Clearly such an event could not have occurred, since Reagan never left the country during the entire war. Cannon and other contemporary journalists eventually found out that Reagan's unit in Culver City had helped to edit and repackage grim footage from the liberated Ohrdruf camp in eastern Germany—footage that was not in Reagan's personal library but shown in American theaters with titles like *The Nazi Murder Mills.* But for Reagan, who spent a lifetime in film, the movies and their plots were reality, even something as bleak and bloody as the reality of World War II. "Yes, I know all about the bad things that happened in that war," the president told a French journalist in 1985. "I was in uniform for four years myself."

The Holocaust story is not out of character. The boy who grew up in a world of imagination and found the perfect adult venue for escaping reality in the world of movies lived in a space where fact and fiction were a constant blur, even after he later gained the highest office in the land. One academic during the 1980s, the late Michael Rogin, who taught at the Gipper's much-despised Berkeley, developed a specialty of finding links between Reagan's speeches and policies and the movies that he had acted in or merely watched. Rogin wrote, "Ronald Reagan found out who he was by whom he played on film. Responding to type-casting that either attracted or repelled him, making active efforts to obtain certain roles and to escape from others, Reagan merged his on-screen and off-screen identities."

But whatever power that Reagan saw in film and storytelling to help win World War II was amplified when he turned his growing rhetorical skill to the conflict he is ultimately associated with, the Cold War. Here again, good timing—although it may not have seemed that way to Reagan at the time—

played a critical role in helping him create his unique persona. In his years following World War II, a time punctuated by his divorce from Wyman, Reagan's movie career, which had never achieved the stature of contemporaries like Jimmy Stewart, began to sputter. That's when General Electric arrived to help change Reagan's life story—and his politics.

Still America's largest industrial company in the twenty-first century, GE arguably was—and still is—at the cutting edge of some of the critical trends and ideas that have helped to shape post–World War II America, including the growth of the military-industrial complex, wooing its postwar and post-Depression middle-class workforce behind strong defense policies and a less regulated, less unionized economy, and using the growing influence of mass media as a tool in that ambitious mission.

The "free world is in mortal danger. . . . If the people were not convinced of that, it would be impossible for Congress to vote the vast sums now being spent to avert that danger," General Electric board chairman Charles Wilson said in April 1951. He added: "With the support of public opinion, as marshaled by the press, we are off to a good start. . . . It is our job—yours and mine—to keep our people convinced that the only way to keep disaster away from our shores is to build America's might."

That speech was delivered to the Newspaper Publishers Association, but General Electric was already beginning to see the power of the new medium of television, and how it could help in that mission. In the same year as Wilson's speech, the company also turned to a new advertising agency, Batten, Barton, Durstine & Osborn, or BBDO, which in turn hatched the idea of a television program called *General Electric Theater*, which would help brand the company for an eager new TV-viewing public. And so, in 1954, GE turned to Reagan, who had started to flirt with television as his film career slowed down, to host that program. His role expanded dramatically over the next eight years—becoming not just a company pitchman but a tireless promoter, speaking to rank-and-file GE workers as often as a dozen times a day. In doing so, Reagan shaped a new patriotic political message with a huge assist from the great unheralded ideologue of the 1950s, Lemuel Boulware.

In the late 1940s, with trade unionism on the rise, Boulware devised a communications strategy for GE that involved going over the heads of the union leaders and selling the company's workers on a new politics that shunned traditional bread-and-butter issues, to convince them that a blend of anticommunism and free-market capitalism was the only thing that would let them keep what they had. This new conservative vision was sold through newsletters, company magazines, and eventually through Reagan's appearances. Boulware's stated goal was to make General Electric's tens of thousands of employees into "mass communicators" who would not only help sell their next-door neighbors on the notion that what was good for GE was good for America, but would elect public officials who understood the same. It was training these "mass communicators" that turned Ronald Reagan into the Great Communicator.

As noted by Thomas W. Evans in his book *The Education of Ronald Reagan: The General Electric Years and the Untold Story of His Conversion to Conservatism,* Reagan himself referred to his time at General Electric as his "post-graduate education in political science." While the transition from matinee movie marquees to what was known as "the mashed potato circuit" would have likely made many a well-known actor bitter and resentful, not so the boundless optimist Ronald Reagan. A fearful flyer who traveled frequently by train, Reagan read up on his politics and spent years refining and honing what eventually became known as "The Speech." He changed and grew during these fairly isolated years to become the Ronald Reagan that all of America would come to know a generation later. He now was a teller of homespun tales and timeworn anecdotes— some true, some not so much—that were rooted in his small-town values yet sold his audience on a bright future, one that would be lit by General Electric. A Hollywood gossip columnist named Sheilah Graham joked famously about someone listening to Reagan's pitch for General Electric's nuclear submarine and saying that "I didn't really need a submarine, but I've got one now."

What emerged was a man who had undergone a political conversion during his eight years in the wilderness, from a solid New Deal Democrat to a Goldwater conservative very much at home in the far-right movement rooted in the freshly constructed, sprawling suburban tracts of places like Southern California's Orange County. Although his work for GE was nonpartisan, after his tenure there was over Reagan threw himself into Senator Barry Goldwater's 1964 GOP presidential race. By then, Reagan, fifty-three and not quite retired from acting, had developed a network of conservative allies that included his family—the physician stepfather of Nancy Reagan was a close Goldwater friend, while Reagan's older brother Neil, known as "Moon," helped craft political TV advertising—and wealthy far-right Republicans such as car dealer Holmes Tuttle. They all wanted to see Reagan run for office. Indeed, as it became clear that Lyndon Johnson was headed for a record landslide in 1964, those millionaire Southern California backers successfully pushed for a prime-time national TV address that would be delivered not by the candidate but by Reagan, whose allies already viewed him as having a rosier political future than the acerbic, blunt-speaking Goldwater.

"A Time for Choosing," the title that was given to the ultimate version of "The Speech" that Reagan delivered on October 27, 1964, was clearly the tipping point; from that day forward, Reagan was no longer a movie actor who dabbled in politics, but a politician who used to be in motion pictures. As with several other key moments in Reagan's mythology, the speech plays better in the history newsreels than it did in the newspapers, where it received little attention. Those who did watch that night received a sneak preview of the man they would come to know over the next twenty-four years: the overarching themes of reducing government and of militant anticommunism, the notion that "we are at war with the most dangerous enemy that has ever faced mankind in his long climb from the swamp to the stars." But the message is punctuated with the smallish anecdotes that Reagan collected, some stirring, some harsh. He told of a woman in Los Angeles who was pregnant with her seventh child and filed for divorce, because the $330 in monthly welfare benefits was greater than the $250 her husband made as a laborer, and he added: "She got the idea from two women in her neighborhood who had already done that very thing."

One passage in this speech still widely celebrated by conservatives a third of a century later is jarring. "We were told four years ago that 17 million people went to bed hungry each night," Reagan said. "Well, that was probably true. They were all on a diet." In fact, the Ronald Reagan that we saw in the fall of 1964 wasn't the 1980s model—the hair was more slicked back, face less jowly and more angular, and there was more of a scowl than a smile. Indeed, "the sunny optimist" Reagan was mostly angry in the middle 1960s. Today it is mainly political junkies who remember that without that simmering rage, cloaked in the often harsh rhetoric of backlash of that tumultuous decade, Ronald Reagan might today be only an answer to a movie trivia question.

But in the same 1964 month that Reagan delivered "A Time for Choosing," the Berkeley campus of the University of California erupted in dramatic protest in the so-called Free Speech Movement against campus restrictions on rallying support for civil rights protests in the Deep South. Just ten months later the streets of the Los Angeles neighborhood of Watts burned in the dramatic riot that claimed thirty-four lives and left nearly a thousand buildings damaged, destroyed, or looted. This was not "Morning in America," and it was largely the angry Reagan, not the sunny one, who rode the waves of white middle-class backlash and resentment to an upset defeat of incumbent Democratic governor Pat Brown in 1966. At large campaign rallies, Reagan called the student protesters "bums" and told cheering crowds that students at Berkeley engaged in "sexual orgies so vile I cannot describe them to you." Critical Reagan biographer Michael Schaller noted that the 1966 campaign was unusual for its time in shunning detailed policy stances in favor of appealing to the raw emotions of the electorate; Reagan "focused voter attention on symbolic issues like freedom, personal autonomy, and 'traditional values.' " It was the blueprint for the rise of the modern conservative movement, and it worked, propelling Reagan to a nearly million-vote landslide victory.

What Reagan had accomplished to this point is truly remarkable. The man who had fought World War II not on the front lines but from a Hollywood studio had now become governor of the largest state in America without ever truly engaging in the trench warfare of politics—the fine arts of compromise and deal-making—or ever having to run a large bureaucratic enterprise like the one he now faced in Sacramento. Indeed, Reagan's most memorable flash of his legendary self-deprecating humor in that 1966 campaign came when someone asked him what kind of governor he'd be: "I don't know—I've never played a governor before." On January 2, 1967, Reagan took the oath of office in a ceremony that was orchestrated with help from the Walt Disney Studios. The next day, Reagan started to "play" a governor for real, and a surprising thing happened.

Reagan's eight years in Sacramento provided him with plenty more opportunities to exercise his rhetorical skills against welfare cheats and hippies, whom he famously described as those who "look like Tarzan, walk like Jane, and smell like Cheetah"—and he acted tough on that front as well, firing university president Clark Kerr in 1967 and dispatching the National Guard to violently clear out People's Park in Berkeley in May 1969. But when it came to the day-in, day-out grind of actually governing—managing the large bureaucracy, balancing the books, and dealing with the Democrats in the legislature—Governor Reagan surprised everyone with his pragmatism and with his ability to compromise. The result was policies that were often moderate, occasionally even liberal. The man who said in his 1966 campaign that "a tree is a tree—how many more do you need to look at?" later endorsed the Redwoods National Park and signed other environmental protections, such as a Wild and Scenic Rivers System for California. The man who promised voters in that first campaign that "there's no more leeway for squeezing the people" ended up enacting in 1967 what was the largest proportional tax increase in the history of an American state—some $1 billion on a $6 billion budget—when he confronted a huge deficit and was unable to whack essential services. Presented that same year with legislation that cleared the way for many more women in California to legally obtain an abortion, Reagan wavered for days and finally, under pressure from some legislative allies, signed it into law.

Lou Cannon, who covered Reagan's rise in the Golden State and followed him to Washington in the 1980s, said in an interview for this book that as governor Reagan was simply establishing the pattern that persisted through sixteen years as a chief executive, as someone who was willing to compromise, sometimes considerably, to get things done or to make a problem go away. "Reagan at every juncture—every juncture—is practical," Cannon said, adding later that this is "not the Reagan that's being celebrated at the Reagan Library. I'm not saying they're wrong things, or dishonest—but I'm saying that they're only part of the story."

In mixing rhetorical red meat with closed-door compromise, Reagan found a winning formula, helping him win a relatively easy reelection victory in 1970 and keeping his name in the mix of GOP prospects for the White House. In 1968, his efforts had been easily trumped by Richard Nixon, who was just as plugged into white middle-class resentment but with a lot more political chits—triggering the chain of events that gave Republicans presidential incumbent candidates in 1972 and in 1976. But Reagan challenged Gerald Ford anyway in 1976, gambling that GOP primary voters would perceive Ford, Vice President Nelson Rockefeller, and Henry Kissinger as insufficiently conservative. Now a private citizen again, Reagan turned up the right-wing verbal heat on what should have been a back-burner issue—giving back the Panama Canal to its host country—and zigzagged when he came up a few delegates short, saying that he, too, would pick a liberal Republican, Senator Richard Schweiker of Pennsylvania, as his running mate. He lost that summer, but so did Ford that November—and Reagan, now in his late sixties, kept on running.

The mid to late 1970s were very much like the 1950s for Reagan, a second era of exile from center stage. Again, arguably by accident rather than design, he sharpened his verbal skills, now with a weekly radio commentary. Freed of the messy compromises of the budget bottom line and from hectoring legislators of both parties, the radio gig allowed Reagan to retreat to his tidy and simpler narrative world of broad ideas punctuated by a story or two—honing the rhetoric that would carry him to the White House in his third attempt. Writing his commentaries in longhand, Reagan offered opinions that are surprising at times—saying of marijuana that "if adults want to take such chances that is their business"—and of course dealt with the ongoing threat, that "Communism is neither an economic or a political system—it is a form of insanity—a temporary aberration which will one day disappear from the earth because it is contrary to human nature." In baseball terminology, the 1970s radio years were like another spring training for Reagan, and he worked hard on his fundamentals.

In politics as in show business, timing is everything. It happened for Reagan in 1954, when GE gave him the unexpected chance to develop political skills, and it happened again in 1966, when his personal sharp-right turn was in step with the public backlash to urban riots and campus unrest. But never would Reagan benefit from being in the right place at the right time as much as he did in 1980, when a nation that was exhausted from nearly two decades of nonstop turmoil would be receptive to a simple message of returning to the rose-colored memories of the lazy-creekside-and-Sunday-school America that Reagan evoked in his ever-refined speechmaking. Plagued by record gas prices, by the devastating effects of stagflation (high inflation and high unemployment at the same time), and finally by the insult and impotence of an unending hostage crisis in Iran, Jimmy Carter tackled America's growing list of problems in the guise of the full-blown policy nerd, and a humorless one at that. The former one-term Georgia governor had been elected after the Watergate scandal on his famous pledge that "I will never lie" to the American people—but he also never promised what would later become famous as "the vision thing" that voters came to crave. And when he sought to rally the American people in some of those darkest moments, Carter could almost be described as "downlifting."

Carter went before the nation on July 15, 1979, in a now notorious televised address, starting out in an almost hectoring tone that America was not paying attention to his detailed energy programs. He then described advice he received from a weekend with supporters, including some from "a southern governor" who seemed to unknowingly predict the rise of Reagan when he told Carter, "Mr. President, you are not leading this nation—you're just managing the government," adding, "Don't talk to us about politics or the mechanics of government, but about an understanding of our common good." Carter didn't quite absorb the message. He lectured again, telling Americans: "Our people are losing that faith, not only in government itself but in the ability as citizens to serve as the ultimate rulers and shapers of our democracy." Even though the word was never uttered by the president, the July 1979 speech is still remembered for the noun that was in the prespeech advice memo that Carter received from his pollster Pat Cadell: *malaise.*

The contrast in styles in 1980 between Reagan, who won the GOP primaries in fairly easy fashion, and Carter is best remembered today in satire, as in a piece in the whimsical *Onion* that recalls the Democrat's pitch as "Let's talk better mileage" and Reagan's mantra as "Kill all the bastards."

Indeed, at times many voters perceived the GOP candidate as direct but perhaps a little scary. That Reagan and Carter remained close in the polls with such a weak economy and with fifty-two Americans still held hostage that fall is a testament to how deeply voters feared the GOP standard-bearer. It was more than just his conservative doctrines. They worried that the man who said of Vietnam in 1965 that "we could pave the whole country and put parking stripes on it and still be home by Christmas" might just be crazy enough to launch the Big One. A large number of voters remained undecided in the days leading up to the November 4, 1980, election—not eager for a Carter second term but not totally convinced they should hand Reagan the keys to the nuclear suitcase, either.

For Reagan, his goal of proving he could stand at the presidential podium required a real debate with the overprepared Carter—an opportunity that was almost ruined because of the presence of moderate-liberal Illinois congressman John Anderson, a Republican who was running as an independent and ultimately got 6.6 percent of the vote. (Carter didn't want Anderson included.) Finally, Reagan and the incumbent agreed to debate one-on-one, in a showdown that was held less than one week before the election, on October 28 in Cleveland.

In every way, the debate was the grand climactic scene of the unconscious movie that Reagan had been crafting for sixty-nine years, needing only the perfect one-liner to send home the cheering audience. His instincts were perfect even as they baffled his close advisors, who spent the days in the run-up to Cleveland drilling the candidate for what they expected would be a flurry of facts from the Carter camp, especially on nuclear weapons. They were fearful that Reagan might lose if he looked unprepared. But as biographer Lou Cannon observed in writing about those key practice sessions, the candidate "spent his time practicing one-liners in the belief that viewers would be more apt to remember a deft phrase than a technical argument." At the end of one of his practice sessions, Reagan told his aides he'd come up with the perfect rejoinder, witty and relaxed.

Carter showed up in Cleveland and acted out his own part, malaise-spreading moralistic Sunday school teacher—dull, pedantic, stiff. Late in the debate, after he had already embarrassed himself to many voters with a riff about getting advice on nuclear weapons from his then twelve-year-old daughter, Amy, Carter gave a long, complicated, and nearly forgotten answer to a question on health care. Few remember that the allegation that he made concerning Reagan—that he had opposed Medicare when it was enacted in the 1960s—was correct. Even fewer remember Carter's ensuing appeal for a national health-care system, the policy that was favored by a majority of Americans then as it is today, at this writing by some 60 percent of Americans, including many Republicans and independents. Said Carter:

> Now, we have an opportunity to move toward national health insurance, with an emphasis on the prevention of disease, an emphasis . . .

The camera cut quickly away from Carter, who stood rigid as he talked, looking almost funereal in a dark suit coat and tie. It showed a longer-distance view of Reagan, who laughed broadly, swaying his broad shoulders back and forth as the president continued with his vision of health care for Americans:

> . . . on outpatient care, not inpatient care; an emphasis on hospital cost containment to hold down the cost of hospital care for those who are ill, an emphasis on catastrophic health insurance, so that if a family is threatened with being wiped out economically because of a very high medical bill, then the insurance would help pay for it. These are the kinds of elements of a national health insurance, important to the American people. Governor Reagan, again, typically is against such a proposal.

The moderator, Howard K. Smith of ABC News, called out plaintively, "Governor?" and the camera quickly panned back to the loose-limbed Reagan, who threw his head back and grinned from ear to ear, tearing Carter's wordy, preachy moment apart with the jujitsu of his relaxed body language, and then acted out the scene with the heroic one-liner exactly as he had rehearsed it in his mind.

> There you go again.

America still lacks the national health-care program that Carter spoke about.

But six days later, Ronald Wilson Reagan defeated James Earl Carter and was elected the fortieth president of the United States. It wasn't even close. He won by 8,423,115 votes, and carried forty-four states. His re-laxed, jocular comeback to Carter was only meant to carry him through November 4, but the one-liner lives on more than a generation later, in spaces that couldn't even be comprehended in 1980—such as the Internet site YouTube.com. Reagan unwittingly had a head start on the highlight reel for his twenty-first-century myth machine, but a much greater challenge lay ahead.

Just as in 1967, he would have to do more than deliver "The Speech." Famously, he would later re-create his rhetorical magic from Berlin to Normandy to the Los Angeles Olympics. But he would again have to do something beyond the power of his words—and that was to govern.

CHAPTER THREE

AN UNTAXING BURDEN

*It's a zero-sum game; somebody wins, somebody loses. Money
itself isn't lost or made, it's simply transferred from one perception
to another.*

—Financier Gordon Gekko, as portrayed by Michael Douglas
in the 1987 movie *Wall Street*

I f any day defined Ronald Reagan's presidency and the distorted legacy that came later, it was the morning that he declared victory in his
Twenty Years War against high income taxes—August 13, 1981, just
208 days into his first term in the White House. And when the day that
cemented Reagan's economic legend finally came, it would be shrouded
in thick, deep, billowing fog.

The grayish-brown California haze poured in waves from the salty
mist over the Pacific Ocean that day, assaulting the steep brushy hills of
the president's 688-acre ranch outside Santa Barbara. It looked as if a big-
spending special effects whiz from one of the studios down Highway 101
had trucked up a van full of fog machines to create a proper mood for the
signing of this law with such a dullish title, the Economic Recovery Tax
Act of 1981.

In fact, the eerie elements were the only piece of stagecraft that came
from Mother Nature and not from the ever-working imagination of Reagan's public relations aides, who weren't seeking to stage a grade-B hor-
ror flick that August but a kind of a Technicolor Western of tax reduction.
Thus it was surely no accident that Reagan showed up to clear away what

he saw as fifty years of tangled tax laws in the same heavy cotton-twill getup he wore for his beloved California brush clearing—a denim jacket, faded blue jeans, and brown boots, the look that would later be bronzed for eternity at the Reagan Library.

He may have been wielding his presidential pen (twenty-four of them, to be exact, doled out to key allies) but he was really playing the role of sagebrush-rebellion cowboy who rode into town to take on the big-spender black hats before galloping home into a hazy Pacific sunset. In fact, several horses from the Reagan ranch did wander in and out of the thick mist, and the president even answered journalists' questions while he petted the head of his dog Millie (whom he briefly called "Lassie"). It didn't take much time as commander in chief for Reagan to get into character—rugged yet avuncular, uncle to many, "Big Brother" to some.

"And this is only the beginning," Reagan told the tightly packed row of reporters and camera crews that day.

But it really was the beginning . . . and end. The follow-through—truly making good on all his pledges, starting in 1964 and running right through his initial unsuccessful lobbying of Congress in 1981 to roll back the growth of the federal government—that he promised on that foggy day would never come. To the Reagan legacy makers, that does not matter, nor do many other actual details of the overall package known as Reaganomics that sought to stimulate the economy but left behind a mountain of debt, in an era in which economic growth was increasingly centered not in the Main Street that Reagan's campaigns celebrated but on Wall Street. To the myth machine, Reagan's 1981 tax cut is not just a mere event between the era of economic malaise brought on by gas lines and 21 percent interest rates and the time when the Dow Jones (with one horrible exception, the 508-point one-day crash in October 1987) soared and stagflation was finally slain—but rather the transformative act that caused those things to happen.

The Reagan tax cuts "marked an end to stagflation and the beginning of an economic renaissance that we all benefit from to this day," a former Reagan advisor and frequent op-ed contributor, Bruce Bartlett, wrote in the late president's favorite periodical, *Human Events,* on the twenty-fifth anniversary of the signing ceremony, in 2006. Immediately after Reagan enacted the tax cuts, Bartlett insisted, "inflation virtually collapsed, just as the supply-side economists expected."

Of course, by that line of reasoning, it would be fair to note that the nation also plunged into a deep economic recession in the days immediately following Reagan's carefully staged signing ceremony, and that some sixteen months after enactment of the Economic Recovery Tax Act and "the beginning of the economic renaissance," America's unemployment rate reached a level unheard of since the Great Depression era, 10.8 percent (in December 1982), as Reagan's own approval rating plunged to a dismal 35 percent. But more than a generation later, Reagan's successful passage of a radical income tax reform is one of the twin peaks of the late leader's distorted legacy, standing tall next to his exaggerated role in winning the Cold War—even as the actual facts are shrouded in a fog as thick as the waves of moisture that assaulted the Santa Ynez Mountains that American morning.

The realities of the Economic Recovery Tax Act of 1981 are these: It would reduce the marginal income tax rates for all Americans across the board by 25 percent over three years; thus the wealthiest Americans, who paid at a 70 percent rate in 1981, would see that drop to 50 percent over that period, while rates on lower-income citizens dropped as well—14 percent to 11 percent in a working-class bracket. So while all people saw a reduction in their income taxes, it was the rich who saved substantial dollars from the Reagan-backed tax law. But that isn't all: during the half-year of machinations that finally led to the passage of the tax act, billion-dollar breaks were tossed in for large corporations and for America's oilmen, among other affluent special interests. Reagan may have signed the law as if he were auditioning for a role in *High Noon,* but the benefits accumulated for the gray-flannel-suited urban cowboys of Wall Street and high finance.

Here's what Thomas B. Edsall reported in the *Washington Post* on that morning in 1981: "In a bill that heavily rewarded traditional Republican constituencies, it sharply reduced and in some cases nearly eliminated federal taxes on such forms of income as business profits, capital gains, interest income and oil revenues, as well as on inheritances. In doing so, it left the government more dependent than ever on taxes on ordinary wage and salary income." He noted another important thing: this radical reform passed Congress with "surprisingly little debate."

Just as the fictional Gordon Gekko would later declare, money was simply transferred from one perception to another.

The mythmakers are right in this sense: undoubtedly, the Reagan 1981 tax cut—and the notion that cutting top tax rates and all taxes on corporations is the only acceptable policy direction—is the enduring legacy that he has bequeathed, at least in terms of public debate, to our modern politics. Even as the federal deficit, briefly reversed to a surplus under Democrat Bill Clinton, soared to new highs as the George W. Bush administration wound down, the GOP candidates battling to succeed him remained locked into a virtual bidding war to outdo the Gipper's historic action. A desperate Rudy Giuliani tried to save his flagging candidacy with a proposal that, as his campaign described it, included a "multi-trillion-dollar tax cut [that] would easily exceed the level of the Reagan or Bush tax cuts," while rivals including eventual Republican nominee John McCain countered with equally ambitious tax-slashing plans.

The legend of Reagan's 1981 tax cut endures almost solely because it was a political turning point, not an economic one. It was, quite accurately, an act of revolution. That was because Reagan was able to use both his personal popularity and the national anxiety over the economic mess to override the liberal coalition that had mostly guided economic policy since the Great Depression, to forge a new coalition of Republicans and conservative Democrats so beaten down by close to ten years of economic misery that they were willing to shift course, at least on taxes.

But this radical experiment, despite all the calls to emulate it today, wasn't the thing that turned the economy around. To use a sports analogy, it would be like saying there's a cause-and-effect relationship between the Boston Red Sox' 2007 World Series win and the New England Patriots' 16–0 regular season, since both happened that same fall and involved sports teams playing in New England. The economy of the 1980s is celebrated mainly because the economy of the 1970s that preceded it was so wretched. The stubborn fact of the 1980s is that inflation stalled and employment rose because a turnaround from the abnormally bad 1970s was inevitable, because Reagan allowed Carter's unpopular pick for Federal Reserve chairman, Paul Volcker, to continue squeezing the money supply, and because global oil prices—which had been so crippling when he took office—plummeted in the Reagan years, for reasons beyond the president's influence.

"There was a big inflation problem in the '70s and the Federal Reserve had a draconian policy of squeezing the economy to squeeze the inflation out—and so there was a terrible double dip recession from 1979 to 1982," says Paul Krugman, the Princeton economist and *New York Times* columnist who has taken a critical view of the Reagan legacy. "And then it bounced back on Reagan's watch—but by the end you were just about where a straight line projection of the previous trend would have taken you, so there's no sign that Reagan did anything to accelerate economic growth; the 'Morning in America' only looked good because the economy had been so down before. There wasn't any fundamental improvement—there was a sharp recession and then a sharp recovery that brought you back on the trend."

As for the tax cuts, it was clear in a matter of months that the initial Reagan plan went way too far. How far? Less than one year later, Congress passed—and Reagan signed—what at the time was the largest peacetime tax increase in American history, a revenue booster with the Orwellian name of the Tax Equity and Fiscal Responsibility Act of 1982. That wasn't all: Reagan signed further tax increases in 1983 and in 1984, and in 1986, enacting a broad tax reform plan that is also a major part of his legacy, he ceded a leading role to Democrats who were reasserting their authority on Capitol Hill. Given the nation's skyrocketing debt, it's easy to understand why Reagan lost much of his influence in this area.

Reagan told the nation in his first State of the Union address, on February 5, 1981, that "the federal budget is out of control and we face runaway deficits," yet in the first years of his presidency the nation's budget gap soared from $80 billion, or 2 percent of the gross domestic product, to more than $200 billion, or 6 percent. He lowered taxes but insisted on sharp increases in military spending in the name of his other main focus—building up Cold War defenses—and showed surprisingly little interest in cutting the rest of the government, even adding employees to the federal payroll and a new cabinet agency, Veterans Affairs.

The Reagan-style deficits, briefly reversed ten years after he left office, only to return in grand fashion during the George W. Bush presidency, are part of his economic legacy, as is the long-term evolution of the United States as a debtor nation, beholden to foreign sources of capital. The Reagan administration did find that while it lacked the will to actually shrink government, it could still ease the burden that government imposes on businesses—continuing a trend toward federal deregulation that actually began under Carter but extending it to the financial sector, leading to a huge savings-and-loan scandal and launching a wave of unchecked financial wheeling and dealing that leads all the way to the credit meltdown of the late 2000s. (One of those ensnared in the tangled web of the late 1980s S&L scandal was an obscure Arizona senator, John McCain, one of the Keating Five reprimanded for pressuring regulators to back away from a large campaign donor, a banking magnate in McCain's home state named Charles Keating.)

But Reagan's true lasting gift to American society is the ever-widening gulf between the wealthy and the middle class—even if that's not an achievement that you'll find on a bronze marker at the Reagan Library. The number of millionaires in the United States grew about eightfold during the Reagan presidency, but the number of Americans below the poverty line rose, too. Generally speaking, Americans in the upper-income bracket reaped a healthy dividend during the 1980s while those in the lower and middle classes barely kept pace with inflation. And the greed-ridden spirit of the 1980s took its cue from Washington and never looked back. It is the money-and-status-driven world that by the end of the decade was the stuff of Hollywood (1987's *Wall Street*), of off-Broadway (1989's *Other People's Money*), of literature (Tom Wolfe's *Bonfire of the Vanities,* 1987), and of the corporate boardroom, where the pay of CEOs began its long climb of Everest magnitudes, soaring from 42 times that of blue-collar workers to 85 times the same workers in 1990 (and continuing well past that in the 1990s and 2000s).

It is this indulgent legacy of Ronald Reagan that even his own vice president, George H. W. Bush, felt compelled to run against in 1988, calling for "a kinder, gentler America"—seen by many as a rebuke of greed and division during the Reagan years—and "a thousand points of light" to deal with the homelessness and poverty-related problems that festered on the nation's streets. Just six months after Reagan left office in 1989, the *New York Times'* Anthony Lewis, outraged by the mounting evidence of swindling by savings-and-loan millionaires and benign neglect of America's poor, wrote that "the intangible costs of the Reagan years to our domestic tranquility are surely greater than what can be measured in dollars. They are the costs of hostility to the role of government, of indulgence toward private greed, of insensitivity to the needs of the weak in our society."

Blame Reagan, but give an unintended assist to Jimmy Carter.

The truth is that throughout the 1970s the American economy was in a free fall for a host of reasons, many of them beyond the power of any U.S. president. The decade launched the long-term decline of well-paying manufacturing jobs in America, starting in the Rust Belt states of the Midwest into the Northeast (and including Reagan's old benefactor, General Electric, which laid off thousands of appliance workers at the peak of the 1973–74 energy crisis), and saw everyone blindsided by rising gasoline prices. Throughout the decade, runaway inflation caused by skyrocketing oil costs, the impact of inflation on consumer confidence, and automatic cost-of-living increases in a more unionized America left the nation's leaders seeming impotent, as shown not only by Carter's "malaise" speech but by predecessor Gerald Ford's much-ridiculed "W.I.N." (for "whip inflation now") button, which he donned in 1976.

By the end of the decade, policy makers largely agreed that the only way to stop inflation was through even greater short-term pain: tightening the money supply and letting interest rates soar. By October 1980, a month before the election, the prime rate had risen to 14 percent, causing an exasperated Carter to declare the policies of the Fed chairman he'd appointed, Volcker, as "ill-advised." Thus when Reagan asked voters in that Cleveland debate, "Are you better off now than you were four years ago?" many saw it as largely a rhetorical question.

For Reagan, in the wake of his overwhelming victory that fall, the crisis meant opportunity: his long-awaited chance to push for a radically different agenda on economics, and especially on the high marginal income tax rates that the incoming president had learned to despise as a star in Hollywood. Of all the themes that had driven his political career since the GE days—anticommunism, reducing government, middle-class resentment—it was the tax cut that became the bedrock idea of his 1980 campaign. Bill Clinton's aides may have popularized the phrase "It's the economy, stupid," but the modern concept was pioneered by Ronald Reagan. This was his main TV ad in the 1980 primaries:

High tax rates don't lower prices, they raise them. In the 1970s taxes grew faster than any other item in the household budget, including the price of energy. High tax rates discourage work and production. They add to the cost of living. If we make a deep cut in everyone's tax rates, we'll have lower prices, an increase in production, and a lot more peace of mind.

But as the White House loomed, there was still a war for the economic soul of Ronald Reagan. There was little doubt that the sixty-nine-year-old's heart was with a younger group of economic rebels whom one of its pioneers, former *Wall Street Journal* editorial writer Jude Wanniski, described famously as the "wild men" influencing the would-be president. The group, which also included up-and-coming GOP congressmen Jack Kemp of New York (the former NFL quarterback) and David Stockman of Michigan, also called itself "the Cabal." Its guru was a young economist from the University of Southern California, Arthur Laffer, who developed a tool called the Laffer Curve to explain his theories of "supply-side economics"—later also called "Reaganomics," "trickle-down economics," or in the famous phrase that Republican primary foe George H. W. Bush would come to regret, "voodoo economics." Laffer's ideas are not hard to explain: he believed (and still does) that sharply lowering taxes, particularly the higher marginal rates paid by the upper strata, would stimulate productivity that would actually increase the amount of revenue that the government ultimately raised—thus reducing the need for budget cuts. To Reagan, the man who had peppered his speeches with anecdotes gleaned from *Reader's Digest,* the plan was perfect, bold yet simple (to its critics, simplistic) and concise, easy to sell to voters.

The question was whether the "wild men" would hold sway, especially as the election drew closer and Reagan brought in more established economic experts and Washington hands who were quite dubious about the Laffer Curve, serious men like Alan Greenspan, the future Fed chairman, and Milton Friedman, who'd formerly held the Fed job. The conventional wisdom in late 1980 through early 1981 was that the sensible men would win, and why not—they always had in the past. But the conventional wisdom was wrong.

Reagan, according to Lou Cannon's biography, was heavily influenced by a memo that the young Stockman—whom Reagan tapped as his budget director, a cabinet-level position—and Kemp authored warning of "An Economic Dunkirk," in other words, that rising interest rates (which peaked at an astounding 21.5 percent right before Reagan took office) and other spiraling economic calamities might thwart any efforts to dramatically cut taxes or spending if he didn't move forcefully and quickly. The new president's path was made clear when his new treasury secretary, Donald Regan, took the supply-side plan to Capitol Hill and, according to the *New York Times*, "acknowledged that the highly optimistic forecast was based on Administration economists' views of how Americans are likely to respond to the program and not on any existing model."

But what mattered in those first fresh days of the Reagan presidency were not eggheady economic models but his gut political instincts and those of Reagan's staff—and these were right on the money, more so than any time in the seven years that followed. Reagan chose to make economics the main focus of his first TV address, on February 5, 1981, and virtually every other major speech after that for seven months. Other than the tax cut, initially pegged at 30 percent, the actual figures seemed to matter little; in one major speech blank spaces were left for numbers to be inserted. Facts may be stubborn things, but in 1981 they increasingly became obstacles to the hopeful message that Reagan was determined to deliver, even as Stockman crunched the reality-based numbers and began to see that already whopping budget deficits were about to soar past $100 billion a year, an unheard-of figure at the time.

The president's message was the 180-degree opposite of what was happening behind the scenes. "We're in control here," Reagan said in another televised speech before Congress on February 18. "There's nothing wrong with America that together we can't fix." And Americans responded: that month, some 77 percent told a *Washington Post* poll that Reagan, who'd received only 50.7 percent of the overall vote the prior November, was "inspiring confidence in the White House." That was a complete reversal from the negative sentiment in the final months of the Carter administration.

And all of this came before March 30, 1981, when Reagan was seriously wounded by a bullet from would-be assassin John Hinckley as he left a Washington hotel where he'd just delivered a speech. Reagan, seventy at the time, lost a bucket of blood from the projectile that puntured his lung, was hospitalized for twelve days, and also lost the services of his press secretary, James Brady, who was permanently disabled by one of the slugs. But Reagan recovered fully and quickly, leaving no lasting physical imprint on his presidency.

Politically it was a different story. News accounts that emphasized the president's bravery and good humor—he famously asked his doctor if he was a Republican—sent his popularity, already reaping the benefits of a presidential honeymoon, even higher. When Reagan spoke again to Congress on April 29, little more than two weeks after his hospital release, to push his economic plan, it was in a new role: hero. The Democratic Speaker of the House, Tip O'Neill, said quite bluntly that "we can't argue with a man as popular as he is."

And so they didn't argue—at least not when it came to taxes or one of the other two legs of Reagan's simple agenda, a steep rise in defense spending. Reagan clinched the deal with a flurry of highly personalized lobbying and schmoozing of key swing votes, using some of his Hollywood star power. "Well, when I was in the movies, I'd reach a point each year where after the second movie I'd be in the 90 percent bracket," he told Indiana Republican representative John T. Myers, as recounted in the *Washington Post*. "So I wouldn't make any more movies that year. And it wasn't just me, but Bogart and Gable and the others did the same. We weren't the ones who were hurt. The people who worked the props and the people who worked in the yard, they were the ones who were hurt."

When the tax bill finally passed that summer, forty-eight House Democrats crossed over to the president and gave him his winning margin. Democratic representative Charlie Wilson of Texas—the incorrigible playboy whose exploits from the bedroom to the Afghan minefield later became a Hollywood movie—turned to an influential but demoralized colleague and said of the president's persuasive powers that it could have been worse, that "he might have come out against f——g."

But the third leg of Reagan's political sales pitch, which was steep cuts in nonmilitary spending, something of a sop to more traditional advisors who were dubious of the Laffer Curve, never really materialized, in 1981 or at any other time in the Reagan presidency, setting the stage for the deficit time bomb that Stockman already heard ticking. White House economic policy advisor Richard Darman told Stockman that summer, "I don't know which is worse, winning now and fixing up the budget mess later, or losing now and facing a political mess immediately."

In the meantime, there was a lot that the Great Communicator left out of his speeches that spring and at his August bill signing on the misty mountaintop. To be sure, there was an income tax cut for all Americans, with the greatest dollar value accruing to the wealthy, who saw their rates falling over three years from 70 percent to 50 percent. But there was a lot more in the thousand-plus pages stacked before him, almost all of it bringing benefits to more affluent Americans who owned companies, bought stocks, or left large inheritances when they died. Specifically, the capital gains tax was slashed from 28 to 20 percent, the threshold for estate taxes went way up from $165,625 to $600,000, and corporations received a number of special breaks as part of a gradual long-term drop in the importance of big business as a source of tax revenue.

There is one other thing about the Economic Recovery Tax Act of 1981 that doesn't get mentioned during the incantations of the Reagan tax cut mantra today: it was a major unexpected windfall for America's oil companies. As the Associated Press reported while the bill was awaiting the president's signature, "The nation's oil industry hit a small gusher in President Reagan's new tax-cutting package, with special breaks for both independent producers and the energy giants." The breaks, inserted into the bill at the last minute, including a repeal of a windfall profits tax that lawmakers would unsuccessfully seek to restore a generation later, added up to more than $12 billion. One of the few who paid attention was Democratic representative James Shannon of Massachusetts, who said, "That $12 billion is more than all taxpayers making under $30,000 a year will get out of this bill next year. There's no way we can justify what we have done for the oil industry. . . ."

Meanwhile, signs that the tax law wouldn't have the predicted economic impact popped up immediately. Supply-side boosters like Kemp and Laffer had said that Wall Street would soar immediately, but a UPI story on the day after the bill signing was headlined STOCKS GO NOWHERE IN DULL AUGUST WEEK. In fact, the economy dipped back into a recession in September, one month after the bill that was predicted to provide such a great stimulus, and unemployment continued to spike through 1982 until it finally surpassed 10 percent at year's end. Not surprisingly, Republicans lost some twenty-seven House seats that fall. Because of both the tax cut and the economic slowdown, the federal deficit rose to beyond what even Stockman had projected—from $73.8 billion in 1980 to $207.8 billion in 1983. Experts like Michael A. Meeropol said the failure of the Reagan tax law to avert a recession should not be surprising, because it did so little to get money quickly to the lower- and middle-income people who would have spent their newfound cash. He wrote that extended unemployment benefits would have had greater impact.

But Reagan's broader approach survived the deep recession trough of 1981–82, and the economy was indeed flourishing by the time he ran for reelection in 1984. One thing that helped, and is lost in the foggy shroud of mythology, was pragmatism. Confronted with the realities of the budget gap, the president was willing to compromise. As Princeton's Krugman would later write, "In fact, no peacetime president has raised taxes so much on so many people." The Tax Equity and Fiscal Responsibility Act of 1982 was designed to raise about one-quarter of the revenues that had been cut the year before. Reagan himself continued to insist that he was just closing loopholes. "It's been dishonestly portrayed and tagged as the largest tax increase in history," he told the reporters who shouted questions at him. "It's nothing of the kind."

That said, Reagan even signed another tax hike in 1982: the Highway Revenue Act, which imposed $3.3 billion in levies on gasoline just as prices at the pump were finally falling. His Social Security deal in 1983 raised payroll taxes on all Americans, especially the working and middle class, which we continue to pay to this day. Even as he ran for his second term, Reagan went on to sign yet another bill that raised revenues, the Deficit Reduction Act of 1984. The Tax Reform Act of 1986, the other major tax bill of his presidency, was a compromise package that offered as much if not more to Democrats who'd increased their hold over Congress; while it achieved Reagan's goal of pushing the marginal tax rates even lower, the sweeping overhaul also was the largest increase of corporate taxes ever and—uncharacteristically for the rightward-tilting 1980s—strongly aided the poorest families by increasing standard deductions. The measure, Joshua Green later noted in *Washington Monthly*, caused a Reagan economic advisor to invoke the Democratic presidential candidate who told America in 1984 that either he or Reagan would raise taxes, stating: "Walter Mondale would be proud."

Bruce Bartlett, the leading defender of the Reagan tax legacy, conceded in a 2003 article in *National Review* the stubborn facts that *Reagan raised taxes every single year* of his presidency except for his all-important first year in the Oval Office and his last, 1988, when his vice president,

George H. W. Bush, was locked in what looked like a close race to succeed him. And of course Bartlett blames everyone except the fortieth president. He claims that "when all the political and economic elites of this country gang up on a president to raise taxes, history shows that they always get what they want."

But the truth is that Reagan was an active participant in the various tax hikes that took place all throughout the 1980s. Unlike those who would come claiming Reagan's legacy in the 2000s, Reagan did live in the reality-based world when he had to, and the reality was that the kind of cuts in social programs that would have been needed to bring the federal budget into line—given the 1981 income tax cut and the size of Reagan's military buildup, which increased defense spending in real dollars by 40 percent over the course of his first term—just weren't achievable. Steep reductions in federal programs simply weren't supported by the voters or their representatives in Congress.

As it became clear in the weeks after enactment of the 1981 tax cut that the deficit was rising to a then-unprecedented $90 billion and beyond, Stockman wrote in the margins of a White House memo: "No easy way to correct with speeches—need hard action. . . ." By 1982, even the conservative Business Roundtable was urging higher taxes, after Wall Street, far from the boisterous rally recalled by the mythmakers, plunged toward bear market territory on the deficit projections. Ultimately, Reagan, under pressure from both parties on Capitol Hill, agreed to lobby for the myriad business tax increases and fees enacted in the 1982 measure because his cherished income tax cut was preserved, allowing the president to proclaim a moral victory. The largest weekly point increase in the Dow, up until that time, came in the week after Reagan agreed to *raise taxes*.

Even with the tax hikes, the federal debt skyrocketed during his presidency, from $700 billion to $3 trillion. That staggering number suggests the government shortfall would have been far worse had Reagan not turned to his pragmatic side—the same instinct that led him to reverse course and enact a $1 billion tax increase as governor of California in 1967. "The rest of the story is that Reagan was a guy who cut deals," biographer Lou Cannon notes. "He was practical on the margins." To Cannon, who covered Reagan in Sacramento and then during both terms in the White House, the act that defines his governing style is one that rarely gets mentioned in the pop history and mythology: his backing down from a radical and unpopular reform of Social Security, and his willingness to submit to a bipartisan process that kept the retirement system solvent.

As outlined by Cannon in his main book on the Reagan presidency, *President Reagan: The Role of a Lifetime,* the botched-and-then-fixed handling of Social Security was a dramatic illustration of the danger of the president's trait of delegating the finer points of policy to underlings. In this case the underling was Stockman, who arrived at the White House believing that a "Reagan revolution" would usher in what he wrote would be a "brave new world" that would not only kill the Great Society reforms of Lyndon Johnson, like Medicare, but cut deeply into the safety net— including Social Security, which he had once described as "closet socialism." Stockman was able to sell the president, in May 1981, shortly after the assassination attempt, on a plan that would have slashed Social Security costs by $110 million by soft-pedaling the political ramifications of his plan's steep and almost immediate cut in payments to early retirees.

The ensuing uproar when the proposal was leaked in the *Washington Post* not only led the Reagan administration to back off but caused the president to ask future Fed chairman Alan Greenspan to chair a bipartisan commission to come up with a long-term plan for making Social Security solvent. To achieve that, Reagan agreed to a lot of things that don't sound anything like what we today call Reaganism—including higher payroll taxes on workers, which is one of the reasons why middle-class Americans never reaped the same financial benefits of the president's policies as were gained by the wealthy. When Reagan took office in 1980, middle-income Americans with children paid 8.2 percent of their pay in income taxes and 9.5 percent in payroll taxes, while in 1988, when Reagan left office, it was down to 6.6 percent in income taxes but up to 11.5 percent in payroll taxes.

In other words, the man hailed as the greatest tax cutter in American history actually increased the government's tax bite from blue-collar workers. Still, many see the Social Security move as a mark of responsible leadership. "That commission worked out a compromise that did some things the Democrats wanted and some things the Republicans wanted," says Cannon, chuckling at a much later quote from Karl Rove, who scoffed at the deal because it saved Social Security for only a couple of generations, still more than any subsequent president has been able to do.

The Social Security episode is important to Reagan's lasting legacy—arguably every bit as much as the 1981 income tax cut. It also seriously undercuts the Reagan myth by showing that when it came to governing, it was the president's often practical side that ruled the day, and that it was this, not his radical conservative instincts, that had the lasting positive impact. It was also a key turning point, because from that day forward, there was no more bravado about rolling back FDR's New Deal, nor was there ever any serious attempt to reduce the size of the federal government. The flaming torch of the "Reagan revolution" was actually doused pretty quickly.

In fact, the federal government grew in size under Reagan. The feds' civilian workforce increased during his two terms from 2.8 million to 3 million, even though his successors George H. W. Bush and especially Bill Clinton showed that government could be slashed (down to just 2.68 million by the time the budget-balancing Democrat left the White House). While the Gipper rode into Washington with tough talk about wielding an axe that might slash two cabinet agencies (Education and Energy), he left eight years later having added one, Veterans Affairs. Today, Reagan's biggest mythmakers will insist that he slashed federal spending. But he didn't. While Reagan was in office, federal spending grew by 2.5 percent per year, even when adjusted for inflation. As a share of America's gross national product, federal spending barely moved during the Reagan years, dropping just a couple of tenths of a percentage point.

"The major failure of the Reagan Administration was the failure to discipline spending," William A. Niskanen, who served on Reagan's Council of Economic Advisers until 1985 and then chaired the conservative Cato Institute, told the *New York Times* in 1987. "We have a bigger government, with higher spending. We've slowed regulation down, but we haven't reversed it. In other words, there was no Reagan revolution."

So the 1980s were a time of lower income taxes, especially for the rich (but higher payroll taxes on working families), runaway federal deficits and borrowing, an increasing trade imbalance, and ultimately, after the brutal recession of 1981–82, an improving U.S. economy. The period of economic expansion that began in early 1983 lasted for ninety-two months, one of the longest on record. The dark clouds of out-of-control inflation lifted during his eight years in office, dropping from an annual rate of 10.4 percent in 1980 to 4.2 percent in 1988, while the jobless rate shrunk over the eight years. Mortgage rates also dropped, and public confidence in the economy in many ways improved, especially during the first two-thirds of his administration.

But how responsible was the Reagan White House for the economic gains that took place from 1983 through 1990? Economists cite three key reasons for the improving financial outlook—none directly attributable to supply-side economics or the broader policies that were dubbed Reaganomics.

First, and arguably foremost, was the work of a presidential appointee—not of Ronald Reagan, but of Jimmy Carter. That would be the man that Carter had tapped in August 1979 to chair the Federal Reserve Bank: economist Paul Volcker. Shortly after assuming the job in the middle of America's stagflation crisis, Volcker applied the most obvious cure: a tight money supply that brought about a fairly rapid drop in inflation—at the price of high interest rates, followed by the record-high unemployment of 1982. Here, at least, Reagan gets an assist: for resisting public pressure to force Volcker to change course. The Fed chairman's bitter inflation pill infuriated the supply-siders in the Reagan White House and also political allies such as Tennessee senator Howard Baker, who blurted out at one frustrated moment in 1981 that "Volcker's got his foot on our neck, and we've got to make him take it off." But Reagan, who struck up a friendship with Volcker during his first few days in office, made a sound decision not to interfere. A generation later, fighting inflation is still the main priority of U.S. fiscal policy.

The second reason, critical but rarely mentioned, has even less to do with Reagan. The oil prices that went up so dramatically in the 1970s, leading directly to the stagflation crisis as well as the political climate for ousting Carter, went down just as dramatically in the 1980s, especially during Reagan's second term. Some of that was inevitable. The conservation measures that were launched during the 1970s—smaller cars and fuel-efficient factories and homes—helped keep demand lower in the following decade, and the higher prices also led to a surge in exploration and new discoveries, with many of the new oil fields outside of the control of the OPEC oil cartel. In fact, OPEC's ability to control production collapsed and Saudi Arabia dramatically increased its production, which led to a steep drop in oil prices in 1986. The cost of crude oil would stay low into the 2000s, overlapping the economic revival that conservatives attributed to Reagan.

Finally we have the laws of economics and the business cycle. The economic slowdown of the late 1970s and the 1981–82 recession were so severe that the inevitable rebound looked like a roaring freight train, both in real terms and even more so when compared to the malaise of the Carter years. Stockman, of all people, put it best in his book of disillusionment, *The Triumph of Politics:* "There was nothing new, revolutionary, or sustainable about [the growth of] the later 1980s. The cycle of boom and bust had been going on for decades and . . . its oscillations had reached the high end of the charts. That was all." Robert Solow, a Nobel Prize–winning economist from the Massachusetts Institute of Technology, said in 2004, after Reagan died, "As for Reagan being responsible [for the 1990s boom], that's far-fetched. What we got in the Reagan years was a deep recession and then half a dozen years of fine growth as we climbed out of the recession, but nothing beyond that." The sharp rise of the gross national product in 1983—7.5 percent—is strong evidence of an economy that was finally ready to break out to the upside. It's also important to remember that the 1980s weren't just a time of government tax cuts, but of pent-up high-tech innovation. For all the hoopla that accompanied Reagan's August 1981 tax bill, a more important development may have happened the day before, and with a lot less fanfare: IBM's rollout of its first personal computer.

That's not to say that Reagan's economic policies didn't have an impact—they did, certainly, and do to the present day. Remember that he rode into Washington promising not only to slash everyone's taxes and reduce government but to ease up on what he described as oppressive government regulations. The irony is that most experts say that Reagan's legacy on deregulation is overhyped and that Carter, who deregulated America's airlines in 1979, and the subsequent Clinton administration accomplished a lot more in this area. But there was one key exception: the easing of rules on the financial industry—with disastrous consequences.

"All in all, I think we hit the jackpot," Reagan said on October 15,

1982, when he signed into law a bill that lifted many restrictions on the savings-and-loan industry, giving thrifts the power to make larger real estate loans and to compete with money market funds. Some seven years later, after Reagan was safely out of office, the S&L industry was on the receiving end of the largest bailout in American history, with American taxpayers footing the bulk of the $160 billion tab even as the nation was still dealing with the original Reagan federal budget deficits. The "jackpot" that Reagan had spoken of quickly became a fool's gold rush into high-risk commercial real estate ventures, many of them tarnished by corruption.

But the S&L scandal and Reagan deregulation were part of a broader emphasis in the 1980s economy on manufacturing financial deals rather than manufacturing durable goods, an anxiety that was voiced in 1987 by novelist Tom Wolfe's bond trader Sherman McCoy, a self-proclaimed "Master of the Universe" who can't explain to his own son exactly what he "makes" for a living. It was a trend that only accelerated in the years after Reagan left office—a direct line leading to the subprime mortgages crisis and the tricky financial instruments that led to the collapse of the brokerage house Bear Stearns and huge losses elsewhere around the globe, all fueled by weak or nonexistent government regulation in the United States.

"A largely unregulated financial sector now dominates our economy, while manufacturing, once the keystone of American economic might, has dwindled to distinctly secondary status," American Prospect editor Harold Meyerson wrote in a 2008 op-ed on the long-term pain caused by Reagan-inspired policies. "As unregulated financial sectors are wont to do, Wall Street embarked on an orgy of speculative investment and debt accumulation."

In fact, during the 1980s, a decade so well remembered for that economic boom, America actually lost manufacturing jobs, with estimates ranging from 300,000 to 1.8 million. Some of that was because the flurry of corporate takeovers encouraged widespread layoffs, and a lot of that was the beginning of the long-term flow of blue-collar jobs across the border and then overseas to Asia. The simple truth is that by the end of the Reagan presidency, Americans were feeling extremely anxious about their long-term economic security. Just go back and read what people were saying in the late 1980s. It sounds nothing like the rose-colored nostalgia for that era's economics that would be expressed on the campaign trail twenty years later.

"Portentous change, in the form of a new global economy, was squeezing American families, evoking anxiety that nostalgia could no longer soothe," the *Boston Globe* wrote in late 1988, summarizing Reagan's second term and the race to succeed him. "Kaisha and keiretsu—the Japanese words for that country's great companies and conglomerates—emerged as new and menacing symbols of a transformed world, threatening to relegate America to second-rate status: an empty industrial core within a ring of exorbitant military armament." Indeed, if America was grateful by the late 1980s for the amazing turnaround that the Reagan administration had wrought in the nation's economy, we had a strange way of showing it. For example, the *Washington Post* ran a multipart series in April 1987 on the country's diminished economy. It wrote then: "In less than a decade, the world's largest creditor nation has become its leading debtor, foreign competition has humbled America's mightiest companies, hundreds of thousands of manufacturing jobs have disappeared and middle-class living standards have declined in many communities."

Those huge budget deficits that began with that 1981 Reagan tax cut weren't as harmless as later mythmakers would claim—most famously Vice President Dick Cheney, who reportedly said privately in 2002 that "Reagan proved that deficits don't matter." Deficits did matter. By the end of Reagan's presidency, the growing federal debt had triggered a chain of events that caused interest rates to begin rising again, bringing foreigners in to buy up the U.S. debt, which at that time strengthened the dollar and began the flood of cheaper imported products into America. The United States had been a creditor nation since 1914, fueling its rise as a global superpower, but under Reagan's watch it quickly reverted to the world's greatest debtor nation. By 2008, the amount of U.S. debt held by overseas central banks, primarily in China and elsewhere in Asia, had swelled to a staggering $2.3 trillion, leaving America at a grave risk that not necessarily friendly outsiders could determine its financial fate.

In an ironic twist, Reagan's irresponsible fiscal policies also set a broader tone for America's citizens, that in a country that was once a nation of savers it was now okay, even encouraged, to live beyond one's means. Economist John W. Sloan, writing about Reagan's supply-side economics, noted that the architects of the 1981 economic plans projected that personal savings, beaten down in the stagflation years, would rise from a national average of 5.4 percent to nearly 8 percent. But instead, savings fell during the 1980s to 4.5 percent and continued to drop. Sloan also notes that consumer debt rose sharply in the decade, from 74.9 percent of after-tax income to 96.9 percent. "Fortunately for the administration's pro-growth policy, however," Sloan wrote in the book *Deconstructing Reagan*, "the capital-short, consumption-driven U.S. economy was bailed out by an unforeseen boost in foreign investment, which was attracted to our low-inflation, high-interest safe haven."

Some of that transfer from a savings society to a credit-card economy was likely born of necessity. In stark policy terms, the lasting legacy of Reaganomics is the steep drop in the marginal tax rates for the top earners, from 70 percent to 28 percent when he left office (eased up and down to the current 35 percent). What that has done for the broader U.S. economy is still a topic for debate, but the impact on the widening gulf between rich Americans and poor Americans is not. By any measure, it began expanding steeply at the start of the 1980s and has never stopped growing.

In many ways, what happened in the early 1980s was a remarkable yet largely unrecognized turning point in American history. As Paul Krugman and other economists noted, the original great divide between the rich of America's Gilded Age and the poorer masses in factories and on farms was mended, to an amazing extent, in a period called the Great Compression, triggered at the time of FDR's New Deal and the industrial buildup to World War II. For the next two generations, America's growth and prosperity was shared by a broad middle class. Then came the era that Krugman and others call, in contrast, the Great Divergence—of America's wealthiest and the working class. The economic data that the Reagan mythmakers tout to show America's economic miracle of the 1980s and beyond don't reflect how unevenly the nation's prosperity has been shared, then and since. The median income of an average American family, in real dollars, grew by just 13 percent from 1979 to 2005, but for the wealthiest 0.1 percent the comparable number is 296 percent. That simply didn't happen in other industrialized Western nations. (Measured another way, the *Philadelphia Inquirer* reported in 1991 that incomes during the 1980s rose 44 percent in noninflation-adjusted dollars for people making from $20,000 to $50,000, but 697 percent for those making from $200,000 to $1 million and 2,184 percent for those who earned more than $1 million.)

The poorest Americans fared even worse during the decade. The president who is today hailed as the modern savior of the American economy saw poverty actually increase while he was in the White House. The percentage of individual citizens living below the poverty line in this country rose sharply from the tail end of the Carter presidency through the first two years of the Reagan White House, peaking over 15 percent, or higher than when Lyndon Johnson had been moved to launch his War on Poverty in 1964. The numbers only eased down slightly during the rest of Reagan's presidency, even when those other economic indicators like the Dow took off.

But there was something else that took off during the Reagan years: a sense that greed was taking over America. Indeed, a speech that was arguably more renowned at the end of the 1980s than Reagan's Berlin Wall address was first delivered in real life by billionaire financier Ivan Boesky and then more famously in fiction by Michael Douglas's Gordon Gekko in *Wall Street*: "Greed, for lack of a better word, is good."

Just as you can argue that the madcap government borrowing during the Reagan years inspired workaday Americans to stop saving and start maxing out credit cards, likewise the era of lowering taxes on the wealthy seemed to motivate a runaway private sector windfall for top executives. The pay for corporate CEOs has gone from 30 times what their employees made in the 1970s to about 300 times higher today.

William Safire, the conservative *New York Times* columnist, wrote his own defense of greed in January 1986, when he claimed that "by competing to make our pile bigger, we engage in the great invisible handshake that enlarges pies, lifts all boats and enriches us without impoverishing our neighbor"—an argument completely out of line with the economic data from the 1980s. Many commentators who took a more jaundiced view of the greed epidemic of the decade argued that Ronald and Nancy Reagan set the tone. As *Newsweek* wrote in a 1988 cover story, "The '80s Are Over,"

The public seemed fascinated by the air of unembarrassed extravagance that floated around the Reagans: Mrs. Reagan eventually spent $25,000 on her Inaugural wardrobe. A planned redecoration of the White House family quarters was to cost $800,000. The price tag for new White House china would be $209,508. What a *relief* the *Reagans* were! The new First Family's imperial life-style seemed to open a tap in the national consciousness, and all the longings for luxury that had been repressed in the parsimonious Carter years came flowing out. Once again we were allowed to be fascinated with wealth and power—a guilty pleasure the previous administration had been determined to deny us. Like hungry kids turned loose in a candy store, we went straight for the buttercreams.

Those who could afford buttercreams, anyway. As is the case with much of the Reagan legacy, his defenders tend to migrate away from the true grit of facts and back toward his lofty words and even more so, to his undeniable optimism: he told Americans his heartfelt belief that brighter days lay ahead, the public took it to heart, and hence that confidence alone was critical to America's economic turnaround.

"There's a great deal of psychology in economics," Reagan told Cannon once, and that was clearly a core belief of his presidency, ranging from his pet peeve of negative stories about joblessness on TV's nightly news to urging America at the depth of the recession in 1982 to "seize these new opportunities to produce, to save, to invest, and together we'll make this economy a mighty engine of freedom, hope, and prosperity again."

But if Reagan deserves credit for that brand of leadership, for setting a tone of robust optimism about the economy, then by that same token doesn't he also deserve blame not only for his policies that tamped down the middle class and the poor but also for a deep failure in moral stewardship? Didn't Reagan's leadership encourage gaudy conspicuous consumption as a nation moved inexorably toward not one but two Americas, and by inspiring not just everyday Americans but America itself to live beyond our means, to create a mountain of debt that is still around for his grandchildren?

The other takeaway from Reaganomics is that his economic legacy would have been even worse had the Gipper's unheralded pragmatic side not been a moderating force for most of his final seven years in the White House—if he had not compromised to salvage rather than destroy Social Security, or not left the core "safety net" of the New Deal untouched, or not agreed to some tax increases that avoided an even greater debt burden for those who came after him. That's an important fact to remember before considering the issue that is truly at the foundation of the Reagan myth: his foreign policy, and his leadership in the Cold War. That is a plotline where "tear down this wall" bravado is a distraction from a real moral of the story, one that so undercuts the dominant neoconservatives of the 2000s—because it is all about accommodation and talking to enemies.

At its core, not surprisingly, is a movie that was made in Hollywood—but is one of the most liberal movies of the 1980s.

CHAPTER FOUR

WARRIOR DEFUSED

> ... *[Reagan] said that killing civilians in a strike against terrorists would be "an act of terrorism itself."*
>
> —Lou Cannon, *President Reagan: The Role of a Lifetime*

The event that permanently altered the course of Ronald Reagan's foreign policy—and thus world history—wasn't the president's calling the Soviet Union an "evil empire," or when he asked Mikhail Gorbachev to tear down the Berlin Wall, or his ability to persuade Congress to spend billions more on defense. Instead it was the production and national broadcast of a TV movie that was conceived in the studio haciendas of the liberal Left Coast and quickly adopted by an American peace movement as its own.

The producers of ABC's *The Day After*, a two-and-a-half-hour movie broadcast on November 20, 1983, insisted their project was a public service to educate Americans about the effect of a thermonuclear war between the United States and the U.S.S.R., not a political jab at the Reagan White House. "We never intended the film to be a political statement," Brandon Stoddard, the president of ABC Motion Pictures, who commissioned the film, told *Time* magazine. "The movie simply says that nuclear war is horrible. That is all it says." Indeed, *The Day After* was in many ways a fairly formulaic TV disaster pic—everyday Americans shown in all their day-to-day middle-class decency and foibles, planning weddings and saving sick people in a hospital, normal lives interrupted by unfathomable events. In this case, however, the catalyst was not an earthquake or towering inferno, but a nuclear exchange that killed tens of millions of people.

The filmmakers set the story in the American heartland; the epicenter is Lawrence, Kansas, where area hospitals are depicted as overwhelmed with the burned and those slowly dying from radiation. There are food riots, and a revival service in a burned-out church captures the absurdity of trying to live normally after an atomic apocalypse.

But it was also absurd to think that a movie in 1983 about nuclear war could be seen as apolitical, not when the film was conceived and produced in the early years of the Reagan presidency, when his tough talk toward the Soviets and his record increase in military spending had focused both America and the world on the possibilities of World War III more so than any time since the Cuban Missile Crisis of 1962. Tom Shales wrote in the *Washington Post* some six weeks before its airing—watched by an estimated 100 million people, still a record for a made-for-TV movie—that "the fact that the telecast is engendering this kind of tumult already could itself be seen as a sign that the mind-set of the country is shifting back to a '50s Cold War mentality, a drift accelerated by the Soviet attack on a South Korean commercial airliner last month and by the Reagan administration's perceived preference for swords over plowshares. Suddenly the Soviet Union is 'evil' again. . . ."

Indeed, that very fall, the Reagan administration was pushing its plan for the installation of intermediate-range nuclear-equipped Pershing II missiles in Europe—where they could be used in a regional conflict very much like the one described early in *The Day After*. That January, *Time* had featured a Pershing II launch on its cover with the headline "Nuclear Poker: The Stakes Get Higher-and-Higher." The military buildup was hardly one-sided: the plan to install the Pershings and cruise missiles in Europe was a response to a Soviet intermediate missile called the SS-20. Nor was it solely Reagan's doing, since planning had actually begun during the Carter administration. But Reagan's election and the concurrent arms race gave enormous power to a grassroots outcry for a so-called nuclear freeze that would halt the introduction of any new atomic weapons. There were mass protests against Reagan's proposals in Europe, and in June 1982 a million people gathered in New York's Central Park to rally for disarmament, still the largest protest event in U.S. history. Not surprisingly, backers of the freeze movement saw the showing of *The Day After* as a massive publicity boon, especially when advance copies leaked out to antinuclear activists.

"What this movie does is put the lie to the whole notion of 'limited nuclear war' for 25 million viewers in one swat," said Democratic U.S. representative Edward Markey of Massachusetts, who was the chief sponsor of a nuclear freeze resolution before Congress and who saw an advance copy. "Support for the president's 'peace-through-strength' program is centered in the Midwest. But when people in Kansas and vicinity—Arkansas through the Dakotas, that half-moon path where our ICBMs are planted—see this film, they'll never again think of fallout shelters as a way of protecting themselves in a nuclear war." Hundreds of groups, including some ad hoc ones, such as the campaign called Target Kansas City/Let Lawrence Live, rallied around *The Day After*, while conservative supporters of Reagan's defense buildup fumed (typical was the Eagle Forum's Phyllis Schlafly, who groused: "This film was made by people who want to disarm the country and are willing to make a $7 million contribution to that campaign"). When the movie was delayed and then cut from four hours to two and a half, there were even rumors—unproven and probably unfounded—that the White House was involved. Indeed, many saw *The Day After* through the prism of Reagan. It's said that in an early version of the film, the voice of the president addressing the nation after the war was a Reagan imitator, later removed as obviously too inflammatory. A woman named Irene Boyd who headed the education office of the Nashville Catholic Center cried as she told *Newsweek* after seeing the movie, "We have set ourselves up for this by voting for Reagan's defense budget. It reminds me of an image of Jesus saying: 'Why can't they see?' "

All those peace activists watching *The Day After* in church basements that fall night never could have imagined in their wildest dreams that one of the show's 100 million viewers was the one citizen who could truly make a difference: Ronald Wilson Reagan. In fact, the father of modern American conservatism was influenced by this supposedly liberal TV movie, greatly—and so were his policies.

Of course, it didn't hurt that ABC stumbled into the best possible format for lobbying Reagan, the narrative arc and dramatic scenes of a motion picture. Unbeknownst, surely, to the filmmakers, key administration officials such as budget chief David Stockman and defense secretary Caspar Weinberger had learned by 1983 to craft visual presentations for the president on complicated issues, finding such a simple narrative the best way to win Reagan's support. And a full-length film was an even better way to get through to the nation's movie buff in chief, who famously told chief aide James Baker that he didn't read his briefing book before a key summit because, "Well, Jim, *The Sound of Music* was on last night." Also, the imagination-prone Reagan had suffered much of his adult life from worries over the prophecies of a world-ending Armageddon as depicted in *The Day After*, a personal concern that didn't disappear when he was handed the keys to the nuclear "football."

That may be why Reagan was in fact more receptive to at least the goal, if not the tactics, of the nuclear freeze movement than anyone realized in 1983. The president was taken aback by the size of the protests in Europe and at home during his first term; he surprised close aides by endorsing a proposal for a so-called zero option on the continent, which would mean no Pershings and cruise missiles in return for removal of the Russian SS-20s, and in October of that year, at the height of the buzz over *The Day After*, he startled his secretary of state, George Shultz, by declaring: "If things get hotter and hotter and arms control remains an issue, maybe I should go see [Soviet premier Yuri] Andropov and propose eliminating all nuclear weapons." And that was before Reagan watched *The Day After*.

"It is powerfully done, all $7 million worth. It's very effective and left me greatly depressed," Reagan wrote in his diary after he saw the film, which had been sent to him to screen in advance at Camp David. He added: "Whether it will be of help to the 'anti-nukes' or not, I can't say. My own reaction was one of our having to do all we can to have a deterrent & to see there is never a nuclear war." Coincidentally, in early November, in between Reagan's private screening and the national telecast, a massive ten-day NATO training exercise in Western Europe called Able Archer so terrified the Soviets—who thought it could be a prelude to an actual attack—that the U.S.S.R. went to its highest level of alert and, according to the experts, the world came closer to war than at any time since the Cuban Missile Crisis. On January 16, 1984, the president reemphasized in a nationally televised speech that "my dream is to see the day when nuclear weapons will be banished from the face of the Earth."

And in the second half of his administration, Reagan may have worked harder than any president before or since in trying to convert his imaginative vision that he personally could save the world from a nuclear Armageddon into a reality. When a crisis of aging Soviet leadership was finally resolved in 1985 with the ascension of Mikhail Gorbachev—himself soon motivated to seek sweeping change by the nuclear power disaster at Chernobyl—the two world leaders embarked on a series of remarkable summits aimed largely at nuclear arms reduction. When they met in Reykjavik in October 1986, they even entertained a radical proposal to eliminate all nuclear weapons, although it foundered on Reagan's refusal to give up another cherished personal vision: his notion of a high-tech weapons shield. That meeting did lay the groundwork for an agreement fourteen months later to eliminate all of those intermediate-range nuclear weapons in Europe. Today you can see the Pershing II and the SS-20 right next to each other—in the Smithsonian Institution, where most would agree such lethal weapons belong. When the agreement was reached for the Intermediate-Range Nuclear Forces Treaty, Reagan sent a remarkable telegram to the director of *The Day After*, Nicholas Meyer. It said: "Don't think your movie didn't have any part of this, because it did."

The story of *The Day After* is fascinating and humanizing—and understandably isn't part of the Reagan myth so vigorously pushed by a new breed of conservative activists and politicians in the 1990s and the 2000s. It simply doesn't match up with the tough-guy legend of that bronze cowboy greeting people at the front door of the Reagan Library. In fact, the tale of Reagan's quest for arms control, which succeeded in reducing the world's nuclear arsenal if not eliminating it, is arguably the most positive legacy that the fortieth president left to the world, but by the late 2000s it seemed that Americans only wanted to listen to a small part of the story, the first part, the leading-man bravado. It's certainly true that Reagan came to the White House backed by a generation of tough talk on communism, that he called the Soviets "an evil empire" (in a comment to ultraconservative fundamentalist preachers that he expressed regret for just weeks later), and asked Mr. Gorbachev to tear down that wall. And he did spend billions of dollars on new weapons systems—most actually conceived during the Carter years—with money his government didn't have.

But in the end, the rhetoric wasn't the ultimate policy, despite what the legacy builders came to say. The tough talk gave him cover to do what seems practically forbidden in today's political environment—talk to his supposed enemy, the Soviet leader Gorbachev, and seek compromises,

what some of his onetime allies on the right even went so far as to brand
a Neville Chamberlain–like "appeasement." The notions that have come
to dominate the American political landscape since the start of this century—never negotiating with enemies, and sustained lethal use of U.S.
military might to sustain hegemony as the world's lone superpower—
were mostly alien ideas to Ronald Reagan.

Indeed, the real Ronald Reagan probably would have been clobbered
on foreign policy questions in the GOP's 2008 presidential debates—even,
and maybe especially, the ones held at the Reagan Library in Simi Valley.
Why? His strong belief—see the quote at the beginning of this chapter—
that military responses to terrorism that kill civilians, even unintentionally, are not appropriate—is just one example of ways that Reagan generally
abhorred direct military interventions, and for a combination of reasons.
One key factor was his oft-overlooked political pragmatism; it's easy to
forget years later that Reagan became president less than six years after
the fall of Saigon, and he knew that the lingering bad taste from Vietnam
made most proposals for using troops abroad unpalatable (Reagan, in fact,
promised "no more Vietnams" in his 1976 campaign). Beyond that, Reagan had real concerns about the image of America as a bully in the world,
notions that unfortunately seem almost quaint in hindsight, and was
practically squeamish about risking U.S. lives. The result was the so-called
Reagan Doctrine, which did seek to halt the spread of Soviet influence
around the globe—but only by funding and advising regional surrogates.
His only offensive use of ground forces in eight years was an operation
using overwhelming force against a lightly defended Caribbean island,
Grenada, while behind the scenes it was typically Reagan himself who
stood down generals who suggested using American troops in conflicts
such as Nicaragua, as a response to an attack on U.S. Marines in El Salvador or in Beirut, or to overthrow dictators such as Panama's General Manuel Noriega; Reagan tried for years to convince the Panamanian strongman
to peacefully stand down, while it took his successor George H. W. Bush
just eleven months in office to send in the Marines.

On July 7, 1985, six months into Reagan's second term, Lou Cannon
wrote a piece for the *Washington Post* headlined WHAT HAPPENED TO REAGAN
THE GUNSLINGER? NOW HIS PROBLEM IS CONVINCING SKEPTICS HE ISN'T A PUSSYCAT. His
critics in the piece were conservatives, furious that the president has ig-

nored a 1981 pledge of "swift and effective retribution" to terrorist attacks. The story noted that the right-slanted *Wall Street Journal* editorial
page called him "Jimmy Reagan" (as in Carter) when he didn't respond to
the death of navy diver Robert Stethem, whom Hezbollah terrorists
dumped on the Beirut airport tarmac in the June 1985 hijacking of TWA
Flight 847. Perpetual right-wing crank Richard Viguerie, initially a huge
Reagan booster, now said, "With each new crisis, Reagan has less and less
credibility with both friends and foes."

Truth be told, there was a lot about Reagan's foreign policy for conservatives, liberals, and even moderates not to like. The "Reagan Doctrine"
of supporting surrogates to wage war in Central America may have saved
the lives of American soldiers, but it also meant a tacit endorsement of
human rights atrocities committed in the name of U.S. interests, such as
the Salvadoran death squads that murdered thousands of civilians or the
Nicaraguan Contras, instructed in a notorious CIA training manual how
to "neutralize" judges and government officials. And as the whole world
learned just a year after Reagan was essentially called "a pussycat" by the
Washington Post, Reagan's personal empathy for Americans held hostage
in the Middle East played a part in the low point of his presidency, the
revelation that his administration enthusiastically sought to trade arms
to a hostile Iran for their release. In fact, the Iran-Contra scandal (some
of the profits from the arms dealing went to finance the Contras after
Congress moved to prohibit such aid) managed to combine several of
Reagan's worst foreign policy traits: his determination to fund the antigovernment rebels that he called "freedom fighters" at all costs, and his
tendency to follow his soaring rhetoric by leaving the dirty details to aides
who were prone to make a mess of things. Third World issues were often
ignored and festered—most notably Islamic extremism—during the Reagan years, when so much of the focus was on dealing with the Soviets, on
the problem as he had largely defined it since the early 1960s and the GE
"mashed potato circuit."

But out of this muddle, it is Reagan's stewardship of America's Cold
War policy, and the fall of the Soviet's Iron Curtain just ten months after
he left office, that has come to define his presidency for those who are
casting bronze statues and looking for extra granite space on Mount Rushmore. A distorted legend, too, is increasingly carved in stone: by moving

away from 1970s philosophies of peaceful coexistence, or détente, and insisting that democracy and free markets would triumph over communism, Reagan himself made that result happen—helped by his 45 percent increase in defense spending. Indeed, the first graffiti on the Berlin Wall was barely dry when his backers began awarding credit.

"One enormous reason all that [change in the Soviet bloc] is happening is because of the policies of Ronald Reagan, which all those liberals made a career of lambasting," the Republican Senate majority leader, Bob Dole, blurted out during a heated floor debate the first week after the opening in Berlin. The irony is that in the days immediately after the wall's collapse and the end of the Cold War, most Americans credited the dropping of the Iron Curtain . . . to Mikhail Gorbachev. A poll published in *USA Today* just four days after the tumultuous events in Berlin found that 43 percent of Americans gave the credit to the Soviet leader, and only 14 percent named Reagan (it was far more pronounced in Germany, where 70 percent credited Gorbachev and only 2 percent hailed the former U.S. president).

But as the conservative media echo chamber grew in the years that followed, including the rise of Rush Limbaugh and a new breed of right-wing radio talkers, so did the notion that it was Reagan, his defense buildup, his call for a "Star Wars" defense shield against incoming weapons (which to this date has never materialized), and his stirring rhetoric that single-handedly won the Cold War.

By the time former Reagan aide Pat Buchanan addressed the Republican National Convention in Houston in 1992, a gathering that shocked many pundits for the party's sharp turn to the right, Reagan's bold actions—including Grenada—had caused the communist dominoes to fall around the world. "Fellow Americans, you ought to remember, it was under our party that the Berlin Wall came down and Europe was reunited," Buchanan thundered. "It was under our party that the Soviet Empire collapsed, and the captive nations broke free." He said that every president is remembered with one sentence, and Reagan's was that he "won the Cold War." Over time, the legend grew even less complicated, and others said it less eloquently. The myth grew more simplistic as it was handed down to the next generation. At a Republican presidential debate on Fox News in 2007, Rudy Giuliani adapted an earlier quote from

Margaret Thatcher when he said, "Ronald Reagan won the Cold War without firing a shot, but it was because he pointed like a thousand missiles at Soviet cities." It was reported that the remark received warm applause.

Are the legacy makers right? Is Reagan's one sentence really that he won the Cold War, and was it really by pointing "like a thousand missiles" at the enemy? Among most historians and writers, the verdict is mixed, divided between those who believe that Reagan's defense spending did help speed up the collapse of the Soviet Union—as *Newsday*'s Marie Cocco best phrased at the time of Reagan's death in 2004, it "perhaps helped to nudge a terminal patient into death"—and those who think the influence of his administration's policies is greatly hyped, that the desperate need within the U.S.S.R. for internal political reforms, including openness, and for an economic overhaul of a nation that was missing the Computer Age, problems finally understood and tackled by Gorbachev, were the main reasons.

Historian Robert Dallek, writing in 2007 and adopting a view that was held by many, said that Reagan deserves a sliver of credit for America's success in the Cold War, but as one of a string of presidents who essentially held fast to a broader strategy in place for four decades, the "containment" strategy as adopted by Harry Truman from his foreign policy expert George Kennan in the late 1940s. The essence of that plan, Dallek noted, was "that the Soviet Union was a contradiction in terms—that it was doomed to self-destruction, that it could not be an effective, productive consumer society, that it invested so mightily in its military side, that at some point it was going to fall of its own weight."

As we have seen in Reagan's prepresidential years, his fervent anti-communism dates to his days in blacklist-era Hollywood following World War II, and was strengthened during his years of rallying General Electric workers behind the common cause of the Cold War as he honed his speech. Indeed, his core belief—that the Soviet Union and other communist states were doomed to failure because of their lack of political freedom and economic opportunity—dovetails with the chief tenets of Kennan's containment strategy. It was Reagan's view—to his credit, prophetically correct—that the Cold War would not be so much won by the West as lost by the U.S.S.R. and the contradictions of communism, which he espoused in his radio commentaries of the 1970s and in several well-known speeches of his first term. In 1982, he spoke to Britain's Parliament and said a line that is frequently still quoted today, that "what I am describing now is a plan and a hope for the long term—the march of freedom and democracy which will leave Marxism-Leninism on the ash heap of history as it has left other tyrannies which stifle the freedom and muzzle the self-expression of the people." Ironically, it was into that same London speech that Reagan had hoped to drop the phrase "evil empire"—but that would not happen until nine months later, in March 1983, when the president traveled to the all-American setting of Orlando, Florida, and addressed an audience that was more receptive, the National Association of Evangelicals.

Some of Reagan's later rhetoric was clearly a reaction to détente, the policy launched by his fellow California Republican, Richard Nixon, in the early 1970s. It sought to defuse Vietnam-era tensions between the U.S. and the U.S.S.R. through a series of treaties and two pacts aimed at controlling the arms race, the Strategic Arms Limitation Treaty, or SALT, and its successor, SALT II, negotiated between Leonid Brezhnev and Jimmy Carter in 1979 but never ratified by the U.S. Senate. But did Reagan really shift American policy to match his high-minded-yet-tough verbal salvos? This is critical, and it is here where the picture becomes a lot less black-and-white than his patter about the Soviets as "the focus of evil."

Through much of Reagan's first term, his policies toward the Soviets were largely along the direction set by Carter. Although Reagan had criticized the SALT II treaty on the campaign trail in 1980, he announced, just a couple of weeks before his "ash heap of history" speech, that he would abide by the limits of the nuclear pact "as long as the Soviet Union showed equal restraint." Also, it was Carter and not Reagan who really initiated the large increase in the American defense budget, in 1979, when the Soviets invaded Afghanistan and when détente really began to fade, nearly two years before his GOP successor was sworn in. (It also seems fair to note that Reagan even undid one of Carter's harsher anti-Soviet moves, a grain embargo that was bitterly opposed by farmers in the heartland states that the Republicans carried in 1980.)

Reagan's contribution to the direction initiated by Carter, as is well-known, was to take this first change in course—to again spend more on the military as the nation's Vietnam anxieties faded—and to bring the power up to warp speed. As historian Michael Schaller notes in *Deconstructing Reagan*, the new president embarked on a $1.5 trillion five-year spending spree after taking office that was a mind-boggling 50 percent increase in real dollars, raising defense spending as a share of the U.S. gross national product from 5.7 percent to 7.4 percent. Indeed, Reagan came into office with an enthusiasm for defense spending that defied any logical concerns about whether it could be actually paid for; budget director David Stockman later acknowledged that amid pressures to slash virtually every other federal program, defense "got a blank check."

The new weapons that were funded during the unprecedented peacetime buildup were aimed at the kind of cataclysmic conflicts long envisioned with the Soviets, and thus were not particularly useful for the more conventional wars that actually were waged by the United States in the years after Reagan left office. And the Pentagon spending spree would become a huge contributor—along with the tax cuts that mainly benefited the wealthy and corporations—to the massive budget shortfalls that turned America into the world's largest debtor nation. The worst part is that many of the weapons didn't even do what the taxpayers were paying them to do. During the Reagan years, the government spent more than $28 billion to build a hundred B-1 bombers that proved to be so flawed that the Air Force continued to use the aging B-52s that the B-1s (whose contracts were spread out among a number of key political states) were meant to replace. The MX missile, a long-range nuclear weapon later given the Orwellian name of Peacekeeper just months before 1984 actually arrived, would eventually cost taxpayers more than $30 billion, despite a political decision to locate them in existing silos where they'd be easier targets.

Despite the "blank check" awarded to the military and the billions of dollars of waste that predictably followed, it is this defense buildup, along with the 1981 tax cut, that is hailed by Reagan's boosters as one of the two great policy achievements of his presidency, the bold actions that met up with his soaring rhetoric. To believe the myth manufacturers, you must also believe that America's $1.5 trillion spending spree on weapons and Reagan's tougher talk are what caused the Berlin Wall to tumble in 1989 and the Soviet Union to dissolve two years later. But did they?

Today, there are essentially three camps on this question. The most extreme pro-Reagan and nuanceless argument comes from the Pat Buchanans, the Rudy Giulianis, and the Grover Norquists of the world, the version where Gorbachev and anyone else is a mere character actor and the Gipper is all but knocking down the Berlin Wall single-handedly the way that actor Harrison Ford later pummeled the terrorist hijackers in *Air Force One*. The second, more reasonable school of thought, embraced by some historians and pundits with less of an ideological axe to grind, is that the combination of Reagan's harsh words and his determination to lavish an unlimited number of dollars on the Pentagon for weapons that targeted the Soviets did have an impact on the Kremlin—speeding reforms in the face of Reagan's seriousness, increasing Gorbachev's willingness to cut deals, and ultimately leading to the U.S.S.R.'s collapse.

Here's how a leading Reagan historian, Jeffrey W. Knopf of the Naval War College, viewed that hypothesis in an article titled quite simply "Did Reagan Win the Cold War?" Wrote Knopf: "The Soviet Union never increased its military spending to match the Reagan buildup and hence avoiding exacerbating the defense burden on the Soviet economy." In other words, Reagan did not bankrupt the Soviet Union, as the distorters of his legacy would like you to believe. But Knopf adds that "the buildup and the more assertive stance were most significant for how they affected Soviet thinking."

In particular, there to this day is considerable debate about the impact of Reagan's dream for a high-tech shield against a nuclear attack—his Strategic Defense Initiative, or SDI, best known in the popular imagination as a "Star Wars" defense system. Reagan had dreamed of such a system even before becoming president. He may have been influenced, some have argued, by a 1940s Warner Bros. movie that Reagan had starred in called *Murder in the Air,* in which a device called an "Inertia Projector" has the power to stop incoming enemy planes in midflight. If true, the idea that so captivated a mind moved by boyhood imagination and then by B movies jumped to the world stage after Reagan received a 1983 visit from renowned nuclear scientist Edward Teller, who told the president of new advances in x-ray technology that suggested such an advanced weapon, which might shoot down incoming nuclear missiles, was now theoretically possible. Within weeks, Reagan went before the nation to announce his intent for SDI, which he said would "give us the means of rendering these nuclear weapons impotent and obsolete."

Make no mistake. The Soviets, as we now know from declassified documents, saw the Strategic Defense Initiative as a serious escalation and potentially a return to the worst days of the Cold War. Richard Ned Lebow and Janice Gross Stein, who relied on the Soviet papers to write *Reagan and the Russians* in 1994, said that hard-liners in the Politburo such as Soviet armed forces chief of staff Marshal Sergei Akhromeyev did indeed call for their own defense buildup in the face of the SDI plan. Soviet official Aleksandr Yakovlev told them that "Star Wars was exploited by hardliners to complicate Gorbachev's attempt to end the Cold War."

That is a telling remark. It suggests that not only did the Kremlin not jack up its own defense spending to match Reagan's, but that the Star Wars plan and other tough talk may have, for a time anyway, tamped down early talk of Soviet reforms, especially when the younger and change-oriented Gorbachev arrived on the scene, because Reagan's words complicated the new leader's relations with his own hawks.

One of the strongest proponents of this argument, ironically, was the father of the "containment" strategy, George Kennan. Still going strong in 1996 (he was ninety-two at the time), when he wrote *At a Century's Ending*, Kennan argued, "The more American political leadership was seen in Moscow as committed to an ultimate military, rather than political, resolution of Soviet-American tensions, the greater was the tendency in Moscow to tighten the controls by both party and police, and greater the braking effect on all liberalizing tendencies within the regime. Thus, the general effect of Cold War extremism was to delay rather than hasten the great change that overtook the country at the end of the 1980s."

So if Reagan's military buildup didn't cause the Berlin Wall to tumble and lead to the end of the Soviet regime, then what did? Here we have the third camp. Many experts think the U.S.S.R.'s economy collapsed not just because of excessive military spending but because of much deeper structural inefficiencies, as well as corruption. And the last straw may indeed have been a technical advance from here in the United States—not SDI, but the PC, the personal computer. When the high-tech revolution began to really take off in the West during the 1980s, the lack of entrepreneurship under communism became glaring. So did the desire of people behind the Iron Curtain to join the surge of consumerism during the Reagan years. Reagan's official biographer, Edmund Morris, wrote in *Dutch* that "since at least the time of Brezhnev, Soviet realists had been aware that the West was computerizing itself at a rate that threatened to advance the millennium, while Russian shopkeepers in central Moscow were still using the abacus."

This sorry state of internal affairs is what truly motivated Gorbachev in 1985, when he finally took over the Kremlin from a generation of aging leaders that was making its last gasp throughout Reagan's first term. His drive both for reform and for more openness, or *glasnost*, in Soviet society accelerated after the horrific 1986 nuclear power accident at Chernobyl, which exposed tens of thousands of people to potentially deadly levels of radiation and was an international embarrassment.

"The country was being stifled by the lack of freedom," Gorbachev himself told the *Washington Post* in an interview in 2004, when Reagan died. "We were increasingly behind the West, which . . . was achieving a new technological era, a new kind of productivity. . . . And I was ashamed for my country—perhaps the country with the richest resources on Earth, and we couldn't provide toothpaste for our people." The *Post* asked the former Soviet leader if Reagan had been responsible for winning the Cold War. Gorbachev's response, more than once, to the question of crediting Reagan was "That's not serious." That argument was in essence seconded by another world leader who didn't think Reagan deserved credit for winning the Cold War: Richard Nixon. The ex-president, who often gave Reagan advice on foreign policy, told his aide, the future journalist and conservative radio talker Monica Crowley, that "Communism would have collapsed anyway."

In the end, whatever help that came from the United States and the Reagan White House in speeding the pace of Soviet reforms, finally resulting in its 1991 dissolution, came not from his now mythologized hard-line actions of the early years, the "evil empire" speech, the announcement of SDI research, or the new missiles in Western Europe, but from the softening positions and Reagan's willingness to negotiate in his second term. Anatoly Dobrynin, the longtime Soviet ambassador to Washington, said that if Reagan "had not abandoned his hostile stance toward the Soviet Union, Gorbachev would not have been able to launch his reforms and his 'new thinking,' " but "would have been forced to continue the conservative foreign and domestic policies of his predecessors."

The willingness of Reagan and Gorbachev to meet face-to-face and take the measure of each other was critical. In a sense, both men needed each other by the mid to late 1980s. While the Soviets used the series of summits that began in Geneva in 1985 to beat back their hard-liners, Reagan and his aides saw the push for arms control as a way to counter Gorbachev's growing popularity and also to take some of the focus off the president's troubles at home, when the Iran-Contra scandal broke in 1986. Their storied summit at Reykjavik in October 1986—when the two men actually considered a proposal to scrap all nuclear weapons, but which foundered on Reagan's insistence on keeping SDI—did result in greater friendship and trust between the two. It was a lesson in personal diplomacy that, sadly, would be largely forgotten over the next two decades.

But there is something else that is frequently misunderstood, a generation later, about Reagan, and that is that from the day he took the oath of office, there was a constant struggle between his anticommunist rhetoric and his belief that differences with the Soviets could be overcome with high-level personal diplomacy, gestures that were in part driven by his very real fear of nuclear war and the apocalypse. As he recovered from the April 1981 assassination attempt, Reagan sent Soviet president Leonid Brezhnev a handwritten letter urging that they both consider "the very real, everyday problems of the people we represent." His seemingly contradictory drives existed in his first term, but his antinuclear motivations commanded center stage only after the dramatic events of 1983—the Soviet shootdown of a Korean jetliner, the Able Archer near miss, and the very real personal impact of *The Day After*. And because the delicate issue of arms control really does require two to tango, Reagan's loftier instincts had to wait for the arrival of a like-minded Soviet.

Rarely do those promoting the myth of a tough-talking Reagan note that the very next sentence after that 1983 "ash heap of history" line in London was a plea for nuclear arms reduction: "And that's why we must continue our efforts to strengthen NATO even as we move forward with our Zero-Option initiative in the negotiations on intermediate-range forces and our proposal for a one-third reduction in strategic ballistic missile warheads." (Seconds earlier, he'd even offered to give Brezhnev a chance to talk to the American people on TV—if he could do the same in the U.S.S.R.)

Indeed, we've already seen that some of his harsher, and now more celebrated, rhetoric was often intended for audiences other than the Kremlin; his 1987 Berlin Wall speech came when he was seeking to mollify right-wing critics who thought Reagan was going too far in seeking peace, while his 1983 "evil empire" speech to Christian evangelicals was driven in part by concerns that the nuclear freeze movement was gaining traction with religious voters. Around the time of the Orlando address, the National Conference of Catholic Bishops had endorsed a freeze—at a time when blue-collar Catholics in the Rust Belt were the core of the so-called Reagan Democrats vital to his reelection.

Ironically, with each passing year, the dominant message and sound bites that sum up Ronald Reagan to a younger generation of American voters have been "tear down this wall" and "Evil Empire." Can you imagine a CNN retrospective on the 1980s that interspersed moonwalking Michael Jackson and New Coke with a video clip of Reagan declaring, "My dream is to see the day when nuclear weapons will be banished from the face of the Earth"? Of course not, even though the remarkable reduction of nuclear tensions in the late 1980s is the one hugely positive and lasting development from that era that almost everyone—regardless of political persuasion—can agree that Reagan deserves some credit for.

Indeed, the achievements in arms control from mid-1985 through the end of the Reagan presidency are remarkable. Working with Gorbachev, the two men achieved a paradigm shift away from controlling nuclear weapons to actually reducing stockpiles. The 1987 INF Treaty, in which the sides agreed to take the Pershing and SS-20 missiles out of Europe, was the first ever to eliminate an entire class of existing weapons, while their summits initiated the process that ultimately led to the Strategic Arms Reduction Talks, or START, treaty of 1991 and a string of subsequent agreements that have built upon that framework. It is the weapons deals and the reduction of Cold War tensions that probably allowed Reagan to leave office with a relatively high approval rating, which makes it so odd that his popularity is now used by current leaders in pushing militarism.

Reagan's abhorrence of nuclear weapons doesn't square with some of the more hawkish aspects of his own White House years. These included not only the rhetoric, the pricey weapons, and the initial deployment of the Pershing II, but also his support for bloody crackdowns and counter-insurgencies by right-wing elements in Central America, his 1983 invasion of Grenada (the first major offensive use of U.S. combat troops since Vietnam), and his 1986 bombing of Libya, the only major military response to acts of terrorism that were on the upswing throughout the decade. On the whole, there is a common thread linking these seemingly disparate events: the way they were handled has roots in Reagan's reluctance to risk the lives of American troops or other citizens overseas or expose the military to prolonged conflict.

That was, in a sense, the underpinning of the "Reagan Doctrine," which sought to roll back Soviet influence in developing nations such as Nicaragua, Angola, and Afghanistan through massive support of so-called freedom fighters like the antigovernment Contras in Nicaragua—whom Reagan once called "the moral equivalent of our Founding Fathers" despite allegations that the right-wing rebels had been involved in human rights abuses and drug trafficking. Indeed, Reagan's support of these bloody causes—as well as of the ultraconservative government of El Salvador and its death squads—continues to provoke understandable anger to this day over things as horrific as the murder of nuns and other social activists and the discoveries of mass graves. Robert Parry, who was an award-winning reporter covering the Reagan years for the Associated Press, wrote harshly in 2008 that "though Reagan portrayed the bloody conflicts as a necessary front in the Cold War, the Central American violence was always more about entrenched ruling elites determined to retain their privileges against impoverished peasants."

But the Reagan Doctrine was clearly the result of two separate impulses. Despite all the praise heaped upon Reagan for changing the direction and mood of the country after the angst of the 1970s, there was one area where public opinion was simply not going to change in the 1980s, and that was the desire to avoid another Vietnam, with that divisive debacle so fresh in the American mind. While "no more Vietnams" was an obvious battle cry in 1976, when voters could practically still hear the whirring of the helicopters that evacuated Saigon, that attitude still ruled the day when Reagan arrived in the White House five years later. Reagan biographer Lou Cannon wrote in *The Role of a Lifetime* that the president was a politician first and so understood that the American public would not support a dragged-out war in the early 1980s. Cannon said Reagan told aides and told Cannon himself in an interview that the United States would be condemned as a "colossus of the north" if it sent troops into Latin America, and he complained to an aide about the failures of the Nicaraguan Contras and his battles with military hawks at the end of his administration. Reagan said, "Those sonuvabitches won't be happy until we have 25,000 troops in Managua, and I'm not going to do it."

The list of possible military actions that were proposed by aides or cabinet members and rejected by Reagan is a surprisingly long one. He gave no serious consideration to a suggestion by his first secretary of state, Alexander Haig, that he blockade Cuba to prevent arms shipments in the region, as well as suggestions that he invade Panama to remove the dictator Noriega, under indictment for drug smuggling. In 1988, the president wrote back to a sergeant who'd asked him about invading Panama and said Latin American nations "still let us know they don't want our help if it means action by our military—anything but that." Nothing changed—except the nameplate on the Oval Office—when George H. W. Bush went ahead and invaded Panama just seventeen months after Reagan's response was mailed from the White House.

After the June 1985 hijacking of TWA Flight 847 by Hezbollah terrorists in Lebanon, which included the death of the navy diver Stethem, Cannon wrote in the *Post* that Reagan stunned some of his aides, such as the bellicose Patrick J. Buchanan, with his unwillingness to use force in response to terrorism. "Reagan, always more tender-hearted when dealing with real people than with abstract ideas, decided that retaliation in which innocent civilians are killed is 'itself a terrorist act'—a view he expressed publicly at his June 18 news conference," Cannon wrote. He noted that just two days later the president had to overrule a military response to an attack on Marines in El Salvador, and he wrote that "Reagan asked [National Security Advisor Robert] McFarlane whether an attack could be carried out without killing civilians—a yardstick that surprised Buchanan." In fact, avoiding collateral damage to civilians and their property was a cornerstone of Pentagon thinking, and Reagan's, in the 1980s. It would be the self-proclaimed heirs to Reagan's legacy who came up with the concept of "shock and awe," the massive show of military firepower that kicked off the war in Iraq, where several studies have found that the events triggered by the American invasion have caused well over one hundred thousand civilian casualties, and possibly many more.

Despite the frequent acts of Middle East terrorism, the turmoil in Central America, and the tensions of a Cold War, the United States launched only two noteworthy offensive military operations during Reagan's eight years in office. In April 1986, armed with what it considered overwhelming evidence of Libyan involvement in international terrorism, including a bombing in a Berlin disco that killed two American servicemen, Reagan ordered an air strike on targets including the residence of its ruler Muammar Gaddafi, whose young adoptive daughter was reportedly killed. The Libyan bombing was not broadly supported by the international community—Spain and France forced the long-range bombers to fly around their countries—but it was not as controversial as the one episode in which Reagan ordered the use of ground forces in an offensive strike.

That was the October 1983 invasion of the small Caribbean island of Grenada, which had been ruled since 1979 by leftist leader Maurice Bishop, who became a close ally of Cuba. With the island in turmoil after an October 13, 1983, coup and Bishop's murder, Reagan ordered an invasion of Grenada twelve days later. The reasons he cited to the American public were murky—the postcoup chaos, the construction of a new airport that the United States said seemed to be military in nature, even though it had been planned and carried out by British and Canadian architects starting long before Bishop took power, and the large number of Americans attending a medical school on the island. The evidence that the American students were never remotely in danger is quite strong—in fact, the vast majority of the students didn't want to leave and many parents sent cables begging the United States not to invade—but the subsequent military action did claim the lives of nineteen American servicemen, most because of accidents such as a midair helicopter collision and drowning.

The overwhelming use of American firepower, including the bombing of a civilian mental hospital that reportedly killed twelve civilians, was condemned around the globe, and not just by the usual suspects in the Third World who routinely condemn American imperialism (although the U.N. General Assembly did vote to "deplore" the invasion by a 198–9 vote). One prominent figure even wrote to Reagan that "this action will be seen as intervention by a Western country in the internal affairs of a small independent nation," and that she was "deeply disturbed"—that leader was Reagan's closest ally, Britain's Margaret Thatcher.

But the operation was popular where it mattered most to Reagan—with the American voter, and with his reelection just one year away. Just after the military action, the president's approval rating soared in a *Washington Post*–ABC News Poll to 63 percent, its highest level since the months following the assassination attempt. Whatever the military significance of invading Grenada, the political impact shows the intuitive understanding by Reagan and his aides of the electorate's mood in the early 1980s: battered by Vietnam, desirous of an uplifting story about American goodness and might, but deeply fearful of another prolonged conflict and sustained loss of U.S. troops. The Grenada invasion is inextricably linked now in the American memory with a more lethal U.S. troop engagement—the deployment in Lebanon that resulted in the tragic death by terrorism of 241 U.S. marines stationed as a peacekeeping force in Beirut. Many believed, and still do, that Grenada was a hasty response to change the subject from the horrific news from Beirut and the mistakes that led up to it; the real story is less clear, since a U.S. intervention in Grenada had been in the planning phase since at least 1981. But the psychic link is obvious: while Grenada was the positive (for Reagan and many voters, anyway) expression of the deep post-Vietnam undercurrents, what played out in Lebanon was the negative manifestation, the yin to Grenada's yang.

Indeed, the entire history of the failed policy in Lebanon is a reminder of how much the world has changed since the early 1980s. For one thing, the decision to send a multinational peacekeeping force to Beirut was not at first motivated by Islamic extremism but largely to defuse tensions escalated by Israel, with its 1982 invasion into Lebanon and the massacres at two Palestinian refugee camps inside the Israeli-occupied lands. In fact, Reagan wrote in his diary that he was furious when he called Israeli prime minister Menachem Begin: "I used the word holocaust deliberately & said the symbol of war was becoming a picture of a 7-month-old baby with its arms blown off."

But once the peacekeepers, an international force with U.S. participation eventually increasing to 1,800 troops, set up camp, they essentially became sitting ducks in a complicated, escalating conflict involving rival militias and sects, as acts of terrorism increased. At home, the murky U.S. presence led to mounting criticism—one of the most vocal foes of the Reagan policy was a Republican freshman who had been a POW in Vietnam, John McCain of Arizona, who said on the House floor on September 28, 1983, that "I do not see any obtainable objectives in Lebanon, and the longer we stay there, the harder it will be to leave."

Just twenty-five days after McCain's comments, a suicide bomber drove a truck larded with explosives into the lobby of the main U.S. Marine compound in Beirut, blowing the building off its foundations and flattening it. The official U.S. response to the terror attacks was predictably resolute. Vice President Bush toured the compound on October 26 and said America would not be "cowed by terrorists." Behind the scenes, it was a different story. Reagan's advisors realized that weak public support for the Lebanon mission was masked by the Grenada euphoria and that the situation in and around Beirut was becoming even more dangerous, both for the Marines and politically for Reagan. In February 1984, the White House announced "a plan for redeployment of the Marines" from the Beirut airport to ships offshore—in other words, exactly the same type of response that would be lambasted by conservatives today in the similar crisis of Iraq as "cutting and running."

It's interesting that Reagan's legacy builders unequivocally award him all the credit for winning the Cold War—even though the final acts took place after he left the stage—but don't seek to assign him with blame for the fact that Islamic-linked terrorism, with the United States as a target, grew after America's confused and failed misadventure in Lebanon, and with the seeming lack of a clear policy in the region. Reagan has stood justifiably accused, while he was president and since, of too much focus on the endgame of fighting communism and ignoring festering issues that didn't seem to link back to the U.S.S.R. "I don't think there is a great understanding of what motivates the third-world countries or the frustrations they feel," an unnamed Western diplomat told the *Christian Science Monitor* in 1984. The seeds of America's great foreign dilemmas of the 2000s, from the Iraq of Saddam Hussein (covertly supported by Reagan as a bulwark against Iran), and Osama bin Laden and the Taliban, allies in the U.S.-funded struggle with the Soviets in Afghanistan, were planted and allowed to grow during the Reagan years.

In the end, the loose strands of Reagan's foreign policy are knotted by the same things that fueled his presidency in other areas: the odd force of the inner Reagan and his powerful imagination—where fears of Armageddon and his heroic dream to rid the world of atomic weapons came together in ways that could be noble but also fanciful, as in the billions wasted on Star Wars research—and the high veneer of soaring rhetoric that was often undercut with a lot less fanfare by dirty deeds around the globe. Some of the contradictions were amplified by his tendency to personalize everything, no matter how serious the implications for broader U.S. policy.

It all came to a head when a string of Americans were snatched by Hezbollah terrorists in the mid-1980s, in what was for the most part a response to the intervention by the U.S. Marines there. The policy of the American government was not to negotiate with terrorists, but it was on this issue more than any other that the human side of Reagan labeled by the *Washington Post* as "the pussycat," who couldn't bear to know of the suffering of the hostages and their families, rose to the forefront. "Despite his right-wing image, his ideology and philosophy always take a back seat when he learns that some individual human being might be hurt," David Stockman wrote. Reagan fretted daily about the personal fate of the kidnapped and aides "knew that he had a soft spot for the hostages," his secretary of state, George Shultz, later said, and they manipulated that into a series of events that resulted in the great crisis of Reagan's presidency, the Iran-Contra scandal.

Indeed, three-fourths of the way through Reagan's presidency, the commander in chief was not widely seen as material for bronze statues or the inspiration for so many future Ronald Reagan Boulevards. In death, Reagan might become the icon for modern American presidents, but by 1987, while still in office, he was fighting for his political life.

CHAPTER FIVE

PROSPERO UNMASKED

By the summer of 1987, Ronald Reagan had been president of the United States for more than six years—and a majority of the American people was sick and tired of his presidency, ready for it to be over.

In fact, remember that "malaise" speech—the one that a gloomy and uninspiring Jimmy Carter had given to the American people at the depths of despair over runaway gas prices and a stagnating economy with what proved to be just eighteen months left in his presidency? Well, with an identical year and a half left to go, Reagan, if he had been so inclined, could have revisited the topic. For the final third of the Reagan presidency, pollsters found Americans just as worried about the future, and just as consumed with malaise, as in the bad old days of the 1970s. If Reagan had asked voters in 1987, "Are you better off now than you were eight years ago," the most common answer would have been "Not really."

In early July of that year, a *Washington Post*–ABC News poll found that 62 percent of Americans thought that "things have gotten pretty seriously off on the wrong track." That was the highest number in the five years since the *Post* and ABC had been asking the question, a period that overlapped with the double-digit unemployment rates of the president's first term, and Reagan's pollster Richard Wirthlin, who'd been asking the "right track, wrong track" question since the Carter years, said at the time that the numbers were comparable with the late 1970s. And the "wrong track" number stayed in positive territory for much of the final third of Reagan's presidency.

Whatever euphoria might have been created by Reagan's first-year tax cut, by the drop in inflation, and by the economy's sharp bounce back from the down cycle of the late 1970s and the early 1980s had all but worn off—replaced by voter anxiety over the steady decline of U.S. manufacturing, the erosion of economic clout to overseas rivals, and the reversal that had made America a debtor nation for the first time since World War I. On the foreign policy front, Reagan's talks with Soviet leader Mikhail Gorbachev were at a stage in 1986–87 that left few satisfied; the president's conservative base worried that the arms negotiations were a form of appeasement, while there was not yet any progress for liberals to rally around. And those issues were secondary to public outrage over the Iran-Contra scandal. The scandal confirmed the worst thoughts of critics who viewed Reagan, then seventy-six, as dangerously out of touch, and rocked his supporters' belief in the president's integrity. Reagan's personal popularity and a reservoir of goodwill sustained him—but just barely. "Oh yes, they like me," the president reportedly told his aides. "They just don't believe me."

And Reagan's low poll numbers were before the record 508-point one-day drop in the Dow in October 1987, which jolted public confidence even further. A few days after the 1987 crash on Wall Street, veteran *Washington Post* columnist David Broder wrote that it would surely deepen the ennui he'd uncovered the prior spring when talking to voters, who complained that "companies were closing and jobs were being lost through mergers and acquisitions, shifts to overseas sites or foreign competition. The voters we met were spontaneously linking the worsening of America's competitive position in the world, the wastrel red-ink budgetary practices of the Washington politicians and the wheeling and dealing of the Wall Street takeover artists as symptoms of a national disease: economic excess." Broder went on to add that there "was an increasing disquiet, a sense that we were living beyond our means, a fear that there would be a day of reckoning."

Some in the media, which had given the White House so much favorable ink for six years and had dutifully channeled presidential photo ops, were now using terms like "failed presidency" to describe the Reagan White House. Lou Cannon, the journalist who covered Reagan more closely than any other and always maintained a balanced view, wrote bluntly after the worst of the Iran-Contra revelations that "all the glitter is gone now, all the magic is lost." By October 1987, *Time* magazine was even harsher, writing after the debacle on Wall Street that the president was "the emperor with no clothes" and that "what crashed was more than just the market. It was the Reagan Illusion: the idea that there could be a defense buildup and tax cut without a price, that the country could live beyond its means indefinitely. The initial Reagan years, with their aura of tinseled optimism, has restored the nation's tattered pride and the lost sense that leadership was possible in the presidency. But he stayed a term too long."

The politicians were just as harsh as the press, sometimes worse. "The Reagan era is over," New York's Democratic senator Daniel Patrick Moynihan said with twenty-three months left in Reagan's second term, and lest you blame partisan politics, Republicans were almost as cutting, especially when it came to the Iran-Contra affair. Newt Gingrich, still an outspoken right-wing firebrand in 1987, said of his party's leader, "He will never again be the same Ronald Reagan he was before he blew it. He is not going to regain our trust and our faith easily."

The same observers who'd seemed so awed by Reagan's vitality—from clearing brush at his California ranch to the contagious optimism of his public addresses—now suddenly whispered questions about whether he was healthy enough to serve out the rest of his term. According to one report from a Washington correspondent for the *Sydney Morning Herald*, senior officials complained in 1987 that in meetings Reagan "often seems distracted and draws cowboy doodles on his notepaper." Current aides and old friends were rushing to Beltway journalists with the same re-ports, that Reagan was weak, out of touch, distracted. "He just shouldn't have run for a second term," an unnamed former White House aide told *Los Angeles Times* bureau chief Jack Nelson that July. "He's an old man, just too old to be President. He gets exhausted too easily, and you can't hold his attention. His staff doesn't tax him because they can't." Six months earlier, a neurologist named Richard Restak wrote a remarkable op-ed in the *Washington Post* that asked, "Is the president suffering from senility?" His answer, intended to reassure Americans, was that "if the president can be faulted for his mental performance, it is entirely likely that the flaw results not from dementia but from laziness."

Still, many in the White House press corps, conditioned from six years of overwhelmingly fawning coverage, felt that despite the growing aura of despair surrounding the Reagan administration, its leader's ceaselessly advancing age, and the little time left in his second term, that the man they hailed as the Great Communicator would find a way to recover. Overseas journalists were not so sure. London's *Guardian* wrote in July 1987 that Reagan was "now viewed as an international absurdity." But most important, as the surveys showed, the president was losing whatever hold he maintained with the American people, who'd given him a resounding reelection in 1984, fueled by the economy's inevitable turnaround, public support for the successful Grenada operation, and renewed patriotism keyed by the summer Olympics (where an Eastern Bloc boycott meant a record haul of gold medals for American athletes). A *Newsweek* poll in March 1987 showed that Reagan's approval rating had plunged from 64 percent to 40 percent in just five months, and even more shockingly, nearly one in three Americans, or 32 percent, thought that the Gipper should consider resigning before the end of his term.

This was not the Ronald Reagan of myth but the Ronald Reagan of reality. The Iran-Contra scandal was a tipping point, because it revealed two very different but equally stubborn facts about Reagan's presidency. One was the simple truth that a rogue operation of previously unknown players like the cartoonishly swashbuckling Colonel Oliver North, the midlevel national security aide who had built up the arms-for-hostages operation and illegal fund diversions to the rebels while Reagan was blissfully unaware of the details, showed to the public what had long been an open secret to the Beltway elites—that the slick White House public relations operation masked a highly disorganized decision-making process that started with Reagan's disengaged style and was increasingly manipulated by aides with their own agendas. But more importantly, Iran-Contra seriously weakened the personal bond of trust that many Americans held with Reagan, and that breakage forced many voters to confront an even more basic problem that they and the press had been able to ignore for a term and a half—that majorities disliked his actual policies.

Indeed, Reagan's broad focus on the economy, particularly tax rates, and on confrontation and then negotiation with the Soviets may have been a successful political strategy that carried him through his 1984 reelection and beyond, but by the end of the 1980s Americans were alarmed by the array of other problems that festered on his watch. For one thing, the overarching themes of his presidency were the topics of the GE speech that he'd honed in the 1950s and 1960s, an era when neither AIDS nor crack cocaine even existed, and when homelessness was not a widespread social problem. On AIDS in particular, Reagan's lack of leadership was appalling—it would not be until 1987, when the disease had already claimed thousands of American lives, that the president even uttered the word in a prepared speech. To many, the AIDS debacle was a symbol of how the Reagan years were not "Morning in America" across the board, that in pushing his nostalgic and rose-colored vision of the country he marginalized many groups of Americans. The notion of a "Reagan revolution" in reaction to the Carter malaise years offered political cover for a range of secondary policies that were not at all backed by the American people: efforts to roll back the environmental gains of the 1970s (many of those schemes were thwarted, some were not), and a war on organized labor. Although Reagan didn't achieve the real reductions in federal spending that he'd promised on the 1980 campaign trail—again, a matter of public support and political reality—his program of tax cuts and all-out military spending did manage to squeeze social programs nonetheless. The greatest impact fell on the poor, with poverty rates rising sharply in his first two years and ending his two terms unchanged despite economic growth for other Americans. Social programs like nonmilitary scientific research suffered dearly; on March 20, 1985, the *Los Angeles Times* carried side-by-side articles—one on Congress approving $1.5 billion for MX "Peacekeeper" missiles and the other on budget cuts that were crippling biomedical experiments including a promising study of brain-cell regeneration that sought a cure for Alzheimer's, the disease that would ultimately and slowly kill Ronald Reagan.

Despite all this, if one of those "little green men" from outer space that Reagan was so fond of talking about (even in front of Gorbachev and before the United Nations) had arrived on Earth at the start of our new millennium, he would assume from the media coverage and from the tone of our politics that our fortieth president had also been our most popular. That was driven home in articles and commentaries upon Reagan's death in 2004, such as the *San Jose Mercury News* obituary, which said the late president had "survived an attempted assassin's bullets to become one of the most popular presidents in history."

Except that he wasn't.

Over the eight years of his presidency, Reagan's average approval rating in the Gallup Poll was 53 percent, placing him squarely among the middle of the pack among just the modern presidents, let alone on any all-time list. Not only is Reagan's cumulative approval rating considerably lower than that of Franklin D. Roosevelt, but it also notably trails two other post–World War II presidents, Dwight Eisenhower and John F. Kennedy, neither of whom now have active campaigns to become the fifth face on Mount Rushmore. In fact, three other postwar presidents, Lyndon Johnson, George H. W. Bush, and Bill Clinton, had slightly higher approval numbers than Reagan, even though Johnson was essentially run out of office over the Vietnam War, the elder Bush received just 37 percent of the U.S. popular vote when he sought a second term, and Clinton, of course, was impeached while in office. The modern presidents who polled worse than Reagan were Harry Truman, mired in Korea and a slumping economy, and the disastrous three who came right before Reagan—Richard Nixon, Gerald Ford, and Jimmy Carter—a fact of good timing that proved a boon to the Reagan legacy. In fact, the Gipper's approval rating was under water for most of his first two years in office and again for much of his second term. Nor was it true what was also widely reported at the time of his death, that "Ronald Reagan was the most popular president ever to leave office," as ABC News anchor Elizabeth Vargas put it. FDR was more popular right before his death—not surprising with America on the brink of victory in World War II—but also the much-maligned Clinton had better poll numbers leaving office than Reagan.

Still, there is the fact that Reagan's approval rating, so low in the dog days of 1987, did bounce back to an impressive 63 percent in December 1988, right before he handed the keys to the Oval Office to George H. W. Bush. That high poll number at Reagan's departure would become a cornerstone in the foundation of his future legacy, so in hindsight it's important to understand what was really going on in the American mind as Reagan prepared to retire. For one thing, the personal popularity of this genial man who was dubbed "the Teflon president" for his ability to deflect blame—onto his aides, for example, in the case of the Iran-Contra scandal—clearly inspired what amounted to a reverse honeymoon at the end of the presidency. The press and the public, after a decade of failure and disappointment under Nixon, Ford, and Carter, simply couldn't brook the idea of yet another failed American presidency, which is why Reagan was both rewarded for his unflappable optimism but also ultimately not punished by a weary nation for the constitutional abuses of Iran-Contra, which were arguably worse than Watergate. In a sense, the rise in Reagan's approval rating in his final months was a bit like what Wall Street calls "a relief rally"—relief that a personally likable president who'd shown such severe signs of aging and drift had made it successfully all the way through eight years, the first to serve two full terms since Ike.

But there was something else at work. In the last two years, Reagan clearly moved to the center, even the center-left on some critical issues. In part, he had to. Democrats posted solid gains in the midterm elections of 1986, as the president's popularity waned, and even took back control of the Senate, which they had lost when Carter was trounced in 1980. The solid Democratic majority on Capitol Hill, coupled with an increasingly weakened presidency, forced the pragmatic side of Reagan to the forefront during this final phase of his presidency. He signed on to a sweeping tax reform bill that did strengthen his cherished tax breaks for the wealthy, lowering them from 50 percent to 28 percent, but otherwise was surprisingly progressive; it actually increased levies on corporations and essentially eliminated income taxes for the poorest Americans. Although he tried in 1987 to push fiery conservative appeals judge Robert Bork onto the Supreme Court, he was ultimately forced to settle for centrist justice Anthony Kennedy, who remains a moderating force to this day. Of course, the ultimate move to the center, and the one that may have gained him the most political goodwill, was his pact with Gorbachev to eliminate intermediate-range nuclear weapons.

But on top of that, the American public may well have also been relieved by the end of 1988 that Reagan never fully carried out the conservative revolution that he had promised since his "A Time for Choosing" speech a generation earlier, and that seemed even more likely as he forged a new alliance in his 1980 campaign with a rising movement of Christian fundamentalists based heavily in the Sunbelt. Despite his strong words against legalized abortion, he invested no real political capital either on the so-called right-to-life movement or other pet causes of the religious right, to the point where some early enthusiastic backers soured on the Reagan presidency. As we've already seen, while he squeezed the umbrella of social programs that traced back to LBJ's Great Society, Reagan and his administration didn't have the political will or power to actually reduce federal spending or the government payroll, nor did he dare diminish the core programs of FDR's New Deal. Instead he helped to preserve Social Security for a couple of generations. Given three selections for the Supreme Court, Reagan chose one hard-core conservative in Antonin Scalia, but two moderates in Kennedy and the first-ever woman justice, Sandra Day O'Connor.

Undoubtedly, millions of Americans wanted to like Reagan, wanted the president to leave Washington on a high note—and he did. But in the end, that would not have happened if the promised Reagan revolution had actually succeeded. Instead, many Americans decided after eight years that it was okay to like Reagan the man because his revolution—which most voters never really wanted in the first place—was largely a flop.

That fact, simple yet somewhat counterintuitive, would help conservatives to begin rewriting a distorted legend of Ronald Reagan after a decent interval.

It wouldn't hurt the legacy builders that their conservative icon left behind hours of footage, with the world's most spectacular backdrops, from the steep cliffs of Normandy to the pageantry of the Olympic Games to the red glare of rockets over the Statue of Liberty, to highlight his often soaring words, which in turn celebrated the broad—and noncontroversial—themes of liberty and patriotism, words that were frequently discombobulated from the messy, real-life nitty-gritty world of day-to-day policy.

Reagan's remarkable streak of high approval ratings really was illuminated by the rockets' red glare—the real ones that exploded over Grenada with America's down-and-dirty invasion in 1983. As the president's approval rating moved back into positive territory after nearly two recession-battered years, the Gipper had a remarkable run of popularity and positive press. It lasted some thirty-three months, and it peaked, along with the bounce-back of the economy, right as Reagan stood for his second term against an uninspired challenge from Carter's former vice president, Walter Mondale. In hindsight, the economic recovery, the rally-round-the-flag effect of Grenada and the Beirut bombing, and the Reagan optimism probably would have propelled the Republican to victory in 1984 even with a fairly conventional and lethargic campaign. Instead, the president's advisors sensed a longing for public spectacle, even exhilaration, coming after decades of turmoil and bad news, and they exploited that desire in ways that no president before them had done.

Reagan's emotional speech on June 6, 1984, the fortieth anniversary of D-Day, at the Pointe du Hoc memorial to the Army Rangers who scaled the cliffs of Normandy was heavily promoted by the president's image team, headed by aide Michael Deaver, who leaned on the hosts from the French government to move up the ceremony to coincide with the network morning shows on American TV. The president was more performer than politician that day, misting up as he said that "the air was dense with smoke and the cries of men, and the air was filled with the crack of rifle fire and the roar of cannon."

It was arguably the most effective speech of Reagan's first term, and, as if it were a tie-in to a Madison Avenue marketing blitz, its appeal to narrative and emotion went hand in hand with a revolutionary TV spot that remains a vital part of his legacy to American politics: "Morning Again in America." Going into the 1984 race, Reagan's team, including Nancy Reagan, who took a keen interest in how her husband was portrayed on television, seemed to sense instinctively what few other political tacticians did, that Madison Avenue was latching on to new ways to use emotion rather than facts to sell products, and that these techniques could work just as well for a politician as they could for soda pop. The Reagan campaign assembled an all-star lineup of ad execs and producers called the Tuesday Team for the 1984 campaign; its guru was an iconoclastic San Franciscan named Hal Riney who had no political experience and was tapped because of an ad he'd written for Yamaha motorcycles that was radical for its time in trying to create a mood about the choppers with virtually no information about the product.

"If you're going to sell the soap, you better see the bar first," Reagan reportedly told the ad team when he met them. One lengthy *Washington Post* story describes the style of Riney (who died in 2008 at age seventy-five) as "luscious photography, wryness, understatement, an appeal to the senses rather than the intellect." That would certainly describe the "Morning Again in America" ad, filmed in the small Victorian towns of Riney's Northern California. There is some concession to the realities of 1980s politics, with narration that refers to lower interest rates and infla-tion, but the voiceover (by the avuncular-sounding Riney himself) is clearly secondary to the feel-good video that includes a wedding, a family moving into a new home, and people hoisting American flags, including a young girl who appears to be the only African-American in the spot. The team's media director, Doug Watts, said in an internal memo the ad was targeted at "the slightly upscale voter" who had done well under Reagan. Mondale, in contrast, ran traditional commercials that attacked Reagan for the deficit. In November, Mondale would win only his home state of Minnesota, while Reagan won the other forty-nine.

That same summer, Reagan also basked in the glory of the 1984 sum-mer Olympic Games held in his old stomping grounds of Los Angeles; thanks to the boycott by the Soviets and thirteen allies, these Olympics were to sports what the Grenada invasion was to modern warfare, with the United States winning eighty-three gold medals, more than four times the next closest competitor. Reagan didn't overly politicize his appear-ance at the opening ceremony, but a dozen years later Deaver told the *New York Times* "it was part of 'Morning Again in America'"—the "U-S-A!" chants so prevalent at the games carried over the next week to the GOP convention in Dallas, where Reagan was renominated.

Indeed, the flag-waving worked so well that it was amped up at the start of Reagan's second term, which was the zenith of his public ap-proval. By 1986, the economy was continuing its long, slow climb out of the deep trough of the Carter and early Reagan years, and weakness in OPEC had caused a steep drop in the price of oil, which had driven so much of the 1970s malaise; in April, a majority of the American public responded enthusiastically to Reagan's one and only military answer to terrorism, the bombing attack on Libya. That July 4 weekend, with Rea-gan's approval rating around 70 percent, New York City staged a hun-dredth birthday party for the Statue of Liberty that took the blurring line between pageantry, politics, pomp, patriotism, and the presidency to new and dizzying heights.

ABC had paid $10 million to stage and to produce a Liberty Weekend extravaganza that was like the glory and decadence of imperial Rome rolled together with state-of-the-art computerized wizardry, with lasers soaring over the multihued glow of the century-old statue. Two years later, the *Boston Globe* would marvel at it all, writing in hindsight, "Who cannot recall the pictures from that Thursday night, bouncing off transponders, sucked up by earth stations: the soft summer darkness, the blizzard of fireworks, and Ronald Reagan's face on the tube, melding with an image of glowing Lady Liberty, until the two became one." But the *Globe* also noted it was clear by weekend's end that it had all gone too far, that there were empty seats at the Meadowlands and clearly "the need for restorative pageantry had passed."

But the mainstream media, which seemed in a daze for much of the Reagan years, didn't notice at the time and remained simply agog. In a cover story, *Time* famously wrote that the president "is a Prospero of American memories, a magician who carries a bright, ideal America like a holograph in his mind and projects the image in the air. . . . Reagan, master illusionist, is himself a kind of American dream."

Master illusionist, indeed. But maintaining the holograph was a two-step dance. The positive affirmation of remembering America's war dead and a string of star-spangled festivals couldn't prevent bad news from happening in foreign hot spots or in an increasingly global economy. That meant a White House public relations effort that specialized in changing the subject and keeping reporters focused on the message that the Reagan spin-control teams wanted. Mark Hertsgaard noted in his press study *On Bended Knee* that when polls showed that a steep two-thirds of Americans didn't like Reagan's education policies, he didn't change his program but launched a series of some twenty-five stage-managed events in schools— and the poll numbers soon reversed. Meanwhile, the decision to withdraw the Marines from Lebanon, one of the more important events of his first term, was announced in a handout in California late in a day when the president was on his ranch and other top aides had all left for the day.

The nonstop PR offensive spin got to be too much for one deputy

White House press secretary, Leslie Janka, who quit in protest after reporters were barred from covering the 1983 invasion of Grenada. "The whole thing was PR," Janka told Hertsgaard of the Reagan presidency. "This was a PR outfit that became President and took over the country. And to the degree then to which the Constitution forced them to do things like make a budget, run foreign policy and all that, they sort of did. But their first, last, and overarching activity was public relations."

The Grenada operation indeed proved to be the place where deadly force and PR spin first met. The Pentagon's decision not to embed any journalists with combat troops in the first couple of days of the assault was unprecedented; with the public clamoring for any kind of information about the fight, the only initial video footage of the invasion was what the government fed to the TV networks, which didn't include much in the way of combat, let alone the mishaps that killed nineteen American soldiers. Indeed, Grenada created a new war template—heavily sanitized, easily winnable, boosting the president's popularity—that would later be reflected in the public imagination in satires such as 1997's *Wag the Dog.* Top Reagan public relations aide Deaver later admitted to Hertsgaard that he had backed the Grenada assault in part because "it was a good story" and added that "I think this country was so hungry for a victory, I don't care what the size of it was, we were going to beat the shit out of it."

The jingoistic military moves, the glow of hyperpatriotism, and the pure plays for public emotion, held together by the glue of Reagan's personal popularity and skills as a performer in the public eye, were critical to cementing the president's popularity in the mid-1980s, because of a dirty little secret so rarely reported in the press. The majority of voters disagreed with Ronald Reagan on most of the major issues facing America, from the time he took the oath of office until the day he left.

Two academics, Thomas Ferguson and Joel Rogers, published a remarkable article in *The Atlantic* in May 1986 called "The Myth of the American Turn to the Right," which looked at a number of polls taken from the New Deal through the first five years of the Reagan administration. They showed that, if anything, the American public had grown slightly more liberal, that large numbers thought that business should be regulated and supported the kinds of federal programs that the White House wanted to cut or eliminate. The authors showed that while broad

Reaganesque appeals against big government and for free markets might resonate with voters, "when it comes to assessing specific government programs or the behavior of actual business enterprises, however, they support government spending in a variety of domestic areas and are profoundly suspicious of big business."

They noted a *Los Angeles Times* poll from 1982 on regulation that showed that Americans favored keeping existing rules instead of Reagan-backed rollbacks on a broad range of issues that included the environment (49 percent to 28 percent), industrial safety (66–18), the teenage minimum wage (58–29), auto emission and safety standards (59–29), federal lands (43–27), and offshore oil drilling (46–29). By 1983, the number of Americans who said they favored even stricter environmental regulations, regardless of cost, had increased to 58 percent. Even after Reagan's landslide in 1984, the authors noted, only 35 percent of Americans favored substantial cuts in social programs to reduce the deficit, and as late as 1986, according to a *New York Times*–CBS News poll, "fully 66 percent think the Government should spend money now on efforts similar to those of the Great Society programs to help the poor people in the United States." Ferguson and Rogers found polls showed strong public support during the Reagan years for legalized abortion and the ultimately unsuccessful Equal Rights Amendment, and against prayer in schools. Public support for affirmative action was now in the majority in the 1980s and continued to increase. Support for defense spending, which rose briefly during the end of the Carter administration because of the Iran hostage crisis and the Soviet invasion of Afghanistan, had fallen back down by Reagan's second term, and of course an overwhelming majority favored a freeze on nuclear weapons. The authors presented strong evidence that Reagan's 1984 landslide was predicated on one thing, what a few short years later would be immortalized as "it's the economy, stupid." The 1981–82 recession, followed by the roaring recovery, mirrored the 1936 landslide enjoyed by FDR as he battled the Great Depression.

For six years, Reagan had also survived this remarkable bit of public schizophrenia mainly because of one thing: much of that public liked him and trusted him. They were able to focus on the feel-good hocus-pocus of the photo ops and carefully staged events they saw on the nightly TV news, and in a strange way, you could even say that the American electorate shared with the Gipper his willingness to gloss over the seeming minutiae of actual policy. In fact, it was widely reported throughout the Reagan years, from start to end, that the commander in chief was remarkably disengaged, even uninterested, when it came to what disgruntled media aide Janka called the things "the Constitution" required them to do. Almost every inside account of the Reagan administration, contemporary or historical, describes the president as not only a passive participant, glazed over even, when the discussions of national security issues or complicated budget or tax issues rose to the forefront, but as a man who loathed making hard decisions, who permitted internal infighting to fester, or allowed important details to be worked out by aides without his input.

One of the most scathing accounts of such an encounter with Reagan came from an enthusiastic supporter, the conservative historian and national security aide Richard Pipes, who wrote about his first National Security Council meeting in 1981 in his diary, which was later reprinted in his book and then widely circulated by *Slate*'s Timothy Noah:

> RR totally lost, out of his depth, uncomfortable. After making some commonsensical remarks did not speak for forty-five minutes or so; when he finally spoke up it was to sigh "Oh boy"— meaning "what am I to make of this mess?" . . . He did not listen attentively, looking away or staring at the papers in front of him— except when Jeane Kirkpatrick spoke up and he briefly engaged in a dialogue with her. . . . All this—both the substance and human conflict—is above and beyond him. He has not enough of either knowledge or decisiveness to cut through the contradictory advice that is being offered to him. . . .

Still, the inner workings of the Reagan White House were considered unimportant "inside baseball" by most everyday Americans, and not surprisingly so. But this behind-the-scenes disorganization was critical to understanding the scandal that was nearly the undoing of his entire presidency, that could have killed the Reagan myth before it was ever floated: the Iran-Contra affair.

The scandal has been the subject of numerous books and articles, many written in the years immediately following the crisis, when it was understandably assumed that the misdeeds of Reagan's aides and the president's mishandling of the matter would loom larger over his legacy than it ultimately has. To offer a brief overview, it's important to know that the scandal arose from the ashes of the administration's unfocused policy in the Middle East, was fueled by Reagan's soft spot for U.S. hostages in the region and their families, which overrode his stated no-negotiation-with-terrorists policy, and festered with the help of aides with conflicting agendas, some related to policy and some to profit.

In the days after the Reagan administration pulled the Marine contingent from the Beirut airport, terrorist groups active in the region, particularly Hezbollah, a Shiite organization with close links to Iran, stepped up their hijacking of Westerners in Lebanon, especially of Americans. Most notably, just thirty-eight days after the Marines left the city, Islamic extremists kidnapped and held hostage the CIA station chief in Beirut, William Buckley. Buckley's fate was not immediately known; he was ultimately tortured and killed. But by 1985, some six Americans were held hostage in Lebanon, and administration officials came to believe that dealing with Iran was key to winning their release. At the time, Iran was also engaged in a protracted war with Saddam Hussein's Iraq; the Iranian regime, despite its ongoing hostility to the United States, was desperately in need of military equipment, and some aides saw this as a way to forge ties with moderate Iranians.

But the Iranian operation, encouraged by Israel and operated by a series of upper midlevel aides, including two national security advisors, Robert McFarlane and John Poindexter, and by the colorful Colonel Oliver North, a military aide to the National Security Council, was an unmitigated disaster. It was with North's involvement that the operation migrated into riskier territory, with the American representatives now working directly with the Iranians and the added twist that millions of dollars in profits from the off-the-books operation would now go to aid the Contras fighting the Nicaraguan government. Congress, reflecting the public's disapproval of the Reagan policies in Central America, had passed the Boland Amendment, which sought to block the government from funding these right-wing rebels, but that only inspired White House efforts to circumvent it.

Had Reagan, or any leader, been completely on top of the increasingly complicated Iran-Contra machinations, he would have realized its enormous destructive potential. The Iran-Contra affair was a serious threat to his integrity, since Reagan—elected, let's not forget, in the shadow of the Iranian hostage crisis that had so undermined Carter—had pledged on numerous occasions that he would never negotiate with terrorists. It was also a deeply corrupt enterprise, with several of the American and Middle Eastern intermediaries accused of runaway profiteering. And it was also arguably unconstitutional, because of the secret effort to circumvent the congressional action on Nicaragua. And worst of all, although two American hostages, Lawrence Jenco and David Jacobsen, were freed during the operation, three more U.S. citizens were abducted in the fall of 1986, presumably to replace the ones released. Simply put, the arms-for-hostages ploy didn't even work on its most basic mission.

And when the operation imploded, partly because of an article in the Arab press and partly when an American's plane was shot down over Nicaragua aiding the Contras, Reagan found himself in quite a bind. His initial response—to deny that arms had been traded for hostages—collapsed with the report of the so-called Tower Commission, which he'd asked to investigate it. Now, if he admitted knowing the details of Iran-Contra, he could be accused of taking part in illegal activity (ultimately some fourteen administration officials were indicted) and even increase his possible exposure to impeachment. On the other hand, if Reagan pressed that he was unaware of the arms-for-hostages moves or the Contra funds diversion, he'd be confirming some of the harshest criticisms of his presidency: that he was uninformed and out of touch, and possibly not even up to the job of commander in chief.

It would be the latter. "A few months ago I told the American people I did not trade arms for hostages," he said in a nationally televised address on March 4, 1987. "My heart and my best intentions still tell me that's true, but the facts and the evidence tell me it is not." The words would have sounded utterly ridiculous coming from any other man who'd sat in the Oval Office, but with the one-of-a-kind president who was named Ronald Reagan, his bizarre admission was enough to salvage his presidency, albeit in a greatly weakened state. His approval rating plunged twenty points while the affair played out, but rebounded slightly after the speech. Just fourteen years before, the media, Congress (even some Republicans), and a majority of the public had turned against a president whose administration had trashed the Constitution, committed illegal acts, and covered them up. A scholar could make the case—and some have—that the abuses of Iran-Contra were worse than Watergate, a deliberate scheme to undermine a Democratic Congress. The Reagan administration's violation of laws that barred weapons deals with Iran and aid to the Contras arguably made Nixon's abuses seem more like the "third-rate burglary" that Nixon's aides famously claimed it was.

But the impeachment of Ronald Reagan was never seriously on the table. His apparent befuddled state about the doings of his close aides clearly helped his case, but more important was the desperation of the American people and the pols to see the nation have a successful, completed presidency after the failures of Nixon, Ford, and Carter. As the new Speaker of the House in 1987, Texan Jim Wright would have been obligated to oversee the impeachment of Reagan, and he candidly admitted a few years after the fact that he just didn't have the stomach for that, and that the congressional investigations of Iran-Contra that did take place were therefore rushed. "I hoped that there would not be discovery of an impeachable offense," Wright told reporters in 1993. "I didn't want to focus on such a divisive subject. I may have bent over backwards in error."

In 1990, legendary investigative reporter Seymour Hersh wrote a lengthy investigation of the Iran-Contra probe, focused on how the rules and timing were rigged to avoid finding any culpability for Reagan. Hersh explained the ground rules, set down two months before Reagan himself came clean on what he knew: "At an early caucus in January [1987], according to one participant, the Senators reached one easy consensus. 'We don't want to go after the President,' the participant said. 'He was too old,' with too little time left in office. The Senators 'honestly thought that the country didn't need another Watergate. They were urgently hoping to avoid a crisis.' There was yet another consensus, the witness added: the President did not have the mental ability to fully understand what had happened."

Reagan's own pollster, Richard Wirthlin, had told the *New York Times* in 1984 that the president's bond with the voters was a kind of "social contract"—that is, "the giving of a stewardship to a President based upon trust, confidence and congruence with a system of beliefs, rather than a congruence with a set of articulated policies." The Iran-Contra affair all but shattered that bond.

Even so, Reagan benefited greatly from desire to move on from the turmoil of the 1960s and the 1970s, and from lowered expectations. "If he just stayed out of war, and avoided a major depression, almost anybody would have that rating after what we've been through," the late historian Stephen Ambrose said in 1989 of Reagan's end-of-term rebound. The public's priorities were prosperity and peace, and so the overall, albeit uneven, economic expansion and the rise of Soviet reformers in the second half of the 1980s was pleasing enough to millions of Americans, even as many other problems swirled under Reagan's rule. In the focus on those "slightly upscale voters" who wanted to celebrate "Morning Again in America," millions more were left out of the picture during the 1980s.

Few blacks have fond memories of the Reagan years. Although the anecdotal evidence is strong that Reagan lacked personal prejudice against blacks, the man whose politics were firmed up during the 1960s white working-class backlash to urban riots governed with a callousness toward African-Americans that was breathtaking at times, leading directly to an insurgent 1984 presidential run by the Reverend Jesse Jackson. Notoriously, Reagan kicked off his 1980 general election campaign at the Neshoba County Fair in Mississippi, a stone's throw from where three civil rights workers had been murdered in 1964, and he did so with an appeal for "states rights," which carried the echoes of the segregation era. He met rarely as president with key black leaders, appointed 66 percent fewer African-Americans to federal posts than Carter had, and sought to weaken the 1982 renewal of the 1965 Voting Rights Act, a measure he'd opposed as a California gubernatorial candidate. He did sign the 1983 law making Martin Luther King, Jr.'s birthday a federal holiday, but only after confessing his reluctance to a conservative backer, stating in a letter that "I have the reservations you have but there the perception of too many people is based on an image not reality." Conversely, you could also say that black hostility toward the administration may have been based on reality, not image; in 1988 the National Center for Health Statistics reported the alarming fact that life expectancy for blacks had fallen for two years in a row even as it continued to rise for whites. That had never happened before, and some experts believed that persistent poverty was a factor. Politically, exit polls showed that Reagan's low standing with black voters surely did not improve after four years in the White House. The 1984 exit polls showed him with between 9 and 12 percent of the African-American vote, roughly the same as 1980.

For that matter, few gays feel nostalgia toward the Reagan years, either—particularly because of the crisis caused by the rapid spread of AIDS. Acquired Immune Deficiency Syndrome was first noted by the federal Centers for Disease Control in June 1981, and the disease was named and widely publicized through the media in the following year—but was personally ignored by Reagan for his entire first term. The key agencies that could help in the fight, including the CDC and the National Institutes of Health, were hamstrung by budget cuts. "Our government's response to this disaster has been far too little," the CDC's top AIDS researcher wrote in April 1983. As with blacks, the Hollywood-nurtured Reagan appears to not have been personally intolerant of homosexuals—his gay White House interior decorator and male partner even stayed together in the Reagans' living quarters in 1984. But as with so many other things, it also took a Hollywood event to inspire Reagan to action, in this case the death of his friend Rock Hudson, who succumbed to the disease in 1985. A few years later, Reagan's personal physician, Brigadier General John Hutton, told the *Seattle Times* shortly after the president left office that before Hudson's death, Reagan "accepted it like it was measles and it would go away." (Ironically, Hutton also disclosed that Reagan himself was tested for AIDS in January 1987, because of his blood transfusion after the 1981 assassination attempt.) Reagan didn't mention AIDS in a prepared public speech until 1987, and his proposals were seen by many as too little, too late. By the end of that year, more than twenty-nine thousand Americans—predominantly gays and minorities—had already been killed by the disease.

With so much focus on the core issues of the economy and the Soviet Union, and especially with the passage of time, it's easy—at least not impossible—to forget all the issues that were on the plate of the White House during the 1980s, and how unpopular or unsuccessful many of those policies were. One of the hallmarks of the Reagan years was a rise in homelessness, an issue that wasn't even on the political radar screen at the start of his presidency. What happened was in many ways a perfect storm. The deinstitutionalization of the mentally ill that started in the 1970s added to the homeless problem, but so did federal policies. Some of the programs that Reagan did succeed in shrinking in real dollars were those that might have ameliorated the numbers of people in the streets, including aid to cities and several low-income housing programs that were slashed even as the poverty rate rose in the early 1980s. To many, the twist of the knife came from the president's seemingly callous attitude, reminiscent of his lame joke about America's hungry "on a diet" a generation earlier. There "are always going to be people" who live in the streets by choice, Reagan told ABC's David Brinkley less than a month before he left office. "There are shelters in virtually every city, and shelters here [in D.C.], and those people still prefer out there on the grates or the lawn to going into one of those shelters." Even Reagan's daughter, Patti Davis, said later she was ashamed of her father's attitude.

Crime rose in America's cities as well during the Reagan years, with localities like Washington, D.C., and New York marching toward all-time record murder rates, even as the 1980s were marked by a steep rise in prison populations. The biggest factor in the rising homicides was an inner-city drug epidemic, fueled by growing trafficking of the new, powerful crack cocaine. Ironically, it was Reagan who had come to office with the promise of a war on drugs, calling for "a sustained, relentless effort to rid America of this scourge by mobilizing every segment of our society against drug abuse," but his actual programs tended to fight this war with few federal dollars. Nancy Reagan, with her famous "Just say no" campaign, made the issue her pet cause as first lady, and while her husband backed low-cost punitive measures like mandatory drug testing and ultrastrict sentencing guidelines, he also proposed some $800 million in spending cuts, including aid to local law enforcement, in 1987 as the urban crime and drug epidemic was on the rise. Much of Reagan's narcotics program focused on abstinence and retribution, while shunning drug treatment. Near the end of his term, Reagan's war on drugs was called "a sham" by one of his key allies in the Senate, New York Republican Alfonse D'Amato.

On the environment, Reagan's overall record wasn't quite as bad as feared in the first couple of years of his presidency, when many rebelled against fiery right-wing appointees James Watt at Interior and Anne Burford at the Environmental Protection Agency and their efforts to dole out drilling and mining leases on public lands and water down toxic waste rules and policy decisions. But even their more moderate successors dithered on fighting acid rain and on global warming (sound familiar?); one of the administration's last actions, just nine days before Reagan left office in January 1989, was to block the Council on Environmental Quality from directing federal agencies to consider the emission of greenhouse gases in their environmental assessments. On schools, Reagan also shifted gears around 1983 to a more centrist approach, away from his original agenda of abolishing the federal Department of Education and pushing hard for vouchers for private and parochial school parents; he essentially was forced to do this when a federal commission slammed "a rising tide of mediocrity" in U.S. classrooms. Still, there was a strong sense by the end of Reagan's second term that American schools continued to lag other industrialized nations.

By the time Reagan left office, the same polls that showed a rebound in popularity for the president also indicated widespread disapproval of his actual policies. Here are some of the other findings from the same January 1989 *New York Times*–CBS News poll that showed his overall approval rating at 63 percent:

> Mr. Reagan argued that "the poverty rate is down" since he took office, but 48 percent said the number of people living in poverty has increased, while 14 percent said it had dropped. . . . Almost three-quarters of them say crime has increased in the last eight years, and only 4 percent say it has fallen. Fifty-four percent said the Administration has not done a good job of controlling illegal drugs, despite Mrs. Reagan's highly publicized "just say no" campaign. . . . In his speech, the President took credit for sparking a "nationwide, grassroots movement to return quality to our schools," but 39 percent said education has deteriorated in his tenure, while 21 percent said it had improved. Thirty-three percent said the standard of ethics in government had dropped since 1980; only 8 percent said it had improved.

There is something else, though, that may explain why Reagan was able to leave office with the blessing of the majority of Americans: faced with the credibility crisis over Iran-Contra and with Democratic majorities in both houses of Congress, the man who came to office promising a conservative revolution increasingly allowed his pragmatic side to take over. In many ways Reagan governed from the center toward the end of his presidency.

Reagan was never the radical right-winger that some had feared. We have already seen that with the New Deal programs of Social Security and Medicare, but nowhere was it more the case than with the reactionary social agenda sought by the up-and-coming religious right, which received considerable media coverage for working to elect Reagan in 1980. The alliance between the Republican Party and Christian fundamentalists such as Jerry Falwell and Pat Robertson was indeed a major achievement for Reagan and his team, but it was purely a political victory, not a successful policy drive. In fact, Reagan, focusing on the economy and Soviets, most likely held an innate sense that moderate voters supported the rhetoric of "family values" but not actual changes in federal laws governing conduct. In fact, some conservative religious activists grew to become highly critical of Reagan; homeschooling advocate Michael Farris said bitterly that the administration offered "a bunch of political trinkets." Reagan published a 1983 book about his opposition to abortion (the first time a book was ever published by a sitting president) but he never truly lobbied for a constitutional amendment to ban the practice, and he started the strange tradition of speaking to large annual anti-abortion rallies by speakerphone, from a couple of blocks away, rather than in person. Likewise, a constitutional amendment to allow prayer in schools was a Reagan applause line in speeches, but not a policy objective.

In fact, perhaps unintentionally, Reagan ensured the long-term future of legalized abortion in America when he named Sandra Day O'Connor as his first nominee for the Supreme Court, not to mention the first woman ever nominated, in fulfillment of a 1980 campaign promise. Given a short list of female candidates when a vacancy arose, O'Connor, a largely unknown Arizona appeals court judge, was the only candidate he interviewed for the job even though she'd once co-sponsored a fairly progressive family-planning bill as a state lawmaker. The president wrote in his diary:

"Already the flack is starting & from my own supporters. Rite to Life people say she's pro-abortion. She declares abortion is personally repugnant to her. I think she'll make a good Justice." In fact, O'Connor would ultimately uphold a woman's legal right to an abortion, with some restrictions, over a twenty-four-year career on the court. Indeed, the next two Reagan appointees to the Supreme Court were staunch conservatives: Antonin Scalia and Robert Bork. But reflecting to some extent Reagan's political weakness during his final years in office, Senate Democrats and even some moderate Republicans such as Pennsylvania's Arlen Specter rose up to defeat Bork in 1987, only the second time in American history that a nominee had been voted down for purely ideological reasons. In response (after an almost comic interlude in which his second choice, Douglas Ginsburg, withdrew after exposés of past marijuana use), Reagan finally moved to fill the vacancy with a moderate Gerald Ford–era appointee to the federal bench, fellow Californian Anthony Kennedy. Reagan was in part motivated by a fear that the seat might otherwise remain vacant until after the 1988 election. Like O'Connor before him, Kennedy has proven to be a centrist swing vote in the middle of a divided court.

But choosing Kennedy, albeit under pressure from Senate Democrats, was just one of the ways that an increasingly pragmatic Reagan moved toward the center near the end of his presidency. Despite the widespread criticism of his AIDS and homelessness policies, he did eventually make some belated moves on both issues. In July 1987, for example, the president signed the McKinney-Vento Homeless Assistance Act, the first federal law to ever target the problem. As noted earlier, the Tax Reform Act of 1986 was a compromise with lawmakers that—in return for an additional steep cut that boosted Reagan's war against marginal tax rates on the wealthy—was in many ways a progressive document. Not only did it include measures that closed loopholes and otherwise raised hundreds of billions of dollars in new revenue from corporations, but it also expanded a popular program for liberals, the Earned Income Tax Credit, which freed many poor families from paying any income tax.

But Reagan's biggest move to the center-left in the 1986–88 period, as we've also already seen, was his epic push for nuclear agreements with the Soviets. Indeed, in the depths of Iran-Contra, many pundits saw this avenue as the president's only path to political salvation. As the *New York Times* noted in January 1988, "Significantly, Mr. Reagan still seems to have succeeded most where he has allowed himself to be driven toward the center, notably in his emerging dialogue and negotiation with the Soviet Union." Not only did the Senate ratify the landmark INF Treaty removing missiles from Europe during Reagan's last year in office, but the lame duck president and Gorbachev soldiered on in the final months of his presidency; that summer in Moscow they reached a Ballistic Missile Launch Notification Agreement to warn each other of a major missile launch, thus further lessening tensions. Their work would ultimately lead, after Reagan had left office, to a Strategic Arms Reduction Treaty, START I, similar to a plan that Reagan had proposed back in the early 1980s. The interplay between the surprising reforms in the Soviet Union driven by Gorbachev and the willingness of both sides to pursue arms deals played an important role in Reagan's surge in voter approval in those final months. So did the realization that the October 1987 stock market crash had not derailed the broader economy. As some—most notably writer Joshua Green in a contrarian *Washington Monthly* piece called "Reagan's Liberal Legacy"—have pointed out, the widespread public dissatisfaction on other key issues would have been even worse had Reagan not moved toward the center on so many issues.

"Had he not saved Social Security, relented on his tax cut, and negotiated with the Soviets, he'd have been a less popular, and lesser, president," Green argued. "An honest portrait of Reagan's presidency would not diminish his memory, but enlarge it." Yes and no. The truth is that after watching the president-by-way-of-Hollywood in what Cannon called "the Role of a Lifetime," there was little hunger in 1988 for a Reagan sequel. Despite the haze of mythology, there can be little doubt of how Americans felt about the Reagan presidency when they had just lived through it. They still liked the guy, but they didn't like much of what he'd actually done.

In October 1987, a *Washington Post*–ABC News poll asked Americans to choose between these two statements: "After eight years of Ronald Reagan, we need a president who can set the nation in a new direction," or "We need to keep the country moving in the direction Ronald Reagan has been taking us."

Some 55 percent of Americans wanted a new direction from Reagan, wanted the "American Prospero" to take his magic tricks and leave the stage. Indeed, the tumult of Reagan's White House years, and America in the 1980s, was almost over, and a new direction was coming, slowly. But the war for Reagan's legacy was just heating up.

CHAPTER SIX

ROLLING BACK REAGAN

The myth of Ronald Reagan began to take its toll before the Gipper himself had even left the Oval Office. Its first casualty was the man who replaced him: his own vice president, George Herbert Walker Bush.

It had been the senior Bush who, running against Reagan in the 1980 primaries as the former CIA director and party chair with a Wall Street pedigree, so famously attacked his rival's supply-side tax cuts as "voodoo economics." Of course, Bush's line resonated more with editorial writers than with voters in New Hampshire or other primary states in that topsy-turvy political year, and so when Reagan threw Bush a surprise political lifeline at that summer's Detroit convention and tapped him as running mate, Bush went from harsh critic to effective salesman of Reagan's policies at home and overseas (including a seeming record number of funerals), earning Bush both Reagan's backing and front-runner status for the Republican nomination in 1988.

But Bush faced huge obstacles in succeeding Reagan, beyond the simple fact that other sitting modern vice presidents such as Richard Nixon in 1960 and Hubert Humphrey in 1968 had also tried to take over from their bosses in an election and failed. On the one hand, poll after poll going into the 1988 contest showed it would be an uphill fight for any Republican, that the uneven economic gains of the 1980s and the continued battering of the blue-collar middle class had created enormous anxiety over runaway debt and the loss of jobs overseas during the final two years of the Reagan administration; a majority was now telling pollsters that the nation was on the wrong track and needed a new direction.

On the other hand, Bush, despite the backing of Reagan and most party insiders, had a hard time at first convincing his fellow Republicans he should even get the party's nod. Standing in the shadow of the Gipper only illuminated the ways in which he didn't measure up to the Reagan legacy—a tongue-tied and awkward patrician out of Yale's secret societies with a detour through the Texas oil patch, a scion of those country club Republicans who'd been undercut by the Sunbelt-based movement of Goldwater and Reagan. To many voters, he was summed up by a notorious *Newsweek* 1987 cover, "Fighting the Wimp Factor" (arguably, the headline was the greatest self-fulfilling prophecy of all time). What's more, the promise of the Reagan revolution had energized a youthful movement within the GOP—Young Republicans who came of age not during the Vietnam era but the Carter malaise. These new activists loved Reagan but loved Reaganism even more, seemingly oblivious to any evidence of its most outlandish contradictions, especially the idea that you could cut taxes sharply and eliminate a budget deficit at the same time.

The poster child for the new Reaganism at the time of that 1987 *Newsweek* article was a thirty-year-old Harvard grad named Grover Norquist. An up-and-coming College Republican during the Carter years, Norquist, inspired by the California property-tax slashing referendum known as Proposition 13, became an antitax, antispending zealot. In 1978, Norquist and his colleagues were knocking on doors pushing a constitutional amendment for a balanced budget. The fact that Norquist's idol Reagan had created the largest budget deficits in American history and also agreed to a series of tax increases beginning in 1982 didn't stop either Norquist or his fellow tax reformers from plowing ahead. By 1988 their goal had shifted slightly toward badgering the candidates into a radical pledge that no would-be president—not even Reagan himself—had made before, to not increase taxes under any circumstances. In the months leading up to the 1988 race, Norquist had some enthusiastic allies in the right places, including a young supply-side diehard named James Pinkerton on Bush's staff and the vice president's iconoclastic political strategist, Lee Atwater. At the time, the Bush team feared their toughest challenge in the 1988 primaries might come from New York's energetic quarterback-turned-congressman Jack Kemp, who had burnished his supply-side credentials in the late 1970s even before Reagan. A decision was made to lurch to the right on taxes.

When Bush announced his candidacy in October 1987, even as some economic analysts were arguing that the rising national debt and its impact on interest rates had caused the 508-point drop in the Dow that month, he flat-out declared, "I will not raise your taxes, period." Even though Kemp's 1988 campaign faded quickly, Bush found the tax issue a useful political bludgeon against the main rival who did emerge, Kansas senator Bob Dole, even as there were still moments during the first part of the year when Bush equivocated on completely ruling out raising levies. That was with good reason, because a few key Bush aides looking beyond politics and beyond November were telling the vice president that Reaganomics was driving the American economy into yet another recession unless the government's massive borrowing could be curtailed, and that spending cuts alone would not achieve that. An unnamed Bush aide told the *Washington Post*'s Bob Woodward, who wrote the definitive account of the forty-first president's fiscal missteps and antitax promises, "People brought this up at the time, said, 'You know, if you make a statement like that, how are you going to govern?' "

It was an excellent question, but it was overridden by a more serious problem in the summer of 1988: that Bush would also not govern at all if he lost the general election to the Democratic nominee, Massachusetts governor Michael Dukakis. The fact that Dukakis was a bland and remarkably uninspiring technocrat would ultimately prove key to his undoing, but in early 1988 that oddly seemed a central part of his appeal, with so many voters ready to jump off of the ideological roller coaster and the perceived fiscal mismanagement of the Reagan years. The vice president's political aides insisted that Bush—recalling how the tax issue had permanently wounded the Democrats' 1984 candidate, Walter Mondale—would need to counter with a statement that was bold and memorable.

Another Bush political advisor, Roger Ailes (who later became head of Fox News), said that what Bush needed at the GOP convention in Dallas that summer was to slay once and for all "the wimp factor." The vice president should instead summon what Ailes called "the Clint Eastwood factor." But in invoking the Hollywood tough guy cowboy-cop and his penchant for crowd-pleasing one-liners, Ailes wasn't really seeking to re-create *Dirty Harry* as much as he was channeling the Gipper, who famously once quoted Eastwood directly in a challenge to congressional Democrats to "go ahead, make my day."

They brought in Reagan's best speechwriter, Peggy Noonan, who after consulting with supply-side guru Kemp, came up with a line that would electrify the party's young base of right-wing activists like Norquist while carrying echoes of the incumbent president's best rhetoric. Noonan wrote: "The Congress will push me to raise taxes, and I'll say no, and they'll push, and I'll say no, and they'll push again. And all I can say to them is: Read my lips, no new taxes." It was, at the same time, both the birth of the Ronald Reagan myth and the defining moment for George H. W. Bush—yet it still almost didn't happen. His more pragmatic aides, especially Richard Darman, a top budget advisor in both the Reagan and Bush 41 presidencies, kept crossing it out, and Bush himself, according to Woodward's sources, said "You know, do we really want to?" He ultimately rehearsed the line numerous times, stumbling over the dramatic pausing that made the pledge resonate with the audience, a problem that the Great Communicator no doubt would have knocked out of the park. (Noonan reportedly muttered of Bush: "He speaks in gusts!") But Bush trailed Dukakis by as much as seventeen points that summer, and the "read my lips" line was testing off the charts with the campaign's focus groups. The GOP camp was desperate.

The one-liner was the one sound bite that anyone remembered from Bush's 1988 bid for the White House, and his play on the electorate's fear of new taxes—along with arguably the most vicious negative campaign in modern American history—propelled Reagan's vice president to political glory. The fact that voters had endorsed the Gipper's designated successor in November 1988, along with Reagan's 63 percent approval rating during his lame-duck transition two months later, are two cornerstones of the Reagan myth, remembered long after the nastiness of that year—such as baseless rumors that Dukakis's wife had once burned an American flag—faded from the nation's collective consciousness.

But when Bush took office in January 1989, his administration faced an annual budget gap that Congress estimated would run as high as $141 billion, and Wall Street was already getting jittery. According to Woodward, leading Republicans held a meeting at a downtown Washington hotel, where Bush pollster Robert Teeter stunned the others in the room by asking, "How long do we have to hold the tax pledge? Can we give it up this year?"

Ed Rollins, a former Reagan campaign aide who now headed the National Republican Congressional Committee, reportedly was furious. "What do you mean, give it up?" he asked. "You can't give it up."

Replied Teeter: "Well, Darman says the numbers don't work."

Darman was right, and George H. W. Bush, in grabbing so eagerly for the brass ring of Reagan's political magic, had already laid the foundation for yet another failed American presidency. The myth today is that Americans didn't want Reagan's "Morning Again in America" to end, but the reality is that much of the nation's political energies for nearly a decade, from 1987 to 1997, would be devoted to undoing the gnarled economic legacy of the fortieth president, as well as the havoc wreaked on America's cities. By the time the senior Bush left office in 1993 after one of the weakest showings by an incumbent president in U.S. history, the nation had been plunged into a recession while awash in government red ink and lingering high interest rates, angry white blue-collar males were desperate for an alternative to the GOP, and a major American city had exploded in a deadly riot.

In fact, the years that immediately followed the end of the Gipper's presidency (January 20, 1989) was more an era of Reagan reaction than anything else. You would have been hard-pressed to find anyone beyond the hard-core right wing of the Republican Party—the activists like Norquist and ex-Reagan aide Pat Buchanan, who tried to blame Bush's failings on straying from Reagan's agenda rather than the economic time bomb that had been left for him—talking about Mount Rushmore for their hero. The simple fact is that once Reagan and his upbeat, likable persona boarded Air Force One for the hills of Los Angeles, it would be nearly sixteen long years until the day when a Republican would again tally the most popular votes for president, and that would be just barely, for an incumbent "war president" of an America embroiled in Iraq and still reeling emotionally from a terrorist attack.

That's hardly a "Reagan revolution."

It would take a Democrat with a different kind of populist vibe, Bill Clinton, to make good on some of the key failed 1980 campaign promises of Reagan: to bring the federal budget into balance and even, albeit briefly, to a surplus, to finally shrink the government payroll in Washington, to help bring interest rates to a historically low level and oversee an era of longer, more powerful, and more broad-based economic growth than Reagan's 1980s, and to even see optimism return to America's embattled cities. Even so, conservatives did continue to wage a revolution into the 1990s on the playing field where they had proved to be the most success- ful in the 1980s: the political one. The Reagan era may have spawned debt as far as the eye can see, but it also gave rise to a cadre of right-wing activ- ists who were mastering new tricks in an age of new media, establishing beachheads in a rising format called talk radio and eventually on cable TV news. In Reagan's personal popularity (which rose, understandably, with his 1994 announcement that he was suffering from Alzheimer's disease and was leaving public life) and the short attention span of a media-overloaded nation, these conservatives would discover a way to control the past. And by using the Reagan myth to control the past, the right could control the present.

The 1988 handoff of political power to George H. W. Bush helped in launching the Reagan myth. As we've already seen, the nation's mood at the beginning of the 1988 campaign season was extremely restless. A majority of the voting public believed that America was on the wrong track at the end of the 1980s, that the decade had been dragged down by greed and rampant consumerism, that a narrow band of millionaires was running wild while the nation's working class was ever downsized, and that the country was living beyond its means. They told pollsters they wanted a different course than the one laid out by Reagan. And his would- be replacement sorely lacked the glue still holding up Reagan's ever-shaky revolution: the charisma of the man himself.

The seeming desire of the public for change in 1988 inspired a throng of candidates in both parties to enter the presidential race. The Demo- cratic field seemed especially robust, even after the early front-runner Gary Hart was knocked out of the race by a sex scandal, a foreshadowing of the so-called politics of personal destruction. Jesse Jackson continued to build on his remarkable success in enrolling black voters in reaction to Reagan's policy, and Al Gore was a young southern moderate with a very different approach than the Gore who would win the Nobel Peace Prize a generation later. But the party ultimately turned to the mild-mannered Dukakis, who was viewed at the height of his popularity as a kind of anti-Reagan: Harvard-style brainy, detail oriented, embodying a different slice of the American dream, the striving immigrants, someone who showed he could get things done through his "Massachusetts miracle" of helping turn a troubled Rust Belt state into a high-tech beacon. Dukakis told voters that "this election isn't about ideology. It's about competence." On July 21, 1988, Dukakis came to Atlanta to accept the Democratic nomination, declaring: "And my friends, if anyone tells you that the American dream belongs to the privileged few and not to all of us; you tell them that the Reagan era is over and a new era is about to begin." His lead in the polls seemed insurmountable.

Bush and his campaign used several tactics to turn things around. The "no new taxes" pledge—and its plain-talking echo of Reagan's signature issue—was a key part of the plan, but Bush also sent out vague but memorable clues that he wanted to keep the essence of the Reagan program while changing some of the things that voters increasingly did not like about the 1980s. Aware that growing inequality was beginning to alarm moderate swing voters, Bush spoke of "a thousand points of light," his idea that caring communities and the private sector could help out America's neediest without undoing the tax and spending changes wrought by Reagan. More importantly, as insider trading scandals swirled on Wall Street and voters grew wearier of the nation's dividedness, Bush talked vaguely of "a kinder, gentler America." The GOP candidate never exactly spelled out what he meant by that, but to insiders at the Reagan White House it was clearly a thinly veiled, if mild, rebuke of his own administration. Nancy Reagan reportedly turned to a friend at the GOP convention in New Orleans and asked, "Kinder and gentler than who?"

But Bush's campaign proved to be anything but kind and gentle. His political advisors concluded that spring that the only way Bush could woo an electorate that seemed hungry for a change in 1988 was to make the prospect of a Dukakis presidency seem even scarier to the so-called silent majority. They would use symbols of patriotism as a bludgeon. Panels of focus groups of so-called Reagan Democrats from the Northeast who were planning to come home to the Democratic Party were told that Dukakis had vetoed a bill requiring students to recite the Pledge of Allegiance, that he was a "card-carrying" member of the American Civil Liberties Union who opposed the death penalty, and was tied to a prison furlough program that had allowed a black inmate named Willie Horton to kill again. As recounted by Haynes Johnson in *Sleepwalking Through History*, half of the focus group members had flipped over to Bush by the time the sessions had ended. Atwater later said the plan was "to paint him as a frostbelt liberal who is out of the mainstream." The smiling stamp that Reagan had placed on the conservative movement had never fully calmed the angry cauldron of white blue-collar resentment bubbling just below the surface, and with Bush those feelings would boil back toward the surface, a function of his political desperation. The tactics were ugly, including not just the infamous Willie Horton ad and the false whispers that Kitty Dukakis had burned a flag in a '60s protest, but even the suggestion that Dukakis was mentally ill. That was cruelly aided by Reagan himself, who told a news conference, "I'm not going to pick on an invalid." In the end, the biggest boost to Atwater's sleazy tactics was none other than Dukakis, who proved to be a remarkably weak candidate, slow to respond to the GOP attacks while creating his own "wimp factor" with a ridiculous romp on a tank. His core belief that ideology didn't matter was fundamentally flawed, as shown on Election Day, when Bush carried forty states with 426 electoral votes. In 1980, Reagan brought his conservative movement to power on the simple fact that he was not Jimmy Carter; but in 1988, the GOP had lost its ability to ask the middle class if it was better off than four years ago, and so Atwater, Ailes, and company had created a new template for future conservative campaigns.

The way that Bush held on to the White House didn't stop Reagan from feeling his record had been vindicated—even if the facts told Americans otherwise. "So I leave as I came, dead set against any new taxes," Reagan said in his January 7, 1989, weekly radio address, ignoring the series of some thirteen different tax hikes he signed from 1982 to 1987. Reagan told a television interviewer that week that he wanted to repeal the Twenty-second Amendment, which barred him from seeking a third term and the repeal of which he said would be a tool to aid future presidents in controlling the budget. Finally, on January 11, the Great Communicator gave his farewell address from the Oval Office. He said he regretted the deficit, but "tonight isn't for argument." His main message was pure patriotism; just weeks after an election decided less on jobs than on the Pledge of Allegiance, he was pushing for an even greater emphasis on the red, white, and blue: "We're about to enter the nineties, and some things have changed. Younger parents aren't sure that an unambivalent appreciation of America is the right thing to teach modern children. And as for those who create the popular culture, well-grounded patriotism is no longer the style."

Nine days later, the Reagan era was officially over. Minutes after Bush took the oath of office, Reagan walked down a red carpet on the east side of the Capitol and into a waiting Marine helicopter that whisked him to Andrews Air Force Base for the long flight home. Some 1,500 greeted him at the base in suburban Maryland; one held up a sign that read "Air Force One Flies Once More for the Gipper." Waiting on the tarmac was SAM 27000, the same blue-and-white jumbo jet that would eventually loom over the Reagan Library and a future generation of debating would-be presidents. The jet would take private citizens, Ronald and Nancy, toward a $1.5 million mansion in the affluent hills outside of Los Angeles, the purchase money fronted by millionaire friends of the Reagans, the kind of folks who benefited so much from his tax program. During their long flyover from coast to coast, the jet-borne party celebrated the end of the presidency with Korbel champagne and a meal of chicken in lemon wine sauce, rice pilaf, and broccoli florets. Some thirty-five thousand feet below, the American heartland was increasingly anxious and unsettled.

The SAM 27000 flew over people like Larry Prisbylla, a young Pittsburgh steelworker-turned-nurse whose plight had been described in the *Washington Post*—lured into the mills by high pay when he finished high school in 1972, only to see his hours shrink and then his job disappear completely at the height of the 1982 recession. It took four grueling years of college with a wife and a newborn baby to gain his nursing job—at virtually the same pay he'd been making at the start of the decade.

The Reagans' opulent jet streaked away from everyday Americans like Mollie James, who after thirty-three years of work now operated a large metal stamping machine for a company in Paterson, New Jersey, and made about sixteen thousand dollars a year. According to the *Philadelphia Inquirer*, James was just a few months away from losing that job when one of the Reagans' new neighbors in the Los Angeles wealth belt bought out

James's employer, closed the New Jersey plant, and shifted some of the work to Mexico.

As the jet neared its destination in Los Angeles, the Reagans and their entourage glided past citizens like Gil Banfill, a fifty-three-year-old worker at a computer memory disc plant in Orange County who went away for a week's vacation in October 1988 and came back to learn that the high-tech plant had closed down while he was gone. The only job he'd even been offered in the three months prior to the end of the Reagan presidency was one that paid six dollars an hour, barely half of what he'd made before. As the *Los Angeles Times* noted, the unemployment rate in Orange County—the conservative hotbed that had backed Goldwater and then Reagan—seemed low, but most of the new hiring in the 1980s had been low-wage service jobs.

Displaced and disoriented workers were part of the economically divided America that Reagan left behind; so too, were new pockets of prosperity, glistening subdivisions in Sunbelt locales like the exurbs outside of Dallas or Atlanta, mostly white and upper-middle-class enclaves where the low-tax mantra and talk of "family values" in the nation's capital had resonated the most, and where Bush's '88 campaign had piled up some of its biggest majorities. Still, his winning conservative coalition was one held together by the political Band-Aids of flag waving and "no new taxes." All it would take to fracture it would be one large downdraft in the American economy, and with the federal debt out of control and 1980s recovery losing steam, that was exactly what happened.

In fact, the Reagan years had buried several political time bombs for his successor. One of them was the savings-and-loan crisis, the "jackpot" that Reagan had bragged about in the early 1980s. It began to emerge from the shadows almost the day Bush arrived in the Oval Office. By 1989, hundreds of the thrifts that had been deregulated by the Reagan administration had drifted into insolvency, beset by bad management, ill-conceived or corrupt loan practices, and the steep drop in regulatory oversight under the Republican administration. Bush was forced to order a bailout that eventually rose to $150 billion in overall cost, with a good chunk of that billed to America's beleaguered federal treasury. The turmoil in the savings-and-loan industry spilled over into the all-important housing market; by 1991, fewer new homes were under construction than at any time since the end of World War II. Bush told the nation, "Nothing is without pain when you come to solve a problem of this magnitude."

That was especially true when you added this new S&L bill on to the unresolved debt of the Reagan years. In 1990, the American economy moved into a recession as the seven-year expansion of the economy wound down. Compared to other economic slowdowns in American history, the recession of 1990–91 was not a particular deep or long one, but what was unique about this economic crisis was the degree to which Bush appeared hampered and weak. That was because the unrelenting weight of the massive debt left behind by Reagan offered Bush none of the traditional weapons. In the past, good economic times had swelled government coffers, but Reagan's policies had the opposite impact, swelling the debt to nearly $3 trillion while raising the government's interest payments to $260 billion, or nearly the amount that taxpayers were spending at that time on national defense. As tax payments slowed further, the 1991 deficit alone was initially projected to rise past $300 billion, a new record. Some of the deficit projections in the late summer of 1990 were compounded by a huge military buildup in the Persian Gulf, Bush's response to Iraq's invasion of Kuwait in early August. The aggressive answer to Iraq was popular with American voters, but it placed two extra burdens on American customers: a sense of consumer uncertainty for the many months that hostilities loomed, as well as the first spike in oil prices in more than a decade.

For much of 1990, as the slowdown gained momentum, the size of the debt and the government's initial slowness in tackling it—in part the result of Bush's no-new-taxes pledge—caused the Federal Reserve Board, now chaired by Alan Greenspan, to refuse to lower interest rates. The fact that much of the debt piled up under Reagan was owned by foreign central banks meant that Greenspan and other stewards of the U.S. economy had less room to maneuver than in the past. Likewise, a huge economic stimulus package that had been considered by the Bush White House had to be dropped, because the federal dollars simply weren't available. Some Bush aides even blamed Reagan, albeit off the record. "We may have spent the Soviet Union into oblivion and fueled an '80s boom," an unnamed White House official told the *Los Angeles Times* in November 1991, "but now the economy isn't rolling along, and we're paying the Reagan price."

Richard Darman, the White House budget director who argued against the Bush tax pledge in the candidate's 1988 campaign, had been lobbying for a tax increase from virtually the day that Bush took office. That was in part because a federal deficit law, Gramm-Rudman, enacted by Congress halfway through Reagan's presidency, would mandate politically unpalatable spending cuts otherwise. According to Woodward's later account in the *Post*, Darman crossed the "read my lips" line out of speeches several times, once shouting: "He's going to have to raise taxes. Don't put that in!" Bush's new treasury secretary, Wall Street veteran Nicholas Brady, also believed the deficit would have to be tamed after learning that concern about the rising gap had been partly behind the 1987 stock market crash. Bush did manage to avoid hiking revenue in his first year, but in 1990 the economy had worsened to the point that meeting the Gramm-Rudman law, without a tax increase, would have meant slashing nonmilitary domestic spending by 38 percent and defense by 25 percent. Democrats in Congress sensed the upper hand, and they forced Bush to agree broadly, in writing, to revenue increases; the president's aides noted that the election was still more than two years away. After their meeting, Bush turned nervously to Democratic House leader Dick Gephardt and said, "Well, the fat's in the fire."

It sure was. His aides had badly misread the public reaction, a sign of how successful he'd been in selling the "read my lips" line in 1988. "Read My Lips: I Lied," screamed the front page of Rupert Murdoch's *New York Post*. Bush may have also "misunderestimated"—in the term his son later coined—the impact of the then fairly young revolution in talk radio, which was right-wing with a deeply populist bent, hating all political pay raises . . . and tax hikes. One Baltimore host labeled Bush "Joe Isuzu," a popular TV ad at the time starring a habitual liar. Reagan's former aide Lyn Nofziger said, "If I were a Republican senator or congressman seeking re-election this year, I would feel like I had been betrayed." Many said exactly that, including voters. "I think it stinks," Marsha Barnes of Peoria, Illinois, told the *Chicago Tribune*. "He's just like all the rest. They promise you something, then they get in office and break their word. I won't believe him in the future."

Even so, the deal didn't come close to making the debt disappear. The U.S. interest payments on the debt accumulated mostly under Reagan and Bush were a still-staggering $200 billion a year, equal to 3.5 percent of the gross national product. That was money that couldn't be spent on more productive purposes, such as rebuilding the nation's sagging infrastructure or encouraging high-tech research. The accumulated debt, which had been 25 percent of the gross national product when Reagan took office in 1981, was now more than half of the GNP. The recession of 1990–91, the accompanying job losses, and the lingering debts led many Americans to agree with what the *Los Angeles Times* reported in its business section in 1992: "ultimately, Reaganomics was a failure." Barry Bosworth, an economist at the Brookings Institution, told the newspaper that "Reagan will go down as having done a great deal for the current generation, but as having done great damage to future generations."

It wasn't just the debt. By the early 1990s, experts and the public began to notice that a big chunk of the 17 million new jobs added under Reagan were actually females who had become second earners in the household, as middle-class families struggled to keep pace. Other factors drove greater economic anxiety in the early 1990s. The unprecedented wave of mergers and acquisitions in the *Wall Street* era of the 1980s often led the newly joined companies to lay off thousands of workers to make the economics of these big deals work out; what's more, many of these newly "downsized," as the trend became known, were middle managers, exactly the types of mostly male and mostly white voters who were Republicans or GOP-leaning swing voters in the 1980s. Even the many white-collar voters who didn't lose their jobs in this new economic climate were insecure, looking over their shoulder. The despair of the American middle class was best captured by two Pulitzer Prize–winning reporters for the *Philadelphia Inquirer*. Donald Barlett and James Steele, who spent much of those years on an investigative project that was later turned into a book, titled simply *America: What Went Wrong?*. They placed a lot of the blame for the economic woes of the middle class—not just job losses but shrinking pensions, diminished buying power, and high payroll taxes—on decision makers in Washington who had rigged the rules for large corporations and their millionaire owners and investors. Here's how

they described their travels across middle class America in the aftermath
of the Reagan years:

> The authors heard a constant refrain. It was a litany sounded in
> city after city, from Hagerstown, Maryland, to South Bend, Indi-
> ana; from Hermann, Missouri, to Martell, California. Over and
> over, blue-collar and white-collar workers, midlevel managers—
> middle class all—talked of businesses that once were, but are no
> more. Sometimes the business was glass-making. Sometimes it
> was printing. Or timber. Or shoemaking. Or meat-packing. But
> always the words were the same. . . . They talked about owners
> and managers who had known the employees by name, who had
> known their families, who had known the equipment on the floor,
> who had walked through the plants and offices and stopped to
> chat. They talked about working with—and for—people who were
> members of an extended corporate family. And, finally, they
> talked—some with a sense of bewilderment, some with sadness,
> some with bitterness—of the takeovers, of the new owners and
> the new managers who replaced the old.

Ironically, in 1991, when *America: What Went Wrong?* was first published as a series in the *Inquirer,* George H. W. Bush set a record for the
highest approval rating ever for an American president. He was reaping
the benefit of a remarkably quick and relatively casualty-free (for our side)
military victory over Saddam Hussein, which undid the dictator's 1990
invasion of Kuwait. Foreign policy was clearly the number one passion for
the first ex-CIA chief to become president, and in many ways his more
aggressive approach was a stark departure from Reagan. Bush's 1989 invasion of Noriega's Panama was the complete opposite of the Gipper's
diplomacy-oriented approach to the problem. The war that ousted Hussein's forces from Kuwait in the late winter of 1991, a United Nations
operation with America in the lead, had a similar political impact as Reagan's action in Grenada, but more so because the stakes in the Persian
Gulf were obviously so much higher. With Bush's approval rating peaking
at 91 percent after the war, the best-known Democrats were loath to challenge the incumbent; for a time the Democrats who did traipse around

Iowa and New Hampshire in anticipation of the 1992 election were known as "the Seven Dwarfs."

Ironically, it would be far-right conservatives, particularly the most die-hard Reaganites, and a new breed of angry independent, amplified by the echo chamber of talk radio, who would sense the weakness of Bush before the opposition party did. In August 1991, the conservative Heritage Foundation threw a party to mark the tenth anniversary of the Reagan tax cut; Bush was not even invited to attend. One of the guests, the gung-ho Reaganite Paul Craig Roberts, told the *Washington Times* that "unfortunately in America the Republican Party is showing elements of brain deadness." By then, staunch conservative activist Pat Buchanan, who worked for a short time as a speechwriter in the Reagan White House, was already proceeding with the unthinkable: a GOP primary challenge to the sitting president. Buchanan, an isolationist on foreign policy, didn't like the president's actions in the Persian Gulf, but he and his supporters were mainly energized by Bush's abandonment of his "no new taxes" pledge. "George Bush has defined himself," Buchanan declared as he weighed a presidential bid. "He is a big government man all the way."

But Buchanan would not be the only unusual challenger to the president. The growing universe of male-dominated political talk radio and cable-TV gabfests had a new and unlikely hero in a big-eared, twang-talking, and sometimes awkward high-tech billionaire, a political independent named Ross Perot who had never held public office before. Perot went on TV shows such as CNN's increasingly popular *Larry King Live,* sounding not so much like a billionaire but rather the mad-as-hell Howard Beale in the movie *Network.* Perot carried the same zeal to America's ever-rising, foreign-owned debt that Reagan had brought to the tax issue a dozen years earlier. "Now, let's go down to grassroots America where the people are hurting and everybody's saying, 'Why are we in this mess?'" Perot said in a highly rated February 1992 appearance on King's show. "The first thing I'd like for you to do—all of you—is look in the mirror. We're the owners of this country. We don't act like the owners. We act like white rabbits that get programmed by messages coming out of Washington. We own this place. The guys in Washington work for us. They are our servants." Near the end of the broadcast, Perot told King he would consider running for president as an independent if there was a groundswell of support in all fifty states; thousands across the country indeed urged the billionaire to run, as many believed that only someone from outside the political system could fix the nation after Carter, Reagan, and Bush.

The weak economy and mounting right-wing revolt weren't the only chickens from the Reagan years that were coming home to roost in the second half of Bush's term. By any measure, America's cities, squeezed by a decade of cuts in direct federal aid and in programs to aid housing and local crime fighting, were at the breaking point at the start of the 1990s, overrun by a rising epidemic of crack cocaine and a sharp increase in murders that accompanied it. In the fall of 1990, the city of Philadelphia came within days of filing for bankruptcy and eventually surrendered control of its finances to an outside panel. In New York, the number of homicides peaked that same year, with some 2,234 people murdered; when a Utah tourist visiting for the U.S. Open tennis tournament was stabbed during a robbery on a midtown subway platform, the *New York Post* railed at Mayor David Dinkins, "Dave, Do Something!" The worst was yet to come in Los Angeles, where long-simmering tensions between cops and black residents finally boiled over after four officers were found not guilty in the videotaped beating of unarmed motorist Rodney King; the riots that followed stunned the nation and were arguably even more violent than the bloodiest uprisings of the 1960s: fifty-five people died, and rioting and looting caused $1 billion in damage. There were many root causes, of course, for the sorry state of the nation's cities—some social, and some the fault of inept or corrupt local governments—but the mounting problems added to the growing sense that America's social contract was again coming apart.

Meanwhile, Bush was left to deal with the collapse of Reaganomics without any of Ronald Reagan's personal charisma or ability to connect with the average voters. The slowing economy and layoffs of 1990 and 1991 were often met with glib and upbeat-sounding remarks from the president himself. He may have believed that he was channeling the Gipper's trademark optimism, but words that might have reassured voters when uttered by Reagan sounded hollow coming from Bush's mouth. "I am not a gloom-and-doom person on where the American economy will be before long," the president declared in the fall of 1990. For the angry middle class, such statements seemed to reinforce the impression that this tongue-tied Yale patrician did not, in the famous polling term, understand the everyday problems of "people like me." For many, the archetypal saga of the Bush years would come as the 1992 election drew closer. A *New York Times* story about a Bush visit to a national grocers' convention in February headlined BUSH ENCOUNTERS THE SUPERMARKET, AMAZED. Bush was wowed and baffled by an electronic checkout scanner of the type shoppers had been using for more than a decade.

But Bush's failure to bond with the common man didn't evoke an outpouring of nostalgia for Reagan, either. In March 1990, a *Boston Globe* poll showed that Reagan's popularity (59 percent) was lower than the man whom he replaced and whose presidency was supposedly despised; Jimmy Carter was at 62 percent. Given some of the press coverage and commentary about both Ronald and Nancy Reagan in the first couple of years after they left office, it's almost surprising that the Gipper's number was even that high. That same month, viewers were stunned by the release of Reagan's videotaped forgetful testimony in an ongoing probe of the Iran-Contra scandal. *Newsweek* wrote of a "Diminished Ron" and quoted a former aide who hoped Americans would remember Reagan's overall record and "not in terms of the rather pathetic figure we see this week."

But that had been just the latest in a string of blows to the Reagan mystique. The negative publicity started just months after the Reagans moved back to Los Angeles, when the couple accepted a $2 million speaking fee to travel to Japan on behalf of a media conglomerate; no ex-president had ever cashed in like that before, especially so soon after leaving office. Nancy Reagan's autobiography, *My Turn,* was panned by critics as mean-spirited. (Wrote the *Washington Post:* "So hurtful, so embarrassing, so pathetic that it takes your breath away.") The Internal Revenue Service was looking at whether back taxes were owed for designer dresses loaned to Nancy while she was in the White House. Even their hometown *California* magazine called the Reagans "the couple everyone loves to hate."

But the real damage to the Reagan reputation wasn't so much the gossipy headlines as his political and economic legacy, which was about to be trashed in the 1992 elections. For a time, both Buchanan and Perot made remarkable headway in their once seemingly quixotic challenges to Bush.

In that winter's New Hampshire primary, Buchanan drew 38 percent of the vote, remarkable for a challenge to an incumbent president by an ideologue who'd never held elected office before. It was a sign of the deep division within the GOP coalition built up by Reagan and now lacking the one figure who held it together. Buchanan's challenge wasn't really sustainable beyond the retail politics of New Hampshire, but a so-called angry middle was rallying behind Perot, to the point where one poll in June 1992 showed the independent billionaire leading a three-way race with 39 percent of the vote. But there was also a problem with Perot's challenge: Perot himself. He stunned backers by pulling out of the race during the Democratic National Convention (giving a huge bounce to the party's nominee Bill Clinton), then got back in but made paranoid allegations that the Bush team was planning to disrupt his daughter's wedding. Despite Perot's deep flaws, he did still ultimately manage to get 19 percent of the popular vote, a better showing than any third-party candidate since ex-president Teddy Roosevelt in 1912, and a powerful symbol of voter unrest in the wake of a dozen years of Republican White House rule.

There was a void in American politics, and in the end Bill Clinton stepped forward to fill it. In many ways the youthful Arkansas governor, the first would-be president mainly molded by the turmoil of the 1960s, was a true product of the post-Reagan era. He did inherit some of the Gipper's better traits and appropriated some others; his campaign carried an upbeat tone (billing Clinton as "the man from Hope," the name of his Arkansas hometown) while the Democrat also brought a strikingly similar childhood story, raised middle class in a heartland small town, with a series of Reagan-like moves and even an alcoholic stepfather, perhaps behind his need to be popular and forge a connection with many voters. He also learned from the Reagan years how to tap into the battered political psyche of the white working class, promising to end a clearly broken welfare system "as we know it." But at the core of what Clinton promised America was not so much a continuation of Reaganism as a clean break from it, especially when it came to the GOP's tortured economics. In retrospect, Clinton's 1992 campaign came to be famously defined by a slogan on a chalkboard, highlighted in the documentary *The War Room:* "It's the economy, stupid." The cornerstones of that plan were to try to eliminate the red ink of the Reagan-Bush years, to free up more capital for investment on the home front, and to provide the frazzled workforce with a greater sense of security, in part with a national health-care system that would provide not only for the poor but also for the millions of increasingly dislocated or underemployed middle class.

In March 1992, at the height of the Democratic primary season, the Congressional Budget Office issued a devastating report about the widening gulf between rich and poor over the prior fifteen years, showing that the bottom 40 percent of America had lost earning power since 1977, even as incomes rose by 20 percent for the top quintile, and 77 percent for the top 1 percent. Clinton waved the CBO report at a news conference and declared: "The Reagan-Bush policy of trickle-down economics was a fraud, a damnable lie, and a miserable way to cheat our poorest people." Behind the populist appeal, Clinton's economists were also noting that the upbeat economic statistics that were posted during the 1983–90 economic expansion were driven by massive borrowing and a flurry of consumerist spending, not by gains in productivity. In June 1992, the Federal Reserve Bank of New York reported that America's emergence as a debtor nation under Reagan had sapped the U.S. economy of some 2.5–3.5 percent of its growth potential by the early 1990s. The economist Robert Reich, who later was named Clinton's labor secretary, explained in an op-ed that summer that the real problem was not necessarily that America had borrowed so much money in the prior thirteen years, but in how that money was actually spent:

> Only about 14 percent of the $3 trillion debt compiled by the Reagan and Bush administrations has been invested in America's future productivity. While Germany, Japan and many other nations have been building their human capital and infrastructure by spending more and more on them, the United States government actually has been cutting back on such investments. Adjusted for inflation, federal spending on child health, education, training and infrastructure has declined by a third since 1980.

In the end, the only real debate in the 1992 election was whether Reaganomics failed because it was both unfair and unsound, as the Democrats argued, or whether Bush was a failed president because he had betrayed Reagan with his 1990 tax hike agreement. One other thing was noteworthy about 1992: it would mark the eighty-one-year-old Gipper's final time on the campaign trail, a last-ditch effort to save both Bush and his own legacy at the same time. He told a rally in Phoenix that the economy was beginning to turn around (as it indeed was somewhat in 1992, a response to belated interest rate cuts that were the response to Bush's tax-raising budget deal) and dipped into his bag of what could be called political nostalgia, blasting "despairing voices of the doomsday Democrats who gave us the turmoil of the '60s and the malaise of the '70s." But the old magic wasn't working—some in the crowd chanted angrily "four more days" and "no more Bush." Reagan gave them another one of his classic lines, that "America's best days are yet to come."

In a sense, Reagan was right, but those days would not be under the presidency of George H. W. Bush, who garnered just 37.4 percent of the popular vote on November 3, 1992. In independent-minded Maine, the incumbent president actually came in third place behind Clinton and Perot. On January 20, 1993, Bill Clinton became America's forty-second president and began to put his own unique stamp on the Oval Office. Still, some four years after the departure of the Great Communicator, the Reagan years continued to loom large over Washington as well as the nation. The new Clinton administration aped some of the most successful (if arguably, to a journalist like this author, most frustrating) Reagan tactics when it came to public relations, staying on a message of the day and creating soaring photo ops with a knack for what was now known as "spin" that rivaled the best efforts of Mike Deaver and David Gergen. But when it came to domestic policy, Clinton was arguably the anti-Reagan, seeking to undo the damage of "trickle-down" theory but also tackling the Gipper's greatest unfulfilled promise.

By 1996, Clinton was able to stand before Congress and mimic Reagan by declaring, "The era of big government is over." The difference was that unlike Reagan, the Democratic Clinton administration took the task of reducing the federal bureaucracy seriously—and it succeeded. He named his vice president Al Gore to head a "reinventing government" task force that sought to cut both waste and needless bureaucracy, and that was one of the more successful efforts of Clinton's entire presidency.

Ultimately, the Democrat reduced the government payroll from about 3 million when he took office to close to 2.6 million, a remarkable accomplishment since the overall economy was growing (the Clinton administration was also more enthusiastic than Reagan–Bush 41 in removing regulation, although here the record is mixed). In the big picture, federal spending would fall as a share of the gross domestic product while Clinton was president, from 21.4 percent in 1993 to 18.5 percent in 2001.

That was just a piece of Clinton's biggest accomplishment, which had seemed almost unthinkable around the time that Reagan's presidency was ending: bringing the federal budget back into balance. The new president's first budget plan required a lot of arm-twisting among his own party, and it just barely passed in the summer of 1993. It was, some argued, less ambitious than the deficit reduction plan that Bush had signed off on in 1990; the reality was that the two bills, taken together, were the giant steps that unwound the Reagan budget fiasco. Representative David Obey of Wisconsin declared that were it not for the Gipper's 1981 tax plan, "we would not be here today dealing with a bill like this." The Omnibus Budget Reconciliation Act of 1993 raised taxes on the wealthy, with a top marginal rate of 39 percent, and also restored higher taxes on corporations. Military spending, which was in limbo after the fall of the Soviet Union, was also reduced in the measure, but spending in the areas that had been so underfunded in the Reagan-Bush years—things like transportation infrastructure and scientific research—got a shot in the arm.

The bill was surely controversial at the time. A first-term Pennsylvania Democrat from the suburbs outside Philadelphia, Marjorie Margolies-Mezvinsky, would lose her seat by casting the deciding vote for it. However, most experts came to credit the measure with fueling an economic expansion that was more powerful than the one seen under Reagan. The lower deficit created a cycle of low interest rates and economic growth; interest rates were estimated as much as 2 percent less than they would have been had the deficit not been tackled. As 1994 loomed, the federal budget was on the slow path to a surplus, and the economy would soon lift up more Americans than the 1980s expansion had done.

In August 1993, the newspapers were filled with articles about the death of Reaganomics, and few people were mourning—it was as if the wicked witch had been declared dead. In fact, the week after the budget bill won approval, *Time* magazine ran a picture on its front cover not of Bill Clinton but of Ronald Reagan—upside down! The article was headlined "Overturning the Reagan Era" and declared flatly, "The final budget deal brings to an end a bankrupt period in American politics."

For Ronald Reagan, the verdict of history seemed to be in.

Few people realized that a small band of right-wing activists was already working to overturn that verdict—aided by a moving farewell from the Gipper himself.

CHAPTER SEVEN

ENTER THE MYTHMAKERS

In the fifteen months after Ronald Reagan's image appeared upside down on the cover of *Time* magazine, the eighty-three-year-old retired president seemed to fade slowly from public view. It was now 1994, and it was the thirtieth anniversary of Reagan's bold entry into the political arena with his Goldwater-supporting "Time for Choosing" speech. His era was melting into history. The Soviet Union had given way to what was, for a time, a democratic Russia and breakaway satellites; the once heroic mujahideen in Afghanistan were slowly morphing into al-Qaeda; urban crime, crack abuse, and teen pregnancy were back on the decline; and there were early clues that shrinking federal deficits might aid the economy more than his largely discredited theory of supply-side economics had ever done.

Reagan hadn't completely vanished; surprisingly, he found common cause with Democratic president Bill Clinton on a couple of issues, most notably free trade. He had also, perhaps inadvertently, aided the Democrats in the 1994 midterm election by lashing out at ex-aide and Iran-Contra figure Oliver North, who was now running for U.S. Senate in Virginia and claimed that his former boss knew everything about the arms-for-hostages scandal. "I am getting pretty steamed about the statements coming from Oliver North," wrote Reagan in a publicly released letter that clearly, if for understandable reasons, broke his eleventh commandment about speaking ill of a fellow Republican.

That August, a reporter for the conservative *Washington Times* visited the Gipper at his penthouse office in Los Angeles's Century City. Reagan, though now wearing a hearing aid, seemed to be in great health and great spirits, even if the man who once famously blamed air pollution on trees was now apologizing for the thick Southern California smog. "This is usually a beautiful view, but we haven't seen the ocean for two months," Reagan said. But privately, others who saw the retired commander in chief around that same time were less sanguine about his health, especially his ability to remember things. "He was having a definite memory problem, and he'd say time and again, 'I just can't remember,' " an unnamed associate later told the *New York Times*. Reagan had even mentioned to the friend that Alzheimer's disease had claimed his mother's life, and he wondered if he was slowly meeting the same fate.

He was. In fact, his doctors diagnosed Reagan with the degenerative and ultimately fatal brain disease around the time of that article in the *Washington Times*. On November 5, 1994, Reagan released a handwritten letter to the American people, and even his persistent detractors could not help but marvel at its courage and grace. He said, in what proved to be a self-fulfilling prophecy, that he and Nancy hoped going public with his illness would raise awareness of Alzheimer's disease. The *New York Times* noted that the two-page missive was written in a remarkably steady hand, marred only by two words that were crossed out as Reagan speculated on his eventual death.

"When the Lord calls me home, whenever that may be, I will leave with the greatest love for this country of ours and eternal optimism for the future," Reagan wrote. "I now begin the journey that will lead me into the sunset of my life. I know that for America there will always be a bright dawn ahead." And he was true to his word: the public would never again hear directly from the Great Communicator.

Needless to say, this news changed the discussion about Reagan and the effect of his presidency overnight. It had been just two years earlier that Clinton had regained the presidency with a hard-nosed assault on Reaganomics. But beginning in November 1994, any public criticism of the ailing, terminally ill ex-president—particularly by public officials or in an increasingly cautious news media—would be remarkably muted and would also, out of good taste and human decency, tend to be balanced with praise for his good qualities, such as his optimism and good-naturedness, or his forays into bipartisanship. Clinton, with the best ear and knack for empathy in modern American politics, picked up immediately on the proper tone as he campaigned in Northern California on the date that Reagan's letter was made public. "We disagreed on a lot of things over the years," Clinton told a rally in Alameda. "But he always fought with a sense of optimism and spirit."

It was the beginning of an unprecedented period in American public life. For nearly ten years, Reagan lived on with his Alzheimer's, never again to be heard (although he was occasionally glimpsed on a golf course or even walking the beachfront of his beloved Pacific near Santa Monica). It was one of the tumultuous decades in the nation's history, of boom and a bust, with new technologies like the Internet and new enemies like Islamic extremists replacing the old ones, and much of America's modern course—for better and for worse—traced back to the Reagan years. But Reagan's unprecedented condition created an environment when sharp criticism of things that went wrong in the White House during the 1980s was now rendered, in the new terminology, politically incorrect.

With Reagan guaranteed kind treatment in the increasingly emotion-driven and soft world of TV news, it would be up to historians in the 1990s to try to judge the Reagan presidency with a more dispassionate eye. In December 1996, the historian Arthur Schlesinger, Jr., asked thirty-two well-known historians and history buffs to rate all forty-one American presidents (the discrepancy is that Grover Cleveland was elected two separate times), carrying on a tradition launched by his famous father in 1948. The group rated Reagan as "average-low," essentially the same level as Jimmy Carter and George H. W. Bush and below such modern figures as John F. Kennedy and Dwight Eisenhower. Reaganites cried foul and claimed the survey had a strong left-wing bias, not just because of so many campus types but also because two of the history buffs were Democratic pols of the 1980s, former New York governor Mario Cuomo and outgoing Illinois senator Paul Simon. But just two months later, a broader survey of some 719 historians and political scientists rendered an even harsher verdict. The book *Rating the Presidents* put Reagan just twenty-sixth out of the forty-one presidents, behind Bush 41 and also Clinton, who was wrapping up his first term. The two studies so close together caused a pointed reaction on the right, especially at the Heritage Foundation, which published a response in its *Policy Review* magazine that spring that was headlined, somewhat predictably, " 'There You Go Again': Liberal Historians and the *New York Times* Deny Ronald Reagan His Due."

But it was not just a bunch of historians that had the Reagan revolutionaries on the run in the mid-1990s. It was also the facts on the ground. By the time voters cast their next ballot for president in November 1996, the debate about steep-tax-cut-fueled deficit spending versus a balanced budget with somewhat higher taxes on the rich and corporations seemed to be answered by a still-rising economic tide that was beginning to dwarf the gains that had been accomplished under Reagan. However, the path to that verdict would hardly be a straight line. To the contrary, the right-wing surge still had one final spasm left: the midterm election of 1994, which took place just three short days after Reagan's surprising Alzheimer's announcement. You could say that the GOP won one final election for the Gipper, recapturing both the House and the Senate for the first time since 1954.

The contest was whipsawed by the angry white male middle class, still mad over the economic gyrations and shrinkage of the 1980s and early 1990s, still whipped up by the populist momentum of talk radio, and still mad as hell at the government, which was personified in 1994 by the Democrat Clinton. The new president misread the public mood upon taking office, not realizing that general mistrust of big government was more powerful than voters' expressed specific desire for better health care; his complicated plan, devised by his wife Hillary, not only failed in the Democratic Congress but riled up voters. Exit polls showed that two-thirds of Ross Perot's independent-minded 1992 voters went Republican in 1994. Some GOP gains also marked the tipping point of long-term demographic trends, as population grew faster in conservative Sunbelt enclaves and the slow transition of right-leaning Boll Weevil Democrats into Republicans peaked that year. As a result, both the Republicans and the increasingly large punditocracy in Washington strove to read more meaning into the 1994 results than really existed. Both hyped the GOP preelection pledge known as the Contract with America, which called for laws requiring a balanced budget and allowing a presidential line item veto, as well as ethics reform, a welfare overhaul, tough-on-crime measures, and other conservative items that read like a transcript of an overheated hour on talk radio. Exit polls from 1994 showed that most voters didn't even know about the Contract with America, and when cocky GOP lawmakers tried to actually implement it there was a backlash from moderate voters that climaxed that fall when Republican lawmakers shut down the government in a budget fight with Clinton—and took the blame from most Americans.

"There needs to be cuts, no doubt about it," a thirty-nine-year-old worker at the Grove City Grain and Feed Mill in rural Minnesota told the *Minneapolis Star Tribune* that fall, adding quickly that some of the Republicans' proposed measures were too drastic and too deep, especially in health care and for veterans' services. "I think [the president's] OK. He's doing some learning yet. Maybe he's being a little hard-nosed now, but it's about time." Polls showed that voters overwhelmingly agreed. They disapproved of the tax-and-spending plan that the new GOP majority sought to foist on Clinton for 1996. The combination of tax reduction and spending cuts went further than the electorate wanted to go. A proposed cut in Medicare was especially harmful to the Republican cause, as well as a report that House Speaker Newt Gingrich—the fiery Georgia right-winger with low popularity numbers—was partly motivated by a petty slight over not getting a seat on the Clinton-led government flight to the funeral of slain Israeli prime minister Yitzhak Rabin.

By 1996, the pendulum of American politics had been swinging wildly, but voters wanted a break, and now it was Bill Clinton, not Ronald Reagan, who was in the right place at the right time. The economy was continuing on its long march upward from the end of the recession that crippled the George H. W. Bush presidency, and in the spring of 1996, right when voters were locking in their choices, the gross domestic product surged by an impressive 4.7 percent. The number of new jobs, some 180,000 a month, was outpacing new job seekers, as would be the case for most of Clinton's presidency. The interest rate on 30-year Treasury notes, which had been about 8.6 percent at the height of the Reagan-Bush deficits in 1990, had fallen to 7.6 percent in 1992 and was down to 6.86 percent as voters went to the polls in 1996. That was in good part because the yearly federal deficit was now at its lowest level, as a share of GDP, since 1974. When the Republican nominee, Senator Bob Dole of Kansas, understandably trailing now by 20 percentage points in the polls, proposed a steep tax cut that August, the New York *Daily News* editorialized that "the drums of voodoo economics are being heard again."

The steep, 15 percent tax cut plan was just one part of an effort by the seventy-two-year-old, dyspeptic Dole to run for the White House not as who he actually was—a World War II veteran who saw actual combat and lost the use of his right arm, a lifelong Washington insider and deal maker, with moderate views on some issues such as civil rights—but as Ronald Reagan Redux. Lest there be any doubt, he famously told the Republican National Committee in 1995, as he was mapping out his campaign, that "I'm willing to be another Ronald Reagan, if that's what you want." Dole even chose Jack Kemp, the former New York congressman and Bush 41 cabinet secretary whose supply-side credentials were even more solid than those of Reagan himself, as his running mate. But the truth is that the Reagan Republican coalition, a wildly disparate group that ran the gamut from Yankee country club millionaires to Bible-thumpin' blue collars from the Deep South—was continuing to unravel. Failure has a way of doing that.

Many of the most rabid right-wing Reaganites found it impossible to forgive Dole for his long record as a moderate, which dated to his very first speech on the floor of the Senate in 1969, when he called for more federal aid for the handicapped. "There's just no enthusiasm for Dole among conservative activists," Phyllis Schlafly, the leader of the conservative women's Eagle Forum, told the Washington Times that August. "Most of the people I know are concentrating on congressional and senatorial races." Many of the so-called Reagan Democrats were now back home with their original party as well; Pennsylvania, whose western steel towns were considered a solid part of Reagan's blue-collar backbone, hasn't voted Republican for president since 1988. On Election Day, Clinton won 379 electoral votes to 159 for Dole.

And by 1997 and beyond, the big picture was even getting progressively worse for the conservative activists. In the days leading up to the 1996 voting, Clinton had reached a deal with the GOP Congress on a reform package that made good on his original promise to "end welfare as we know it." Likewise, Clinton had pushed through a crime bill during his first term that added a hundred thousand new cops and helped a new breed of law-and-order mayors finally reduce crime in the nation's cities, including New York, Philadelphia, and Washington. Murder levels in those cities dropped to surprising lows. Progress in the inner cities, in particular, was hailed in a December 1998 article in the New York Times headlined LEGACY OF THE '90S BOOM: MORE JOBS FOR BLACK MEN. It noted that young blacks were getting jobs at higher rates than any time since the 1950s, the crack cocaine trade had collapsed, and wages for the bottom 20 percent of the workforce were rising 3.6 percent a year, aided in part by the minimum wage hike backed by Clinton.

Then there was the Clintonian motto, "It's the economy, stupid." By January 1998, the interest on 30-year Treasury notes had fallen to their lowest level since the government started selling them in 1977, and the rates would continue to fall. By the time Clinton left office, the numbers were staggering: The economy was continuing to expand for the 118th straight month, 22 million new jobs had been created, bringing unemployment from 7.5 percent to 4.0 percent, the poverty rate fell from 15.1 percent to 11.8 percent, and the Dow had more than tripled, from 3,200 to more than 10,000 by 2001. In the last three years of Clinton's presidency, the federal government went from deficits to surpluses, reducing the overall debt load by some $360 billion and fueling optimism about further reductions. But the statistics, while amazing, fail to capture the national mood, at least as it pertained to the economy. The later 1990s will long be remembered as a time of soaring wealth—of overnight Internet billionaires, when bars and restaurants started showing the surging stock prices on CNBC instead of *SportsCenter* on ESPN. That didn't make America a nirvana: there was more greed, of course, and some ridiculous excess, as epitomized by the surge in gas-guzzling SUVs and oversized Humvees that would become symbols of scorn a decade later.

But the overall story line couldn't seem clearer. While Reagan's well-timed optimism had given the American consumer a shot in the arm during the 1980s, his economic recovery had been shown as largely illusory, fueled by an irresponsible borrowing binge and a more than $2 trillion mountain of red ink, leading to a gap between rich and poor, then middle-class anxiety, and finally a crash landing in the early 1990s. Undoing Reaganomics had sparked a real boom—longer and stronger, with lower interest rates and more home ownership, lower unemployment, less poverty, and a more secure middle class. Clinton hadn't only produced the balanced budgets that Reagan had falsely promised in 1980, but with an assist from Al Gore, he had actually reduced the federal payroll. Voters noticed. In April 1997, CNN reported that Clinton was enjoying "a remarkable second honeymoon" as his second term was starting to hit full stride, with 54 percent of voters approving and just 37 percent disapproving of his job performance.

The conservative movement that had flourished during the Reagan years still had a strong toehold in the body politic; right-wing talker Rush Limbaugh had his army of 20 million listeners and a growing legion of imitators; former Reagan and Nixon aide Roger Ailes brought the revolution to cable TV with Rupert Murdoch's Fox News Channel, and the formerly fresh-faced ideologues like Grover Norquist who had infiltrated the Beltway in the 1980s had created a permanent shadow government, attached to the GOP majority in Congress and a growing network of big-business-supported think tanks and publications. But the failures of the mid-1990s—the backlash against the Contract with America plan in Congress, Clinton's reelection, and the ever-rising economic tides—were leading to a highly predictable civil war among the factions who'd been briefly united by the Gipper.

That July, E. J. Dionne wrote a piece in the *Washington Post* on the crisis of the conservative movement, headlined ONE BIG MESS, IN SEARCH OF AN IDEA. He quoted a typical complaint from one of the GOP's leading conservatives in the House, Representative David McIntosh of Indiana: "We don't have an agenda of our own. We've agreed to let Clinton lead and we'll react and that's led to our coalition falling apart." Dionne, citing GOP pollster Tony Fabrizio, spelled out five feuding factions within the Republican Party: supply-siders, deficit hawks, moralists, cultural populists, and progressives (apparently neoconservatives were under the radar screen in 1997). Many on the right felt outmaneuvered by Clinton, who spoke in Reagan-like terms of fighting big government while supporting targeted programs that were popular with voters. Some Republicans debated whether their approach should be one of cooperation with Clinton on tax cuts and budget balancing, as had been the case with welfare reform the year before, or instead confrontation.

Even the most radical right-wing Young Turks like Norquist seemed conflicted at the start of Clinton's second term. On inauguration day, the *Washington Post* found Norquist, then forty, on his way to a counterinaugural ball hosted by the conservative humorists Christopher Buckley and P. J. O'Rourke. The activist was in "a magnanimous mood." Said Norquist: "Bill Clinton has basically agreed with our agenda of less government and less regulation. He is the last Democrat president. In that sense, he's the equivalent of Gorbachev—the guy who managed the collapse of the Soviet Empire. Nobody was mad at Gorbachev. He was our ally. I hope Clinton has a similarly soft landing and walks away unharmed."

Yeah, right.

If Norquist was indeed sincere that night, his magnanimous mood would not last for very long. Within months, he and his allies would find that "idea" that Dionne was writing about—two ideas, really—and both would be real doozies. In the coming months, the most radical elements of the right would wage war not against Clinton's popular policies but against his personal peccadilloes (which, sadly for him, were considerable), and thus undo the Democrat's historical legacy as well as any momentum for continuing his successful policies. The flip side of tearing down Clinton would be the pumping up of a Republican counterhero: not anyone from the current unpopular crew (House Speaker Gingrich had a 24 percent approval rating, and his GOP colleagues weren't much better) but rather the only man who'd united the warring GOP factions and now walked in the limbo of Alzheimer's disease, immune from direct criticism even when millions carried still vivid memories of the divisive 1980s and the subsequent collapse of Reaganomics.

The myth of Ronald Reagan was already looming in the spring of 1997, but what Norquist and his allies proposed was virtually unheard of: an active, mapped out, audacious campaign to spread a distorted vision of his legacy across America.

In a sense, some of the credit for triggering this may belong to those supposedly liberal editors at the *New York Times,* and their decision at the end of 1996 to publish that Schlesinger survey of the presidents. The below-average rating by the historians for Reagan, coming right on the heels of Clinton's easy reelection, was a wake-up call for these people who came to Washington in the 1980s as the shock troops of a revolution, and now saw everything slipping away. The first Reagan salvos came from the Heritage Foundation, the same conservative think tank that also had feted the tenth anniversary of the Reagan tax cut in 1991. After its initial article slamming the *Times,* the foundation's magazine *Policy Review* came back in July 1997 with a second piece for its twentieth anniversary issue: "Reagan Betrayed: Are Conservatives Fumbling His Legacy?"

The coming contours of the Reagan myth were neatly laid out in a series of short essays from the leaders of the conservative movement: that the Gipper deserved all or at least most of the credit for winning the Cold War, that the economic boom that Americans were enjoying in 1997 was the result of the Reagan tax cut (and not the march toward balanced budgets, lower interest rates, and targeted investment), and that the biggest problem with the GOP was, as the title suggested, not Reagan's legacy but a new generation of weak-kneed leaders who were getting it all wrong. The tone was established by none other than Reagan's own son, Michael, now himself a talk-radio host, who wrote: "Although my father is the one afflicted with Alzheimer's disease, I sometimes think the Republicans are suffering a much greater memory loss. They have forgotten Ronald Reagan's accomplishments—and that is why we have lost so many of them."

Michael Reagan, like most of the others, mentioned Reagan's frequent calls for less government—presumably his accomplishment there was simply in calling for it, since he never came close to achieving it. Gary Bauer, another former Reagan aide who later ran for president as an anti-abortion "family values" candidate, took a similar tack on the speaking-out issue, noting that Reagan "spoke of the sanctity of human life with passion"—again regardless of his lack of concrete results on that front. One of the writers argued, "On the international scene, Reagan knew that only America could lead the forces of freedom." The author was former assistant secretary of state Elliott Abrams, who'd pleaded guilty in a deal to withholding information about Iran-Contra from Congress and was pardoned by President George H. W. Bush. Oklahoma governor Frank Keating even went the distance and compared Reagan to the sixteenth president with his argument that "Reagan's achievement can be compared to Lincoln's, because he faced immense challenges in an era characterized by deep and fundamental philosophical divisions among the people he set out to lead." Of course, Keating's analogy implied that stagflation and a left-wing government in Nicaragua were on an equivalent plane with slavery and a civil war that killed hundreds of thousands of Americans on our own soil. This shows the rhetorical lengths conservatives were now willing to go to to salvage their movement.

One of the more down-to-earth tributes was written by Norquist, who said, "Every conservative knows that we will win radical tax reform and reduction as soon as we elect a president who will sign the bill. The flow of history is with us. Our victories can be delayed, but not denied. This is the change wrought by Ronald Reagan." Norquist all but revealed one of his missions in the coming two years: finding a presidential candidate who would assume the Reagan mantle in a way that neither Bush 41 nor Dole ever could. But his second big push was practically a guerrilla marketing campaign to make sure that less engaged Middle America would get the message that Reagan belonged in the pantheon of all-time greats right next to Lincoln, Washington, and FDR. Norquist had learned the lessons of Normandy and the Brandenburg Gate, which was that powerful symbols can mean a lot more than words (especially in a little-read policy journal), that a motorist under the big Sunbelt sky of Ronald Reagan Boulevard will absorb the message of the Gipper's greatness without ever pondering if ketchup should be a vegetable in federally funded school lunches or if "the moral equivalent of our Founding Fathers" in Central America were drug-dealing thugs, the kind of stubborn things that popped up in those newspaper articles ranking the presidents.

The Ronald Reagan Legacy Project was hatched in the spring of 1997, and as in most successful guerrilla operations, there was an element of surprise. There was no formal announcement, nothing to tip off any alarmists on the left. Rather than incorporate the Reagan project as a separate entity, which carried the potential of greater scrutiny of its operations and its finances, it was simply a unit of the group that Norquist had been overseeing for more than a decade, Americans for Tax Reform. The Reagan Legacy Project would not even get its first mention in print until October 23, 1997. By then its first bold proposal had two key backers in Representative Bob Barr and Senator Paul Coverdell, both Republicans from Georgia. They had endorsed legislation that would rename the capital region's busy domestic airport, Washington National, as Reagan National. Of course, among the millions of air travelers who would pass through the facility named for the fortieth president, a disproportionate number would be from the nation's liberal elites, especially in Big Media. Simply put, Reagan National Airport would be a constant thumb in the eye of the Yankee elites who were still belittling the aging Gipper's presidency.

The announcement didn't even get coverage in the hometown *Washington Post* until exactly one month later, when Norquist's behind-the-scenes lobbying push had already bagged the endorsement of the influential Republican Governors Association, including George Allen, governor of Virginia (the airport is in Arlington), and House Speaker Gingrich. With Reagan having been out of public view with Alzheimer's for three years, Barr cast the measure as a feel-good proposal that surpassed partisanship. "People appreciate how Ronald Reagan gave voice to Americans' basic good feelings, including a lot of Democrats," he said. Democrats, in fact, did what you would expect them to do . . . they hemmed and hawed. The mayor of Washington, D.C.—it had the largest presence on the regional panel that ran Washington National—was Democrat Marion Barry, a bitter foe of Reagan's politics, who could only fret that there were a "host of other" people who should be considered, too. Geraldine Ferraro, Walter Mondale's running mate in 1984, said later that Reagan's real legacy was the mountain of debt, but then she offered a verbal shrug: "The man was president of the United States; he served two terms." It almost brought to mind Reagan's cruel remark about Michael Dukakis a decade earlier, that "I'm not going to pick on an invalid."

After a couple of years in the wilderness with the rest of the Beltway right wing, Norquist had found a new cause that not only advanced the movement but was something he could have fun with. "The guy ended the Cold War; he turned the economy around," Norquist told the *Baltimore Sun*. "He deserves a monument like the Jefferson or the FDR—or the Colossus at Rhodes! National Airport is a good place to start."

Norquist was the leader of a new breed, the College Republican–trained version of an ideological bomb thrower. Molded by the 1970s and that political void between the hangover of campus radicalism and the Carter malaise, he was a true believer with an iconoclastic outlook, who called the countercultural drug-overdosing rock star Janis Joplin a hero even as he forged political ties with the Christian right. Like most political junkies, his ideas were a mix of heredity—his father, a Polaroid executive, taught his young son to hate taxes in a suburban Boston ice-cream parlor by taking the first two licks of his son's cone and calling it the income and sales tax—and generational rebellion. But that rebellion was against the liberal norms at Harvard, which he attended in the mid-1970s, even while working on the left-leaning *Harvard Crimson*. When he escaped to Washington in 1978, it was still as an outsider; he would later tell the *Washington Post* that the sight of the more opulent federal buildings there made him "physically ill" because they were built with taxpayer dollars, that they were a kind of "neo-American fascism," that "they took people's money to build those things, people who were just getting by, [they] stole their money and built those things out of marble."

Ronald Reagan came three years later to rescue Grover Norquist, to take a young single Republican nerd and make him a player, albeit a small-time one at first. It was through Reagan's team that Norquist came to launch Americans for Tax Reform in 1986, to win support for that year's overhaul (even though, as noted earlier, the bill raised taxes on corporations substantially—one of the early contradictions among many that would pile up over Norquist's long career). During those days, the geeky twenty-something took strength from Reagan's support of so-called freedom fighters like Jonas Savimbi in Angola, a right-wing rebel backed by South Africa's apartheid government. Norquist's office was lined with pictures of his gun-toting visits to the jungle, interspersed with the Joplin memorabilia.

By the 1990s, Norquist was in a new political mode: survivor. He served as a close ally of Gingrich, helping to draft and promulgate the 1994 Contract with America, but the bitter chain of events that seemed to start the day his heroic Gipper headed into the California sunset—followed by Bush 41 and his betrayal on taxes and then the anti-Gingrich backlash—caused him to again focus on the presidency as the place where the action was. Of course, by now Norquist was not so much a rebel as a conglomerate, enmeshed in a tangled web of alliances, sometimes for money. By 1997, Norquist was a registered lobbyist for what was becoming the most powerful business monopoly of the computer era, the software giant Microsoft, while his tax reform umbrella group was being probed for its multimillion-dollar ad campaign on behalf of GOP candidates in the 1996 elections. The investigation in Congress ended in 1997 after Senate Republicans voted not to continue it. In fact, the very spring that Norquist launched the Reagan Legacy Project, his fellow conservative Tucker Carlson wrote a scathing profile that accused the activist of cynically selling out. The article in the left-leaning *New Republic* (the conservative *Weekly Standard* had rejected it) carried the headline "What I Sold at the Revolution" and said that, among other things, Norquist was now receiving ten thousand dollars a month from the left-wing strongman who controlled the African nation of Seychelles, the polar opposite of the type of anticommunist rebels he once supported.

So perhaps the Reagan project was a little escape for Norquist, a little getting back to his roots, with the kind of in-your-face surprising ploy that had been his youthful trademark. From the start, he handed the task of running the legacy project to a young aide named Michael Kamburowski, who had recently arrived from his native Australia with a kind of zeal for Reaganism that maybe only a newcomer could carry. A decade later, it would come out that Kamburowski, who also lobbied with Norquist on issues such as immigration reform, was here in the United States illegally (and even jailed for a time in 2001), which somehow didn't prevent him from landing a subsequent job as chief operating officer of the California Republican Party. But while he apparently was in the United States as an illegal alien, Kamburowski still seemed to "get" the Reagan Legacy Project from day one, that it wasn't just about honoring Reagan but enshrining Reagan's conservative principles as the American ideal. "Someone 30 to 40 years from now who may never have heard of Reagan will be forced to ask himself, 'Who was this man to have so many things named after him?' " Kamburowski said in 1997 to the left-oriented magazine *Mother Jones*, which was examining Norquist's legacy scheme. The initial media coverage of the idea tended to range from bemusement to amusement. *People* magazine, the ultimate vehicle for connecting with the silent majority of unengaged voters, covered an early effort of the legacy campaign, a six-foot portrait of Reagan made from fourteen thousand jelly beans. The item was headlined "Reagan's Sweet Legacy."

All the sweetness and yuks masked a somewhat startling fact: that by enshrining a national myth about Reagan so soon after his presidency, while he was still alive (albeit incapacitated), and for purposes that were essentially partisan in nature, Norquist, Kamburowski, and their powerful and growing list of conservative allies were pulling off a maneuver that was unprecedented in American history. Other presidents and leaders had surely been mythologized—a walk from Norquist's office near K Street to the National Mall would show that—but not while they were still living, or in a manner so blatantly calculated in the very spirit of a presidency built around effective public relations. This may have been American history, circa 1984, but as if the textbook had been authored by Orwell himself. As young Kamburowski said flatly to the *Hartford Courant* in December 1997, "The left has been far better at rewriting history. Conservatives just haven't paid that much attention to this kind of thing."

It is true that some of America's flesh-and-blood presidents have been mythologized over time, but usually over a long time, and typically as the result of broader social forces than a campaign concocted by a few partisan ideologues. There is no better example than the case of Abraham Lincoln, consistently rated by both historians and the American public as the greatest president, and understandably so, given his leadership of a shattered and then reunified nation in the Civil War, his signing of the Emancipation Proclamation, and his eloquence as expressed in the Gettysburg Address. What most modern Americans fail to realize is that the Lincoln Memorial wasn't officially authorized by Congress until 1911, some forty-six years after his death, and wasn't dedicated until 1922, the height of the era in which the Great Emancipator came to be venerated in American life.

Although Lincoln's assassination had been greeted in 1865 with the expected national outpouring of grief, the sixteenth president practically faded from the political discussion for the next couple of decades. That may seem surprising today, but the generation after the Civil War was largely preoccupied with moving beyond the national catastrophe that had killed so many, not to mention with the rapid industrialization of America. It was not until the turn of the century, thirty-five years after Lincoln's death, that the Civil War leader was widely hailed as a national hero. Barry Schwartz, in *Abraham Lincoln and the Forge of National Memory*, observes that several biographies of Lincoln—particularly one by noted muckraker Ida Tarbell, first published in the pages of *McClure's* in 1893—fostered an image of Lincoln that promoted native-born American values and rural character. His views on slavery and image as a reformer (the suspension of habeas corpus notwithstanding) made Lincoln popular with the fast-growing progressive movement of the early twentieth century, even as tales of his log-splitting youth reaffirmed small-town conservative social and moral values. The image of Lincoln as a national unifier gained considerable currency in the uneasy years leading to World War I, which challenged ethnic unity at home. Even southerners, as best captured in D. W. Griffith's 1915 epic movie *The Birth of a Nation*, romanticized Lincoln as a leader who would have spared the region the perceived indignities of Reconstruction.

The glorification of Lincoln took place in that era of social upheaval from 1900 to 1920, when at least twenty-two Lincoln statues were dedicated across America, some hundreds of hagiographic books were published, and the Lincoln Memorial was designed with a deliberate nod to the ancient gods, with architecture inspired by a Greek temple for Zeus. (In fact, for many years the key Lincoln sites in Illinois were described in the state's signage as "Lincoln shrines.") The Lincoln penny, considered a tribute to the man's humble origins, was released in 1909, the centennial of his birth. Lincoln may be the best example of the role of myth and the nation's presidents, but he is not alone. Most of the other well-known presidential monuments did not arrive at least a half century after their deaths; the Jefferson Memorial on the Mall, in fact, wasn't built until the Great Depression, more than a hundred years after the third president died. More recently, there were urgent pushes to name local facilities for John F. Kennedy and Martin Luther King (King, in particular, is honored with streets in some 730 American cities and towns, frequently in predominantly black neighborhoods), but in both cases the speedy honors were closely tied to public shock and grief over their assassinations.

Reagan, it should be noted again, was still very much alive when Norquist and friends launched their push for memorials and naming opportunities—not just one on the Mall, although that would soon be proposed in Congress, but also for some kind of Reagan highway or facility in each of America's 3,067 counties. Looking at the mythology of Abraham Lincoln, one can indeed see some similarities with Reagan: the idealized working-class heartland roots in Illinois, the sharply divided public opinion while each served in office. But the differences are even more striking. Lincoln, while surely flawed, was a great leader at the most difficult period in American history, who moved to end the worst blot on the nation's collective experience, slavery, while achieving victory in a war that threatened to destroy the very fabric of the republic. Reagan had presided over the end (temporarily, at least) of an energy crisis and the invasion of a virtually helpless island in the Caribbean, and even the most significant actions of his presidency—guiding the nation's high-wire foreign policy as the Cold War ended without a shot—were still a subject of historical debate in 1997, as they are today. In hindsight, the enshrinement of Abraham Lincoln was driven by complex social forces in early-twentieth-century America, and it was for the most part nonpartisan. The Reagan myth was quite different. A posse of political jihadists had a narrow and highly partisan agenda: to patch up a fractured Republican Party and provide a badly needed source of inspiration that might recapture the White House for the GOP in 2000 and generations beyond.

Republican activist Jack Pitney, who had worked on Capitol Hill during the Reagan years, talked to *Philadelphia Inquirer* political writer Dick Polman in early 1998 about the desperate need to reunite the increasingly bitter factions of the conservative movement: the probusiness tax cutters and immigrant-bashing isolationists, the imperial force crowd known as the "neocons," and the Christian right:

> Ronald Reagan has already become the Shroud of Turin for the Republicans. Every political movement needs its heroes, and who else can Republicans turn to: Richard Nixon? Gerald Ford? George Bush? Ike was a hero, but that was because of the war. This Reagan-worship is also happening because there's a leadership vacuum in the party right now. When people can't see the future, they look to the past.

But the Reagan myth didn't take root in a total vacuum. It happened in the sixth year of Bill Clinton's presidency, as the combustible mixing of the incumbent president's all-too-human foibles and an unprecedented and endless GOP investigation of Clinton's personal dealings and relationships, ultimately costing taxpayers some $40 million, struck a certain type of paydirt in January 1998. The former Arkansas governor, who won in 1992 despite long-standing allegations and rumors of sexual misconduct, had conducted tawdry liaisons inside the White House with a twenty-two-year-old White House intern, Monica Lewinsky. The facts emerged through a series of conservative-funded lawsuits and investigations (particularly a civil lawsuit by a former Arkansas state employee

who claimed sexual harassment when Clinton had been governor) famously described by Hillary Clinton as "a vast right-wing conspiracy."
Her allegation, laughed off by a news media then excited by the sensa-
tional facts of an honest-to-goodness White House sex scandal, was
largely revealed to be true, but in 1998 and 1999 the nation's body politic
was too whipsawed to look at the big picture. The Lewinsky scandal consumed America, its fast-growing pop-culture-meets-politics media infrastructure, and its thriving late-night comedy, even as the economy raced
to record heights, the government posted its first surplus in a generation,
and crime and poverty rates approached modern lows—and even as polls
showed that as much as 70 percent of the public didn't want Congress
pushing the Lewinsky matter.

Overnight, Bill Clinton became the Bizarro World Ronald Reagan, the
antimatter version of the 1980s president. Remember, polls in the final
two years of the Reagan White House showed that a majority of Americans continued to like and respect the man but strongly disagreed with
his policies on everything from AIDS and homelessness to the federal
deficit and the surge in military spending. Now, with Clinton, the public
overwhelmingly backed a president's handling of the economy and of
government priorities, but was repulsed by his character. There was no
overt link between the rise of the Ronald Reagan Legacy Project and the
impeachment of William Jefferson Clinton, but there didn't need to be,
because the interplay was so fundamental.

Still, there was considerable overlap between the strongest advocates
of impeaching Clinton—which eventually happened in the GOP-led
House in December 1998, only to fall far short in a divided Senate, where
a two-thirds vote was needed for removal, after a trial in early 1999—and
the Reagan legacy drive. In February 1999, Norquist announced the cre-
ation of what was described as a "nonpartisan" board of advisors to the
Reagan Legacy Project (it included an obscure retired Democratic senator
from Florida who had become Reagan's Central America envoy in 1983).
One of its members was Republican National Committee Chair Jim Nicholson, who that same month said new (and never proven) allegations that
Clinton had raped a woman (Juanita Broaddrick) were "credible," "compelling," and "moving." Another Reagan Legacy board member, Phyllis
Schlafly of the Eagle Forum, had called for impeaching Clinton one month

before the Lewinsky revelations because of an Asian fund-raising scandal. Her ally was Congressman Barr, the lead sponsor of the Reagan airport renaming bill. Another board member, Oklahoma's Governor Keating, had already called upon Clinton to resign in December 1997, telling reporters that the president was guilty of "embarrassing, humiliating, obscene conduct."

The pumping up of Reagan and the taking down of Clinton seemed to draw oxygen from each other in 1998. Robert Dallek, the historian who'd studied so many modern presidents, told the *Los Angeles Times* that year that the correlation was hardly an accident. "So when we pass through an episode like we're going through now, with Bill Clinton and accusations of lying, perjury, sexual misconduct and obfuscation, there's a natural inclination to look back to past presidents and exaggerate their virtues," he said. "You can only have heroes if you also have people with shortcomings."

Just six years earlier, Clinton had recaptured the presidency for the Democrats by running forcefully against the Reagan legacy, but now the sudden turn of events left the White House in no position to stop the Norquist-led campaign even if it had wanted to. Clinton was too weakened politically by the Lewinsky scandal, and Reagan was immunized from political criticism by his Alz-heimer's disclosure. When the Republican-led Congress passed the airport renaming bill in time for Reagan's eighty-seventh birthday on February 6, 1998, two weeks after the Lewinsky story broke, some Democrats urged Clinton to veto the measure, but the response, as an unnamed White House aide told the *Los Angeles Times,* was essentially "We're signing it, forget it—go away."

To reject a specific tribute to a terminally ill ex-president might seem remarkably petty and cruel to a largely disengaged American public, which was content to read about the Gipper's "sweet legacy" in *People* magazine and had no idea who Grover Norquist even was. The early days of the Reagan Legacy Project rushed to capitalize on the manufactured nostalgia for the fortieth president with little regard to the obstacles or to common sense. In Washington, the Reagan legacy builders started taking in big donations to rename the Tenth Street Overlook near L'Enfant Plaza for Reagan and erect a large statue of the Gipper—undercutting a local historian's lifelong campaign to place a monument there for Benjamin Banneker, the nation's first acclaimed African-American scientist. The most ironic tribute to Reagan, arguably, was one of the earliest ones, a colossal edifice in the capital that was exactly the type of structure that Norquist had dubbed "neo-American fascist," a 3.1-million-square-foot "horizontal skyscraper" shrine to the federal bureaucracy that cost a budget-expanding $732 million to construct. In a final irony, the Ronald Reagan Building and International Trade Center would house one of his least favorite departments, the Environmental Protection Agency; even an angry Michael Reagan branded the project "Mount Wastemore."

There was one man who had thwarted any early effort to place a Reagan memorial on the National Mall—Reagan himself. It was he who signed legislation in 1986 that barred any memorial on the Mall until at least twenty-five years after that person's death. The early success of the Reagan National Airport push did lead to other bold proposals that tended to grab headlines. In the 1990s, conservatives, including the movement's father figure William F. Buckley, floated the geologically, if not politically, impractical idea of carving Reagan into Mount Rushmore. Paul Coverdell, the Senate sponsor of the airport legislation, pushed for Reagan to replace Alexander Hamilton—the first treasury secretary who didn't seem to have much of an active constituency in the late 1990s—on the ten-dollar bill. Ironically, that plan seemed to get a boost when it was Coverdell, not Reagan, who passed away first, in July 2000. There were other big successes, including the USS *Ronald Reagan,* a $4.5 billion nuclear-powered aircraft carrier that would be christened in 2001 as the first such warship to be named after a still-living figure. But the big-ticket proposals, including the impractical ones like Mount Rushmore, obscured the remarkable early smaller-scale successes out there in the American heartland in naming schools and roads for Reagan—roughly fifty over the course of just three years—in small towns and sprawling suburbs. This was the true passion of Norquist and the others: not so much honoring the still sentient Ronald Reagan as finding the next one, or at least a reasonable facsimile who would allow the right-wing party to go on.

As 1998 morphed into 1999, after an embarrassing and unexpected loss of congressional seats for the GOP and the failure to remove Clinton from office, Norquist and other movement conservatives came to believe they had found a worthy successor to the Reagan legacy in the most unlikely persona: the son of the very Republican they blamed for betraying the Gipper's legacy in the first place. Enter George Walker Bush of Texas.

It wasn't love at first sight. The younger Bush had snuck into the American political landscape in 1994, ousting Democratic icon Ann Richards as governor in the year of the GOP backlash, helped by some local goodwill earned while he was minority owner and front man for the Texas Rangers baseball franchise. Some political writers identified him as a potential heir to his father's White House legacy (especially when brother Jeb lost his first bid to become governor of Florida that same year) but D.C. insiders still recalled a young man who was rough around the edges, a former party animal who'd only quit the bottle a decade earlier, at age forty. But worse, as far as Norquist & Co. were concerned, was that "W," as the forty-first president's like-named son became known, didn't ride into office with his tax-cutting guns ablaze.

In 1997, the younger Bush's third year in Austin, the Texas governor proposed a tax reform package that would have increased some levies against businesses; Norquist and his Americans for Tax Reform were adamantly against the Bush plan and even ran radio ads in the Lone Star State attacking it. Norquist told friends that year that he could never support George W. Bush for president, and faxed out complaints about Bush to allies in key primary states. But as the 2000 election drew near, Norquist did something that really wasn't so unusual for him: he flip-flopped.

It turned out that Norquist and Bush shared a similar vision of a Reaganist restoration in the White House. Both men had seen, from different perspectives, the devastating impact that the tax hike of 1990 had on Bush 41's career, and both drew the same conclusion: the increase, not his foolish pledge to voters in the 1988 campaign, killed his reelection campaign. In fact, after Bush 41 defeated Bob Dole, who wouldn't sign Norquist's no-tax pledge, in the 1988 New Hampshire primary, and after the ensuing debacle of 1990, the pledge was now a necessary rite of passage for any GOP White House wannabe. By the spring of 1999, ten potential Republican candidates had signed the Norquist pledge—the only one who hadn't was George W. Bush. But when Norquist flew down to Austin for lunch with the Texas governor that March, they were clearly on the same wavelength. For the younger Bush, it was nothing short of Oedipal. He wanted to show the old man what he could do—and his mentor would be Ronald Reagan, not George H. W. Bush.

Indeed, Bush sent a series of signals out to the Republican base, in that preprimary year of 1999, that he would be a president in the mode—or the perceived mode, anyway—of Reagan. As chronicled by Jonathan Chait in *The Big Con: The True Story of How Washington Got Hoodwinked and Hijacked by Crackpot Economics,* son Bush said he would pick a Supreme Court justice in the mold of Reagan appointee Antonin Scalia, ignoring his dad's nominees Clarence Thomas and the surprisingly liberal David Souter. He also chose the new Reagan Library as the setting for a foreign policy address that mentioned the Gipper six times and his father, Bush 41, but once, in passing. He told the *Wall Street Journal*'s Robert Bartley that his father's 1990 tax increase had "destabilized the base." For those who still didn't notice, conservative pundit Cal Thomas wrote that "the Texas Republican is sending a message. A George W. Bush presidency, he signaled, will be Reagan III, not Bush II." Norquist certainly noticed the talk coming out of Austin. He told National Public Radio that "the challenge is that the Reagan revolution was so complete in moving the Republican Party toward a cohesive, more principle-based party that the establishment candidate, Governor Bush of Texas, is also a Reagan Republican conservative candidate."

On June 8, 1999, Bush wrote to Norquist and became the final 2000 candidate to sign the no-new-taxes pledge. In a letter to the activist, Bush wrote that he understood that any kind of tax hike "would reduce productivity, remove money from the pockets of Americans at a time when taxes already take a record peacetime share of national income and hurt our country's ability to provide high-quality, high-paying jobs." Norquist said to the *Washington Times,* "Why believe the son? When President George Bush lost the 1992 election over it, it was a lesson for every Republican running for office."

The GOP front-runner for 2000 had made it very clear to the American public: he wanted to be Ronald Reagan in the worst way.

That is exactly what would happen.

CHAPTER EIGHT

THE GREAT MISINTERPRETER

The 2000 presidential election was decided, and won, by Ronald Reagan.

That became true in a literal way in December 2000, when the ridiculously close race between Al Gore and George W. Bush, and a monthlong uproar about recounts, butterfly ballots, and hanging chads in Florida finally ended up in the U.S. Supreme Court, in the case that became known as *Bush v. Gore*. The facts of the voting and states' rights issues before the justices appeared to matter little; to most observers it seemed a given that the three hard-core conservative justices—Antonin Scalia, Clarence Thomas, and Chief Justice William Rehnquist—would back Bush and stop the recount, while the more liberal Ruth Bader Ginsburg, Stephen Breyer, David Souter, and John Paul Stevens were expected to side with Gore. That left the case in the hands of the two moderate swing justices whom Reagan had appointed, Anthony Kennedy and Sandra Day O'Connor, and it wasn't a shock when the two GOP appointees won another one for the Gipper. The *Wall Street Journal* reported that O'Connor's husband had told guests at a party shortly before the case that his wife was considering retiring from the high court, but was reluctant to do so with a Democrat in the White House.

But in a figurative sense, Reagan—now eighty-nine, completely out of sight in Southern California in the twilight mist of Alzheimer's—stood to gain a major victory if the younger Bush could win the general election. Since the start of the year, Bush had staked his entire bid for the White House on two things: a promise to return character to the Oval Office in the aftermath of Clinton's impeachment, and a platform that could just as easily have been presented at the 1980 convention in Detroit, which tapped Reagan. The cornerstone of George W. Bush's economic plan for the new millennium was something that the American people clearly didn't want right now—but Bush won anyway.

The issue, of course, was a massive, Reaganesque tax cut. Bush started out the 2000 campaign as the GOP's clear front-runner, backed by much of the party's establishment. Moreover, positions on supply-side economics and social issues that would have placed a candidate on the far right in 1980 were now the official party line. Although Republican voters historically backed the favorite of their top leaders—as in the famous saying "Democrats fall in love, Republicans fall in line"—Bush still faced a lively primary field, almost all of whom staked some claim on Reagan's legacy. That included the wealthy magazine publisher Steve Forbes, a flat-tax and supply-side advocate who'd forged ties with the Christian right, and two former midlevel cogs in the Reagan administration: Alan Keyes, who'd served as an ambassador to a United Nations council, and "family values" candidate Gary Bauer, who never failed to remind voters of his Reagan ties as a domestic policy advisor. The most serious challenger to Bush also boasted of his links with the fortieth president—indeed, John McCain and his first wife had been personal friends with the Reagans in the 1970s, and so before the New Hampshire primary he ran TV ads that showed him conferring with the Gipper. "We think we have the best ties to Reagan and we are not afraid to spell them out," a McCain advisor, Mike Murphy, told the Detroit News. But the Arizona senator was really running toward what he misjudged to be the zeitgeist of 2000, as a kind of self-proclaimed "maverick" and "straight talker" who seemed to borrow pages from the playbook of Ross Perot (he stressed his role as a campaign-finance reformer after his ties to a crooked S&L millionaire almost cost him his career in the late 1980s) and even from Clinton (McCain argued that the tax cut backed by Bush was too skewed to the wealthy).

McCain's outside-the-box views made him a political hero to some voters and especially to the media, which reveled in the unlimited access that the Arizonan provided on his campaign bus, the "Straight Talk Express." His quirky approach was a home run with New Hampshire's notoriously iconoclastic primary voters, and when he defeated Bush easily there in February 2000, the Reagan revolution appeared to be truly in its last throes. But the empire struck back. Rush Limbaugh, whose radio audience of 20 million gave him a megaphone like no other, lambasted McCain for days on end. Joining in the scrum was Grover Norquist, who'd been officially converted to the Bush camp and whose Americans for Tax Reform spent a hundred thousand dollars on anti-McCain ads, labeling him as a liberal on campaign finance reform—and on taxes.

Bush, for his part, had jump-started his campaign in December 1999 with an audacious tax cut proposal: $1.35 trillion over ten years, nearly double the size of a GOP proposal that had just been vetoed by Clinton as fiscally irresponsible. Bush's plan had something for everyone, including married couples and the working poor, but the largest beneficiary in actual dollars, just as in 1981, would be the wealthiest Americans, whose marginal tax rate would fall from just under 40 percent to 33 percent. The proposal caused key players like onetime candidate Elizabeth Dole, who had been Reagan's labor secretary, to get behind Bush; she compared the Texas governor to her former boss in January 2000. Said Dole: "Today we rally to another western governor, just as bold at challenging the status quo, just as resolved to restore pride in our institutions, just as determined to be himself."

The tax plan wasn't a direct pander to most voters, bizarre as that may seem. Despite the popular perception that American voters always desire lower taxes, it clearly was not what the electorate wanted in 2000, even with the federal coffers finally showing a surplus. The year before, a series of public opinion polls showed that the overwhelming majority of Americans didn't want to blow the new budget surpluses on a tax cut—not when the economy was booming, and not when the funds could be spent on other useful purposes. In early 1999, some 64 percent of Americans in a *New York Times*–CBS News poll said the surplus should be used to shore up Social Security, while just 12 percent wanted the money given back in tax cuts. In January 2000, a *USA Today*–CNN–Gallup poll put tax cuts low on voters' priority list, behind education, health care, and preserving Social Security. The article in *USA Today* presenting those results noted that a lot of the economic gains of the late 1990s hadn't even been taxed— those in retirement accounts or stock mutual funds—and voters were eager, even excited, about paying down the debts accumulated under Reagan. The public attitudes were throwing conservatives for a loop; the Heritage Foundation held a forum that winter on how to revive support for lower taxes. The only leading right-winger who seemed unconcerned was Norquist; he told the newspaper that if a Republican president were elected with a Republican Congress, the tax cut would happen, regardless. "You win, you do it," Norquist said—and the public would like the results.

He was right about the first two.

Bush's Reagan-inspired tax plan did help politically, not so much in its direct appeal to rank-and-file voters but in encouraging insiders like Norquist and Limbaugh, the GOP lifers, the big donors and the ambitious K Street lobbyists, that the formerly obscure Texas governor was exactly what they were seeking in the next president. The establishment, along with a cutthroat political aide named Karl Rove and some dirty rumors and push polls thrown at McCain in the decisive South Carolina primary, carried W on to the fall election, and into a race that, by normal standards, should have been an uphill climb for the Republican, given eight years of relative peace and prosperity under the Democrats.

But 2000 was an election year with a mixed message. The lingering hangover from the Clinton impeachment left a befuddled Gore campaign confused over whether it should embrace the president's legacy or run away from it; although the vice president provided his liberal base with some red meat in the fall campaign with increasingly populist rhetoric, the overall Gore zeitgeist was too cautiously centrist. The man who six years later would win the Nobel Peace Prize for his fiery advocacy on global warming hardly ever mentioned the issue when he was running for the White House, where he would have actually been able to do something about climate change. Bush, while actively working to hold together his right flank with advocacy for tax cuts, private Social Security accounts, and government aid for faith-based programs, also skewed to the center when speaking to voters, talking vaguely of something called "compassionate conservatism," which seemed to be the 2.0 version of the "kinder, gentler America." The author, who covered the 2000 presidential election for the *Philadelphia Daily News*, watched a lily-white audience of suburban and rural Republicans in a giant hangar outside Rochester, New York, gaze in puzzlement and clap gently that March as Bush spoke at great length about raising inner-city kids' school test scores. An unnamed Republican strategist confessed to the *New York Times* three years later, "Bush instinctively, and Rove intellectually and tactically, knew they should not compete issue by issue. Clinton and Gore had the edge. So you got a values campaign: 'an era of responsibility,' 'leave no child behind' and, of course, 'compassion.' "

The seeming jag to the political center by the 2000 candidates, coupled with the economic boom of the dot-com era (although the bubble on Wall Street did begin bursting that spring), created the dominant mood of the election, at least until the Florida recount woke some people up. That mood was an almost passionate apathy. Barely 51 percent of the U.S. voting age population even bothered to turn out; of those who did cast ballots, nearly 2.9 million predominantly liberal voters went with Ralph Nader, agreeing with him that the two major candidates were pro-corporate clones. The two candidates struck too many voters as a couple of uninspiring yuppies of the baby boomer generation, with little difference between the two. Some flippant journalists summed up that perception by calling the candidates "Gush" and "Bore."

But it wasn't true. One of the two major 2000 candidates would become a leading voice of the progressive movement in America over the next decade—not only its best-known environmental advocate but also an early opponent of the 2003 invasion of Iraq, a critic of the corporate media, a fierce foe of the gutting of the Constitution, even a late convert to supporting gay marriage. The other major candidate, who won in the Electoral College and at the Supreme Court despite a half-million fewer popular votes, became . . . well, he became the George W. Bush that we know today, a president widely despised outside the United States even as he also sets new benchmarks for voter disapproval at home. And the myth of Ronald Reagan shadowed Bush every step of the way down.

Like the Reagan myth itself, the interplay between Bush and his somewhat tortured appropriation of the Gipper's legacy is complicated, and has several facets. On taxes and spending, Bush arguably tried too hard to mimic Reagan's actual program despite radically different circumstances. Unlike Reagan in midpresidency, Bush stubbornly resisted any change in course. That helped turn what was supposed to be a decade of wiping out deficits into a second era of rising debts, much of it held by foreign powers. On war and foreign policy, Bush and his cadre of neoconservative advisors used the Gipper's rhetoric to pursue a most un-Reagan-like approach, launching not one but two protracted wars featuring all of the things that the fortieth president abhorred: U.S. casualties as well as major collateral damage that killed thousands of civilians and turned world opinion against America. Politically, Bush sought to continue his work of the 2000 campaign by holding together the Reagan coalition, but while Reagan had done that largely by sheer force of his personality, Bush won support with expensive programs, such as the millions spent on faith-based grants and sexual abstinence training. So Bush failed even worse than his role model had done in shrinking government. Yet pressed to pay for his expensive wars, Bush nonetheless managed to skimp in the places where it would have made a difference. He failed to regulate a runaway mortgage system, which finally undermined the global economy, and in 2005 he was stunningly unable to grasp the damage in New Orleans from Hurricane Katrina, which killed at least 1,464 people and the soul of a great American city.

The Bush 43 presidency seemed to absorb all the wrong lessons of the Reagan years, and not just that "deficits don't matter," as Vice President Dick Cheney is reported to have said, but also that Congress, the media, and large segments of the public have a high tolerance for abuse of the Constitution. The acts of torture and rendition against terrorism suspects and the widespread electronic spying on Americans under Bush has made the crimes of Iran-Contra seem in hindsight like shoplifting at a convenience store, but there was no real pressure for a Bush impeachment. George W. Bush may have signaled to the GOP establishment in 1999 and 2000 that he was planning to mimic Reagan, but what he actually "accomplished" in that sense was truly stunning. He managed to copy the worst of Reagan's presidency: the runaway debt to fund policies that benefited the rich; a view of the Constitution as merely an occasional hindrance; a probusiness bias that allowed investment banks to implode in the late 2000s, exactly as S&Ls had done in the late 1980s; and a refusal to confront any problem like climate change that could only be addressed through citizen cooperation and sacrifice. The areas where Bush diverged were the areas where the Gipper had done his very best: using rhetoric to motivate and inspire confidence, dealing with mistakes and those times when compromise or even backpedaling were necessary, a willingness to talk to enemies, and an ultimate vision of a peaceful world with fewer weapons.

In the end, the greatest differences between Bush and Reagan were in personality and vision. Ronald Reagan was an American original with a broad strategic vision—antigovernment, antitaxation, and anticommunism, but for personal freedom—which he expressed through skilled rhetoric and, with the help of his clever team, powerful imagery. Voters and opinion makers reacted to that persona, even as Reagan often skated right around the messy details underneath. Bush presented an outward aura of blustery self-assurance but it didn't take a psychology major to sense all the Oedipal insecurities not far below the surface of this son of a president, a son who was an underachiever until his forties, when a longtime heavy drinker abruptly quit the bottle, found Christianity, and sought to quickly reinvent himself. Ronald Reagan became the obvious template for this tabula rasa, especially as Reagan mythology took over the GOP in Bush's formative 1990s. Bush could only convince the world that he was a Reagan-like figure by copying Reagan's policies, even though some hadn't even worked the first time and others were a poor fit in a new millennium.

Bush seemed to thrive on the handful of similarities with Reagan while working hard to ignore the obvious differences. As he prepared to seek the Oval Office, Bush—who was never seen atop a horse—even bought up a ranch in the Texas countryside and developed an uncannily similar love of clearing brush on his lengthy vacations there. Both men, like so many driven to politics, wanted on some level to get the attention of their daddies, even if Reagan's father was a drunk and Bush's was the leader of the free world. Both Reagan and Bush managed to spend a time of war in uniform, yet far away from combat. Both Bush and Reagan were often underestimated—or "misunderestimated," as Bush said in the famous malapropism that seemed to sum up in one word exactly why people "misunderestimated" him. Liberals, the media, and other so-called elitists didn't seem to grasp their appeal, but for different reasons: Reagan was characterized, albeit unfairly, as an amiable dunce, whereas Bush's occasional lack of knowledge seemed fraught with arrogance and perhaps a slice of willful ignorance, since after all, he did have degrees from Yale and Harvard.

Most importantly, Bush and Reagan brought leadership styles that also appeared to be similar but were in fact quite different. Both were prone to making bold, and occasionally unpopular pronouncements, but Reagan's were broadly rhetorical and occasionally undercut by his policy decisions, from his California tax hike all the way through to trading arms with Iran. Bush's proclamations were foolishly rash, from promising to capture 9/11 mastermind Osama bin Laden "dead or alive" to saying "bring 'em on" about attacks on U.S. forces in Iraq. And they were tied to policies that were unyielding, regardless of the underlying and shifting facts. Both brought passive management styles that stayed away from the details, but with Reagan there was also indecision, which in turn led to considerable infighting, not to mention Iran-Contra. Bush also didn't sweat the small stuff, but he was eager to avoid dissent and unpleasant news. Bush was, in another phrase that he made famous, "the decider," even as those decisions left a trail of tears from the foreclosed mortgages of Florida to the bombed-out neighborhoods of a burning Baghdad.

Still, the similarities were beguiling to many when Bush was riding his highest, at midpresidency, just as had been the case for Reagan. Bill Keller, who would soon be named executive editor of the *New York Times* (in part because of the fallout over coverage of the run-up to war in Iraq that was too accepting of the Bush White House spin), famously described Bush, in a nearly eight-thousand-word article in January 2003 (that is, right as Bush was making that case on Iraq), as "Reagan's son." Wrote Keller: "Bush is not, as Reagan was, an original, but he has adapted Reagan's ideas to new times, and found some new language in which to market them. We seem not only to be witnessing the third term of the Reagan presidency; at this rate we may well see the fourth." To make his case, Keller quoted approvingly from some of the Gipper's closest acolytes, even from Mike Deaver, who said "I think he's the most Reagan-like politician we have seen, certainly in the White House." This, of course, was the zenith, when Bush was the "war president" who'd responded to a crisis the likes of which Reagan had not seen, a terrorist attack on U.S. soil that had claimed the lives of nearly three thousand U.S. citizens and demanded a more forceful response than did the kidnappings and scattered acts of violence that Reagan had confronted in the Middle East.

Bush was defined by 9/11, then and now, making it harder even to recall those first eight months of his administration, when he first set out the road map that Reagan had seemingly paved for him. When he arrived for his inauguration in January 2001, the conventional wisdom was unanimous: Bush would be a centrist; he would spend a lot of energy reaching out to Democrats, especially with the Senate now divided fifty-fifty (with Vice President Dick Cheney as the tiebreaker); he would be seeking to establish his legitimacy after the Florida recount and after Gore had polled more popular votes. Indeed, Bush made a few head fakes in that direction—inviting Senator Ted Kennedy to the White House to watch a movie, for example—but the reality was that he had no intention whatsoever of ruling from the center. And the Reagan-inspired income tax cut, the plan that had won over Norquist and the rest of the conservative crowd around K Street, would be Bush's first shot across the bow of conventional Beltway wisdom.

During the late 1990s, as the Dow soared and Clinton's stock plummeted with the Lewinsky scandal, the public had come not only to trust but practically to worship Alan Greenspan, the Federal Reserve chairman, who was given enormous credit for the boom times. And Greenspan had made clear his position that the surpluses should be used as an opportunity to shore up Social Security and not in what he described as a reckless tax giveaway. In July 1999, Greenspan had testified before Congress to warn against a $792 billion tax cut that the Republicans were pushing that summer. "We probably would be better off holding off on a tax cut immediately, largely because it is apparent that the surpluses are doing a great deal of good to the economy," the Fed chairman said. A precipitous tax cut could raise interest rates, he noted. The Republican-led Congress went ahead and passed the bill anyway—the Dow dropped sharply on the day that it passed the House—and Clinton vetoed it.

Now, eighteen months later, and just five days after Bush took the oath of office, Greenspan was asked to testify yet again about a Republican tax bill, and this time the new president was still pushing for his much steeper reduction, amounting to $1.3 trillion over ten years. All of Washington was stunned by what the revered economist said on January 25, 2001. He said he had changed his mind, that a situation in which the government paid down all of its debt in the coming years—as many analysts were projecting in those heady post-Clinton days—actually posed certain risk, that the government might be forced to invest some cash in private assets. "I still hold the No. 1 priority is reducing the debt," Greenspan explained. "The problem is we're going to get that out of the way far sooner than any of us imagined." Democrats were flabbergasted. "In all candor, you shock me," Democratic Senator Ernest Hollings of South Carolina said. "You are going to start a stampede this morning."

What exactly was Greenspan thinking? Years later, it's still not clear. Many think it was nothing more than a nod to the financial guru's political side, that he was offering a kind of honeymoon gift to the new administration. The only tiny window so far has been offered by Bush's then treasury secretary Paul O'Neill, who later became so disenchanted with the White House that he co-authored a 2004 tell-all book about his time there. In Greenspan's testimony, the chairman did refer, in his characteristically obtuse manner, to the idea that certain triggers would kick in to reduce or even eliminate the tax cuts if the federal surpluses started to vanish. But the Bush administration never got behind that idea, and an amendment mandating such triggers failed in the Senate by one vote. A May 22, 2001, meeting between Greenspan and the treasury secretary was later recounted by O'Neill: "Without the triggers, that tax cut is irresponsible fiscal policy," Greenspan said in his deepest funereal tone. "Eventually, I think that will be the consensus view."

It was too late. The Beltway pundits had failed to account for how deeply partisan Congress had become since the Reagan years, with the Contract with America and then the Clinton impeachment. Bush did not have to govern from the political center, because his narrow Republican majority would stick solidly together and even pick off a few red state Democrats here and there. A week after Greenspan's lament, the Bush tax cut passed on Capitol Hill pretty much as he had proposed it when he was a presidential candidate seeking Norquist's blessing back in 1999. The biggest difference was the price tag, which had actually increased by some $500 billion, partly because the economy was now sliding into recession and every adult taxpayer would get an immediate three-hundred-dollar "stimulus check." Indeed, the stimulus check hoopla obscured the sweeping changes in the Bush tax bill. While the broad outline was somewhat different from the Reagan plan in 1981, it had a similar effect in rewarding America's wealthiest. A 2002 in-depth analysis by Citizens for Tax Justice found that 52 percent of the tax breaks over ten years would be reaped by the richest 1 percent of Americans, and their total windfall over the life of the measure as passed would be $477 billion. That figure wouldn't seem quite so outrageous if the federal government actually ran the kind of surpluses that were projected when Clinton left the White House. Instead, the rosy projections were gone in months—by early 2002, not long into Bush's first term, surplus talk was about as relevant as a share of stock in Pets.com, or a new CD by the Backstreet Boys.

"Obviously, we've got budget matters," the president was telling a fund-raiser for Ohio's Governor Bob Taft by May 2002. "You know, when I was running for president, in Chicago, somebody said, would you ever have deficit spending? I said, only if we were at war, or only if we had a recession, or only if we had a national emergency. Never did I dream we'd get the trifecta." He was referring to the recession that slowed the economy in 2001 under the impact of the bursting Wall Street bubble, the second fiscal blow from the September 11, 2001, terror attacks, and finally the war that Bush had then launched in the terrorists' safe haven of Afghanistan. Bush's "joke," which he amazingly repeated on several occasions, may have raised a valid point; it is highly doubtful that a President Gore or any other administration would have achieved the over-the-top projections of a $5.6 trillion budget windfall that were bandied about in early 2001. But Bush failed to tell his audiences that his tax plan had ensured deeper deficits. In January 2002, budget crunchers said tax collections had fallen about $215 billion less than expected because of the recession and 9/11, and now the government was projected to run deficits for the next couple of years. In fact, in the first six full fiscal years of the Bush administration, some $3.33 trillion was added to the federal debt, which is now fast approaching the $10 trillion mark overall. More than three-quarters of the increase in the debt during the Bush years, according to some experts, was attributable to two facts: the wars in Iraq and Afghanistan, and the tax cuts. If that combination sounds odd to you, it should—most past American presidents have raised taxes to pay the costs of a major conflict; Bush would become the first wartime leader to cut them.

In fact, Bush's second tax cut—known as the Jobs and Growth Tax Relief Reconciliation Act of 2003—was enacted in May 2003, when the dust had barely settled from the toppling of the Saddam Hussein statue in downtown Baghdad. It was a package with an initial price tag of another $350 billion over ten years, and it was heavily weighted toward the financial instruments of the very rich, by curbing levies on stock dividends and other capital gains. It was the 2003 tax cut, along with the rising tide of red ink, that prompted dire warnings from O'Neill and Cheney's famous rebuke that "Reagan proved that deficits don't matter." The Republicans in Congress who voted for the Bush proposals also had a highly selective memory of the Reagan years. They successfully tossed the series of rollbacks that started with Reagan and culminated with the Bush 41 and Clinton revenue hikes, straight down the memory hole. Representative Jim Nussle of Iowa, who was chairman of the House Budget Committee, told the *New York Times* in 2004 that while he did believe that deficits were important, what he described as "the basic playbook" on taxes and deficits was the one written by Reagan, and "that is the playbook I follow today." No one was a bigger advocate for Bush's tax policies than the head of the Reagan Legacy Project, Norquist, who insisted that Bush "understands that tax reduction is the central organizing principle of the modern Republican Party." He added that Bush wanted "to have a tax cut every year."

But deficits did matter. While the Fed initiated a long series of rate cuts in the early 2000s, long-term interest rates paid by consumers failed to come down considerably, and most economists said the federal deficits were a major reason for that. Meanwhile, the value of the U.S. dollar, long considered a benchmark of the U.S. economy, started a long period of remarkable decline in 2002, the year that budget deficits began piling up again. The dollar lost more than a third of its value over that time. The last time such a decline had happened was during the 1970s and the era of stagflation under Jimmy Carter. The irony is too much to bear: in trying to re-create the economic gains of the Reagan years, Bush has instead managed to bring back an echo of the despised presidency that Reagan replaced. Because of Bush's large new debt and because of Americans' ever-growing demand for cheap goods manufactured overseas, the culmination of the trend toward offshore manufacturing that really accelerated during Reagan's 1980s, the U.S. economy was, by the end of George W. Bush's presidency, dependent on an influx of some $2 billion in foreign cash, every single day.

The immediate impact of the falling dollar under Bush wasn't immediately clear to many Americans. Those who worked in the shrinking number of U.S. manufacturing plants actually reaped a short-term gain, because American-made goods were now more attractive in foreign markets. But the dollar's decline was also inflationary. All those Chinese-made goods that Americans were used to buying at Wal-Mart suddenly cost a lot more to import, and by July 2008 the U.S. economy was suffering its highest inflation rate in twenty-six years. Gasoline prices at the pump soared past $4 a gallon as a barrel of crude oil reached $147, or more than ten times what it had been during the boom years of the 1990s. Some of the oil crisis couldn't be pinned on shortsighted economic policies, since it was also the result of shortsighted energy policies in America—even ex-oilman Bush was forced to confess we are "addicted to oil"—and elsewhere as rising global demand for petroleum began to outstrip supplies. But some experts say the falling dollar also accounted for as much as a quarter of the run-up in the cost of oil, because most of the world's crude oil is traded in dollars, and when the dollar is worth less, it takes more of them to buy the exact same barrel.

It was all becoming a vicious cycle of higher oil costs, higher food costs, and a slowing economy but with inflation and a weak dollar that made it impossible for the Fed to sharply cut interest rates as it had done before when recessions loomed. And no one could say how and where the downward spiral will stop, because the new wild card in all of this was the massive amount of foreign ownership of the American debt, the dangerous trend that began in earnest under Ronald Reagan and began to snowball once again with Bush—"Reagan's son"—in the White House. By 2008, foreigners owned some 45 percent of outstanding U.S. treasuries, and $11.5 trillion in U.S. public and private debt altogether. Most experts believed that China, which owned about 10 percent of those U.S. treasuries, would never sell them off, since that would cripple its own economy, so heavily dependent on cheap exports to America. That is perhaps true, but the risk of such a precipitous action seemed to grow as the dollar continued to shrink in value. In the 1980s, Reagan had been able to negotiate, with a few close calls like the Able Archer incident in 1983, a world of military mutually assured destruction, or MAD, with the Soviets; now America looked into the abyss of what looked like global economic mutually assured destruction, but with Bush at the helm inspiring little confidence. To some experts, the global financial house of cards, compounded by an explosion in risky mortgages and other borrowing with little or no government oversight, looked a lot like 1931, as the Great Depression lunged toward its worst depths. Leading economists laid the blame directly at America's bankrupt policies.

"The richest country in the world cannot live within its means," Nobel Prize winner Joseph Stiglitz, former chief economist for the World Bank, said in 2007. He feared for the world's economy, and he specifically blamed the Bush tax cuts along with another ill-advised move by Greenspan, encouraging adjustable-rate mortgages when there was clearly a bubble in the U.S. housing market. "It's a real example of macroeconomic mismanagement. The working out of this global imbalance will cause global problems. The depth of the conviction on free markets in the United States is not very great. We have increased those subsidies, doubled them, under President Bush."

If the march toward such a precarious global situation during the Bush years didn't get the attention that it deserved, that could be explained by the fact that America had its mind on other big problems in the 2000s. While the economy did again become the top issue at the end of Bush's second term, most of the time voters were instead focused on two overlapping and interrelated events: the 9/11 terrorist attack and the invasion and occupation of Iraq, which started a year and a half later. The flip side of the Reagan myth was very much at work when it came to U.S. policy in the Middle East and Central Asia. In football terms, Bush's economic plan was like a running game against a stacked defensive line, bulling ahead with tax cuts regardless of the circumstances, unwilling or able to change direction. But his foreign policy was more like a fancy flea-flicker play, appropriating some of the Gipper's prettier words to justify ugly policies that Reagan would not have tolerated.

This warped direction actually traced back to the years immediately after Reagan, when the Soviet Union collapsed for good. To an upbeat public, the end of the Cold War would mean a "peace dividend": the nation could stop diverting so much of its wealth into runway defense spending, and indeed, cuts in the Pentagon budget were a factor in the government surplus that briefly emerged in the late 1990s. But a conservative foreign policy clique, bolstered by so-called neoconservatives who'd been Democratic anti-Soviet hawks in an earlier era, had other ideas. While George H. W. Bush was still president in 1992, defense secretary Dick Cheney worked with up-and-coming neocon Paul Wolfowitz to produce a stunning document, a new national defense strategy that called upon the United States to essentially act as a lone-wolf imperial superpower. A draft document said America would "establish and protect a new order" that accounts "sufficiently for the interests of the advanced industrial nations to discourage them from challenging our leadership," while at the same time maintaining a military dominance capable of "deterring potential competitors from even aspiring to a larger regional or global role."

Not surprisingly, the proposed strategy caused an uproar and was never adopted. Its thrust was something that Reagan—who had pledged "no more Vietnams" and who said just four short years before the draft report that unilateral military actions would make America seem the "colossus of the north"—would have never even considered. But out of power, this coalition of neocons and former officials in Republican administrations, including Reagan's, worked to make the strategy happen. In spring 1997, that same season when the Ronald Reagan Legacy Foundation was formed, a group of right-wing foreign policy hawks also founded the ominously named Project for a New American Century, or PNAC. The initial director of PNAC, Gary Schmitt, had been chairman of Reagan's Foreign Intelligence Advisory Board, but more importantly, its early advisors would become a Who's Who of the incoming Bush 43 administration, including Vice President Cheney, Defense Secretary Donald Rumsfeld, Wolfowitz, who was Cheney's top lieutenant, and Richard Perle, a hawkish former assistant defense secretary from the Reagan era. "The history of the 20th century should have taught us that it is important to shape circumstances before crises emerge, and to meet threats before they become dire," said PNAC's initial statement of principles, and its first act was a futile effort to convince President Clinton in 1998 to overthrow Iraq's Saddam Hussein. In a 2000 white paper on rebuilding America's defenses, Schmitt and others questioned America's resolve to play a forceful leadership role "absent some catastrophic and catalyzing event—like a new Pearl Harbor."

The new Pearl Harbor arrived at 8:46 A.M. on the morning of September 11, 2001, less than eight full months into the Bush presidency. Before the day was through, four planes had been hijacked, taking down both towers of New York's World Trade Center and crashing into a wing of the Pentagon, claiming the lives of nearly three thousand mostly American civilians. Bush's first-day response to the attack appeared wobbly but the next few weeks were arguably the strongest of his presidency, highlighted by a well-received speech to Congress and a military move against Afghanistan that was supported by leaders of both parties and most Americans.

But behind the scenes, Bush and some of the PNAC alums immediately saw an opening for also ousting Saddam, strengthening America's presence in the world's main oil-producing region. "Judge whether good enough [to] hit S.H. [Saddam Hussein] at the same time," Secretary Rumsfeld scribbled on a pad while the Pentagon was still on fire. "Not only UBL [Osama, or Usama, bin Laden]. Go massive. Sweep it all up. Things related and not." By mid-2002, the push for invading Iraq, one of the things not related, was under way, and it became clear how much America and the world had changed. While Reagan had declared publicly that killing civilians in a military response to terrorism was "terrorism itself," U.S. officials spoke in 2002 and into 2003 of a new doctrine of "shock and awe," massive bombing aimed at scaring an enemy population into a speedy surrender.

The main case for the war, as manufactured by the Bush administration, involved Iraq's stockpile of weapons of mass destruction, a threat to America and its allies, and Saddam's supposed ties to bin Laden's al-Qaeda terror network—neither of which, the world learned after the lethal invasion of March 2003, in fact existed. But in building a rhetorical case for support, Bush would lean heavily upon the same template that Reagan had drawn out for the Cold War, despite the lack of similarities between the two struggles. In particular, Bush and his speechwriters, seeking to win backing for tougher measures against nations deemed hostile in the wake of 9/11, looked to the growing aura around the Gipper's "evil empire" speech of 1983, which had been viewed by many at the time as unduly provocative but gained the endorsement of history when the U.S.S.R. collapsed. When Bush delivered his first post-9/11 State of the Union address, he stunned many watching by describing Iraq, Iran, and North Korea as an "axis of evil." Critics immediately questioned the remark, noting that not only did it seem overly aggressive but there was no evidence that the nations were working in concert, as was the case with the original "Axis" powers of Germany, Italy, and Japan, which had signed a nonaggression pact before World War II. (Iran and Iraq, in contrast, had fought a protracted war against each other in the 1980s.)

Delaware Democrat Joe Biden, who was chairman of the Senate Foreign Relations Committee at the time, said that America's allies were confused by the president's "axis of evil" remark, and so was he. "Was it meant to stake out a general notion that we know these guys are bad guys but not the only bad guys? Or was it meant to be an all-inclusive list? Or was it . . . a rhetorical connection between Roosevelt and Reagan—'axis' and 'evil'?" The short answer was, yes. White House speechwriter David Frum, who authored that section of the speech, said he'd been reading up on Franklin Roosevelt's response to Pearl Harbor, in part because he wanted to learn how FDR had convinced the nation to enthusiastically support the war against Germany when it had been Japan that attacked the United States. He believed that the three nations made up what he called an "axis of hate," and he claimed Bush himself changed it to "evil." Was Bush intending to mimic Reagan? A couple of weeks later, Bush toured the border of North and South Korea and was said to be pleased when the South Korean president, Kim Dae-jung, compared the "axis of evil" comments to Reagan's "evil empire" speech. "And yet, [Reagan] was then able to have constructive dialogue with Mr. Gorbachev," Bush added to the reporters at a joint news conference.

What the world didn't know—but was reported four years later in the *American Prospect*—was that a back channel of cooperation to remove the Taliban in Afghanistan and deal with al-Qaeda, which Tehran saw as a threat, had secretly opened between the United States and Iran, and Bush's efforts to sound Reaganesque all but destroyed these links. (A second push for accommodation by Iran did come around the time of the Iraq invasion, but it was also rebuffed.) Rather than encourage and work with moderates in Tehran, the overt U.S. hostility was greeted with the election of hard-liner Mahmoud Ahmadinejad as president and escalating tensions over its nuclear program. In 2008, in a speech to Israel's Knesset, Bush contradicted his earlier suggestion that day in Korea that he could talk to an "evil" nation by comparing the situation with the Iranian leader to Nazi Germany and calling negotiations with a nation such as Iran "the false comfort of appeasement" (an obvious jab at Democrat Barack Obama, who said he would be willing to meet with Iranian leaders).

Meanwhile, Bush continued to struggle to justify his decision to invade one of the other members of the axis, Iraq. The operation had led to an ongoing insurgency and, at times, a religious civil war that not only ripped the oil-rich nation apart but claimed more than four thousand American lives and killed an untold number of Iraqis. Increasingly, he turned to the issues of freedom and democracy to justify the war, and used the type of rhetoric that had worked so well a generation earlier for Reagan. In November 2003, when the anti-U.S. insurgency was beginning to stir and it was becoming clear that the public had been misled about weapons of mass destruction under Saddam, Bush appeared before the National Endowment for Democracy, a group that had been founded in 1983 as a direct response to Reagan's famous "ash heap of history" speech about the Soviets in London that year. The embattled president, suddenly facing a tougher reelection campaign, was now making the push for freedom and democracy as the main focus of his strategy in the Persian Gulf.

Our commitment to democracy is also tested in the Middle East, which is my focus today, and must be a focus of American policy for decades to come. In many nations of the Middle East— countries of great strategic importance—democracy has not yet taken root. And the questions arise: Are the peoples of the Middle East somehow beyond the reach of liberty? Are millions of men and women and children condemned by history or culture to live in despotism? Are they alone never to know freedom, and never even to have a choice in the matter? I, for one, do not believe it. I believe every person has the ability and the right to be free. [Applause.] Some skeptics of democracy assert that the traditions of Islam are inhospitable to the representative government. This "cultural condescension," as Ronald Reagan termed it, has a long history.

He didn't stop there, telling graduates from the U.S. Air Force Academy in June 2004 that "we believe, in Ronald Reagan's words, that 'the future belongs to the free.' " One problem with that argument was that the Reagan administration actually had a long history in the region, and while it perhaps didn't involve "cultural condescension," it didn't involve a clear-cut fight for democracy, either. In fact, as critics of Bush's Iraq policies were quick to point out, the Reagan administration had largely leaned in favor of Saddam's regime during the long Iran-Iraq War, since the spread of Iran's Shiite fundamentalism was its greatest fear in the region. In December 1983, the Reagan administration sent a private citizen as an envoy to Baghdad, where he met not only with Saddam but foreign minister Tariq Aziz and agreed that the United States and Iraq shared "many common interests." That envoy was Donald Rumsfeld, who as defense secretary in 2003 would lead the war to overthrow the now-evil Saddam. Meanwhile, it emerged that throughout the 1980s, the Reagan White House had trodden very lightly around the increasing evidence that Iraq was using chemical weapons in its stalemated war with Iran. While publicly condemning the use of such weapons, which were a violation of the Geneva Conventions, a team of as many as sixty aides in the Reagan-era Pentagon continued to offer intelligence and other assistance to Saddam. The *New York Times* reported in August 2002: "The Pentagon 'wasn't so horrified by Iraq's use of gas,' said one veteran of the program. 'It was just another way of killing people—whether with a bullet or phosgene, it didn't make any difference.' " The enormous irony was that while America had tolerated the existence and even use of what would later become known as weapons of mass destruction in Iraq during the Reagan years, when Bush cited those weapons as a reason to invade, they were no longer there—such weapons and programs were taken down in the years immediately following the success of Operation Desert Storm in 1991.

In fact, the powerful Reagan rhetoric on freedom was almost entirely constructed around the Soviets, communism, and the Cold War prism through which he and his team viewed every conflict, from Beirut to Managua. When it came to the often warring Muslim-led nations of the Middle East and Central Asia, Reagan's policies were less driven by idealism and more by what many have described as realpolitik. (One bizarre example, Craig Unger reported, was when the Pentagon in 1986 stepped up its aid to Saddam precisely so that Tehran would more desperately need the weapons offered in the White House's arms-for-hostages dealings.) Indeed, as the Bush years unfolded, and especially after a majority of the American people turned against his policies in Iraq, an increasingly popular topic for Reaganologists, the academics who study the presidency and the journalists who'd covered the fortieth president or wrote about his legacy, was this: Would a President Ronald Reagan have invaded Iraq in the period after 9/11? Most of the experts conclude that he would not have.

Bruce Bartlett, the former Reagan economic advisor who has written extensively about the legacy of his former boss, has said that Reagan's record suggests he would have taken a much more cautious approach to dealing with Saddam in the 2000s, that he would have been more likely to rely on sanctions and possibly airpower to force concessions before sending in ground troops. Furthermore, Bartlett believes that Reagan would have repeated his actions in Lebanon, withdrawing forces from an untenable position, when confronted with evidence of a similar stalemate in Iraq. "At the peak of the Cold War, this was a very hard thing for Reagan to do," wrote Bartlett on the *New York Times* website in January 2007, citing what happened in Beirut in 1983–84. "He knew it would show weakness and undermine his position in dealing with the Soviet Union. But he realized, as Bush does not, that you cannot undo a mistake by continuing to make it. All you can do is stop making the mistake, cut your losses and move on."

Bush's critics noted something else about the president's Iraq policy that was very un-Reagan-like: his treatment of the U.S. military, from the top brass all the way down to the grunts who actually fight in the dusty desert towns of Iraq. Lou Cannon and his son Carl, the authors of *Reagan's Disciple*, said Reagan tended to leave military strategy to the generals and never would have undercut a high-ranking officer like General Eric Shinseki, who was contradicted in 2002 when he predicted, quite correctly, that more troops would be needed to stabilize Iraq than Bush and Rumsfeld were planning to commit. Meanwhile, Lawrence Korb, a foreign policy expert who was assistant secretary of defense under Reagan, has insisted that Reagan would never have sent volunteer soldiers or members of the reserves and National Guard on lengthy, multiple tours of combat duty in Iraq, as Bush has done. If necessary, Korb argued, Reagan likely would have resorted to a draft to fight the kind of wars that the Bush administration has waged in Iraq and Afghanistan. Korb wrote in the *Washington Times* that "the 40th president accepted the social compact with the troops that said for every day in a combat zone, the military person would spend at least two days at home."

Lou Cannon has pondered the question of Reagan and Iraq for quite a long time, and he says that the more he looks back on Reagan's record, the more convinced he and his co-author son Carl are that there would have been no ground strike against Saddam's forces. "The clincher for me is the Panama thing," says Cannon, recalling Reagan's policy toward General Manuel Noriega at the end of his second term. "He was urged to take out Noriega more than once, but he wouldn't do it." Some of that reluctance, Cannon believes, was because the 241 Marine deaths in Beirut weighed on Reagan so heavily.

Of course, the only man who could have truly answered the question was unable to, living in a hazy twilight that none of the rest of us can truly comprehend. Ronald Reagan remained at home in the hills of Southern California in March 2003, having just marked his ninety-second birthday and his fiftieth wedding anniversary, cared for by nurses around the clock. He knew nothing of the war being waged in his name. CBS's Mike Wallace interviewed Nancy Reagan that June and asked if her husband even still recognized her.

"I don't know," she replied.

CHAPTER NINE

REAGAN'S '08 CAMPAIGN

The phone call that Tony Chapa had been expecting for close to a decade finally came on a Saturday afternoon. Chapa, the head of the Los Angeles office of the Secret Service, was sitting in a veterinarian's waiting room with his sick dog on June 5, 2004, when his cell phone went off. The caller said just two words:

"Operation Serenade."

Chapa and his ailing pooch never saw the vet that day. He quickly dialed a posse of other local law enforcement officials, dropped the dog off at home, and hurried to the posh hills of Bel Air on the west side of Los Angeles. By the time he arrived, there were as many as a hundred people milling around the driveway, and media vans from all over the world.

Ronald Reagan was dead.

Word had already leaked out that the ninety-three-year-old icon was now gravely ill from his advancing Alzheimer's, and on his final day not only Nancy but his two youngest children, Ron Jr. and Patti, were also by his side. "At the last moment, when his breathing told us this was it, he opened his eyes and looked straight at my mother," his daughter later told CNN. "Eyes that hadn't opened for days did, and they weren't chalky or vague. They were clear and blue and full of love. If a death can be lovely, his was."

Reagan was pronounced dead at 1:09 P.M., Pacific Time, and within minutes, hundreds of people sprung into action, from Los Angeles to Washington to even Paris, where President Bush was traveling that day. The beehive of local law enforcement activity was just one aspect of Operation Serenade, a code name for the actions and ceremonies leading up to Reagan's funeral that a cadre of former White House advance men and aides had started devising in the mid-1990s, right after the Gipper had revealed to the world that he was slowly dying from Alzheimer's. In fact, the event was so elaborately planned that when the leader of Operation Serenade, former Reagan advance man Jim Hooley, took a new job with the software giant Siebel Systems in 2000, he remembered to negotiate a sudden-leave provision for the inevitable day when Reagan passed.

It was an amazing end to a little-known aspect of Reagan's presidential years. In the 1980s, the detailed work of his advance team in finding just the right camera angles and backdrop—from the bombs bursting in air over the Statue of Liberty to the cliffs of Pointe du Hoc to the day-to-day photo ops like the crab fisherman on Maryland's Eastern Shore—had helped remake the American presidency, and most owed their later successful careers in corporate America or running campaigns to those heady days in the West Wing. Hooley recalled to the *Wall Street Journal*, which published the definitive behind-the-scenes account of Operation Serenade, that no advance men had ever had such close access to a president before. "We went from being the guys blowing up balloons and getting cars for the motorcades to senior, respected members of the team," Hooley said, adding of Reagan: "He was an actor, and he understood there was somebody who planned the lighting, somebody who built the set and wrote the script."

It was Hooley, his former White House underling Rick Ahearn, and their former co-workers who wrote the script for what became a week of national mourning for their old boss. Most baby boomers now in their prime still remember the dramatic funeral of John F. Kennedy, which took place just three days after he was shot. His widow, Jackie, had planned much of that event, saying, according to presidential historian Michael Beschloss, "I'm worried that Jack is going to be left to these bitter old historians. Jack might not be remembered by history." Public observances for subsequent presidential passings such as Dwight Eisenhower and Lyndon Johnson also lasted just three days or so, or half of the drawn-out Reagan mourning, which involved multiple events in both Washington, D.C., and California.

Exactly twenty years earlier to that very week, Reagan had touched millions with his misty tribute to the boys of Pointe du Hoc; now it was the sound and lighting boys of Pointe du Hoc, circa 1984, who had stormed Normandy to find just the right political backdrop to help reelect a president, who were repaying the favor. The multiplier effect on the Reagan myth—the historical distortions of his presidency that had been pushed by a calculating cadre of conservatives ever since the start of Bill Clinton's second term—was incalculable. For the next week, the carefully planned imagery that sometimes made the president appear larger than life, from "there you go again" all the way to the Brandenburg Gate and back, were running on an endless TV loop, interrupted only by newer and more spectacular imagery, right up to the final moment that Nancy Reagan stroked the flag-draped coffin and whispered a final good-bye exactly as the sun disappeared over the Pacific, at the end of prime time on the East Coast.

Reagan's death and funeral was a "spontaneous" moment of national unity and shared grief that had been mapped out for years, his aides nurturing his image against their fears of a liberal media covering the event. "We need every opportunity to show the media, who might be skeptical, that this is the way that America feels about the guy," Ahearn said. "This is a legacy-building event." Hooley used the same formula that had been so successful for much of Reagan's eight years in the White House, which they called "HPS," for "headline, picture, story," to be cast by them and not by the journalists. His preordained "HPS" for the Reagan funeral, he told the *Wall Street Journal*, was "Ronald Reagan as a man who won the Cold War, who brought back America's faith in itself."

And so viewers saw a funeral procession route with mourners waving some fifty thousand tiny American flags, a touch arranged in advance by Hooley. They worked with a nearby college and even with Waste Management—supplier of portable toilets—to guarantee that the somewhat isolated Reagan Library in Simi Valley could handle the hundred thousand people who eventually filed by Reagan's casket. Ahearn, the *Washington Post* reported, decided that "Reagan's riding boots, fitted in the stirrups of the riderless horse accompanying the caisson for the procession to the Capitol, should be left scuffed but not dusty. He took a little saddle soap to them." Most importantly, the Reagan advance team generated a nonstop flow of images to a media universe that had exploded in the fifteen years since the Great Communicator had left the Oval Office. This in-

cluded three around-the-clock cable channels that had learned that viewers could be mesmerized by an hour of overhead shots of a moving
hearse—in spite of, or perhaps because of, the weird similarity to the images of accused killer O. J. Simpson's Ford Bronco chase a decade earlier.
Even the final sighs and whispers of the Reagan family were captured on
shotgun microphones. "Each gesture was minutely choreographed,"
wrote Richard Goldstein of the week's events, "every tear strategically
placed."

The almost funny part was that all the worrying of the former Reagan
aides about the "liberal media" was for nothing. The powerful Beltway
journalists who covered Reagan on bended knee, in author Mark Hertsgaard's famous phrase, practically lay prostrate upon the Gipper's death.
It was a combination of the normal human impulse to speak nothing ill of
the dead and a kind of warped nostalgia for the close—and often way too
close—bonds between Reagan's associates and the elite reporters who
covered the administration. The so-called liberal media bent over backward to show that it wasn't biased when the conservative Reagan was
president, many believe, and now with his death it performed a full back-
flip.

"I was worried about that," *Washington Post* columnist E. J. Dionne
said at week's end on CNN. "I mean, I think what you've had is a sort of
30-year campaign on the conservative side to say that the media is liberal,
and now I think you're having another reaction from liberals who are saying, wait a minute, when we look at a week like this, a week of praise of
Ronald Reagan, it is very hard to say there is a liberal media anymore."

Hard indeed. Even the right-wing Fox News Channel presents more
liberal Democrats in a normal week than a viewer saw on any of the cable
channels in the second week of June 2004, in which viewers were treated
to a nonstop cavalcade of right-wing all-stars such as Peggy Noonan and Pat
Buchanan, each with his or her own adoring memories of the patron saint
of their conservative movement, each reinforcing the headline, picture,
story that Reagan had won the Cold War and restored America's faith. The
American electorate in 2004 included some voters who were only four
years old when Reagan left office, but such viewers would have little clue
that the 1980s were such a divisive time in American history. One unnamed TV executive in the Reagan funeral aftermath told Jim Hoagland of

the *Washington Post,* "Today history is what we say it is." Fox did invite on one anti-Reaganite, the arch-tongued cartoonist Ted Rall, so that host Sean Hannity could describe him as "thoughtless, mean, hateful."

Thomas Kunkel, dean of the Philip Merrill College of Journalism at the University of Maryland, wrote that "the initial burst of news coverage would have you believe that Reagan was a cross between Abe Lincoln and Mother Teresa, with an overlay of Mister Rogers." Even more troubling, he noted, was the way that right-leaning talk radio lashed out at the few who tried to offer a different perspective on a divisive president. Kunkel added: "Those who weren't remembering Reagan in the politically approved way—who credited him for his gracious demeanor, say, or sense of humor—were derided as patronizing. And those who actually had the audacity to point out that as president, Reagan alienated millions of people at home and abroad, were blasted as unpatriotic."

And so you might think that the week of uninterrupted coverage, which virtually wiped the growing, bloody insurgency against the George W. Bush–led occupation of Iraq off the air and off the front page, was an immense hit with the American viewer, the ones who weren't lining the California freeways with red-white-and-blue flags. But not really that much: viewership did increase modestly, but not as much as for the death of another icon of the 1980s, Princess Diana. Perhaps it was a function of the couch-potato age we live in, or a sign that the Gipper wasn't as much of a people's president as the talking heads implied, but Frank Rich noted in the *New York Times* that the reported viewing crowds of a hundred thousand at the Capitol and another hundred thousand at Simi Valley was actually not so great by historical standards, that an estimated 3 million people had watched the 1923 cross-country funeral train of President Warren Harding, now generally rated one of the worst presidents of the past century. Even reporters who waded into the crowds found opinions as divided in 2004 as they had been back in 1987. "Somebody came up to me and said, wait a minute, why are they honoring this guy?" the *Post's* Dionne noted. "He cut my student loans."

Leave it to a reporter for the international press, Julian Borger of Britain's *Guardian,* to point out what was ignored in the American media, that Reagan's death was not at all a moment of national unity, that the outpouring of grief and show of respect from everyday Americans was overwhelmingly from what had become known in post-Gipper culture as red America, a heavily Christian fundamentalist and conservative crew of talk-radio fanatics and supporters of the Iraq War and President George W. Bush. "They fly the flag on their lawns," he wrote, "and they are almost entirely white." Borger and several other commentators noted the unsurprising fact that virtually none of the people filing past Reagan's casket in the Capitol Rotunda were black, even though the surrounding District of Columbia is overwhelmingly African-American. He quoted one mourner who sounded as if she were channeling Rush Limbaugh when she pointed up at the rotunda where Reagan lay in state, and said, "Americans like straight-talking presidents. They don't like lip-biting, poll-taking presidents. If it was Clinton up there you would have had four people."

One thing about Reagan's death that wasn't scripted was the timing, of course, but it just so happened that it came when George W. Bush was fighting for his political life as he sought a second term. Like his father before him, Bush 43 had soared to astronomical highs in the public opinion polls on foreign policy and war—specifically his initial response to 9/11 and then the initial military successes of the Afghanistan and Iraq invasions—only to fall back as reelection time approached. And so the Bush campaign grasped on to the memory of Ronald Reagan like a lifeline. For the long week of Reagan funeral activities, the Bush campaign website featured a large picture not of its own candidate but of Reagan, with links to the ex-president's speeches and, by week's end, a video that interspersed clips of the eulogy that the current president had delivered with the Gipper's greatest hits, including the Pointe du Hoc speech. Noted the *New York Times* some nine days after Reagan's death, "It was difficult to tell where the 40th president ended and the 43rd began, a blurring further promoted by Ken Mehlman, the president's campaign manager, who told an Iowa Republican Party convention on Saturday that Mr. Reagan's spirit lived on. 'Every time an American soldier, sailor, airman or marine risks his or her life to ensure our security and peace, Ronald Reagan will be there,' Mr. Mehlman said."

It's not clear whether that Ronald Reagan was there on November 2, 2004, the day that Bush eked out a reelection victory against Senator John Kerry. Some journalists actually called the victory a "mandate," ignoring that Bush's popular tally of 51.2 percent was stunningly low for a wartime commander in chief, or that Kerry would have won in the Electoral College if fewer than sixty thousand Bush backers in Ohio had voted Democratic instead. Holding together the fragile Reagan coalition was clearly the key to Bush's victory that day. In past presidential campaigns, the ideal strategy was moving toward the political center in the fall, to attract the ever-shrinking pool of moderate voters who swung between the two parties. Bush, as guided by his political guru Karl Rove, took a completely different route, hewing to the political right and working to energize his base, with a major focus on millions of Christian fundamentalists who historically had been more dependable at turning out for church on Sunday than to the polls on Tuesday. (In the decisive state, Ohio, a gay-marriage amendment was placed on the ballot to gin up interest for the religious right.) The glorification of the Reagan legacy and the establishment of Bush as the still-rightful heir to that mantle was critical to bestowing conservative legitimacy on the incumbent, even more so because by 2004 some so-called true conservatives were already beginning to grumble about profligate spending by the Bush administration on everything from those faith-based grants to prescription drugs for seniors. If Bush were to have been judged solely on his own merits in 2004, the public might have viewed him merely as a tongue-tied bumbler who had preemptively invaded a nation that hadn't attacked the United States and who had no real plan for its occupation, who had turned a budget surplus into a flood of red ink in a matter of months. But it looked differently if you perceived Bush as the latest in a line of saviors from the malaise of Jimmy Carter's 1970s, as what Keller of the *New York Times* had described as "Reagan's son." In the nineteenth century, a different breed of "radical Republican" held sway for decades by "waving the bloody shirt" of the Civil War against the Democrats; now, more than a century later, the new Grand Old Party could wave the oil-stained shirt of Carter's stagflation from a dirty-laundry basket that also held Monica Lewinsky's stained blue dress from the Gap. And Ronald Reagan was their new Abraham Lincoln.

And the Reagan magic still worked.

Indeed, the Reagan myth became so critical to the conservative movement that the distortions of exactly who he was and what his legacy was became much more elaborate and more sophisticated during the early

2000s. In many ways, the era was propitious for building an impenetrable legend about him. As we've already seen, the fact of Reagan's lingering illness for the first half of the decade, followed by his death and a new era of good feeling for his widow Nancy (still an icon to conservatives, she unexpectedly became popular on the left by breaking with Bush and the hard-core right on embryonic stem cell research, with its potential for treatment of Alzheimer's and other illnesses), made it awkward and difficult for Democrats and the media to offer blunt criticisms. What's more, the fact that Republicans, after Bush's narrow ascension, now controlled Congress and the White House for the first time since the 1950s made Reagan's rise in the 1980s feel more like a major historical turning point than it had when Clinton, who'd successfully fought to undo Reaganomics, was in the White House. The GOP majority also provided a powerful platform for pushing the Reagan legacy to convince the public that Reagan on Rushmore was merely a matter of solving the geology. As years passed and the public's political memory became hazier, it became remarkably easy to simplify the history of the American economy into Before Reagan and After Reagan: B.R. was gas lines and 21 percent mortgages and A.R. was that simple tax cut that sent the Dow from triple digits all the way above 14,000. The reality, that Reaganomics nearly destroyed the American economy before Bush 41 and Clinton intervened, seemed just too complicated.

A generation of Reagan-era ideologues stepped into America's memory hole with a flood of books and recollections about the Gipper that, in a way somewhat reminiscent of how Lincoln was recast as the homespun man of the prairie in the late nineteenth century, reintroduced him as someone different than he had seemed to contemporaries when he was actually in the White House. He was no longer an ex-actor turned Great Communicator following a script, but rather a political thinker, and a man of God, with an extraordinary character. By the middle of the decade more than a thousand books had been published about Ronald Reagan, and the number continues to soar. By and large, the new generation of volumes didn't come from policy types. Those books, such as the tell-all that disgruntled chief of staff Donald Regan wrote during Reagan's second term, had been unflattering, focusing on White House infighting and the president's disengagement. Now the bestselling Reagan tomes sprang from the fiercely ideological speechwriting shop, the once-young vanguard of the Reagan revolution who had written the sound bites that refused to die, even as the policies and issues of the 1980s that had once given them a context faded into obscurity.

But there was a flip side to all of this: in the 2000s there were many who did in fact still remember the darker sides of the Reagan legacy, the seeming indifference to social issues such as homelessness and AIDS, and to minorities and gays, not to mention the near disaster of Iran-Contra. For the Reagan myth to really take hold, it would require more than just a wave of positive nostalgia. One had to make sure that any portrayals with a negative edge—even balanced ones—were crushed. And that is exactly what had happened in 2003, a year before the ex-president's death, when CBS sought to air a miniseries, *The Reagans,* on the eve of Bush's reelection drive.

Perhaps CBS didn't fully understand the politically charged minefield it was stepping into when it commissioned the two-part program, which had been slated to air in mid-November of 2003. The producers of the miniseries had aired successful shows about Hollywood subjects a tad less controversial, such as Judy Garland and Dean Martin and Jerry Lewis, and now they were giving the Gipper the standard movie-of-the-week treatment, somewhat following reality but with some invented scenes and dramatic dialogue, playing up the highest highs and the lowest lows. The first major piece on the upcoming drama, in the *New York Times* in October 2003, written with access to the final script, described a movie that for all its Hollywood ridiculousness and excess, was probably a more balanced and nuanced portrayal than what Americans would have seen that year on reality-based CNN. It did reportedly emphasize his moments of forgetfulness and his conflicts with staff, but it also was said to give Reagan "most of the credit for ending the cold war and paints him as an exceptionally gifted politician and a moral man who stuck to his beliefs, often against his advisers' urgings." Co-producer Craig Zadan told the newspaper: "It's not painted in black and white, but in blacks, whites and grays, many variations of gray."

But there were no acceptable shades of gray for Ronald Reagan in 2003—especially not when the scriptwriter threw in one admittedly made-up line of dialogue on the still hot-button issue of AIDS, in which the Reagan character, as portrayed by actor James Brolin, rebuffs Nancy Reagan on the issue by declaring "They that live in sin shall die in sin." That didn't sound like Reagan to those who knew him, and indeed there was circumstantial evidence that the Hollywood-nurtured Reagans were both personally at least tolerant of gays, if administration policy didn't at all reflect that. Some noted that Reagan did say to his official biographer Edmund Morris that "maybe the Lord brought down this plague," because "illicit sex is against the Ten Commandments." But that's not the quote in the movie, and so by inventing some extra drama, as Hollywood does with virtually every "based on a true story" production, there was more than enough ammunition for the Reagan mythmakers to shoot down *The Reagans*.

It might not have happened in an earlier time, but by 2003 there was not only an extensive infrastructure of conservative talk radio but also the growing power of the Internet, which both the left and the right were learning to harness for political clout. Now just the word that Hollywood—a punching bag for the conservative movement going back to the 1960s—was tackling the Reagan legacy was enough to energize the right wing weeks before the show even aired. It didn't help that the star Brolin was not only a liberal himself but married to a left-wing Hollywood icon, Barbra Streisand, or that actress Judy Davis, who portrayed Nancy Reagan, told the *Times* that "if this film can help create a bit more questioning in the public about the direction America has been going in since the 1970's, I guess then I think it will be doing a service." One of the first dire warnings came from Reagan's own son Michael, who wrote in an online column that "I fully expect this mini-series will be largely unfavorable to my dad" and that "Hollywood has been hijacked by the liberal left."

That was before the right started playing hardball. Brent Bozell, head of the conservative Media Research Center, wrote letters to the hundred most prominent TV advertisers urging them not to support the broadcast of *The Reagans*, which he described not as a gray, balanced portrayal but as "a partisan attack against one of America's most beloved presidents." An obscure Republican political consultant named Michael Paranzino launched a website called BoycottCBS.com and became a frequent guest on Fox News Channel, while grassroots organizing led to some eighty thousand angry e-mails sent to CBS. What's more, even the chairman of the Republican National Committee at the time, Ed Gillespie, entered the fray with a demand that CBS allow a historical review of the program or else post frequent warnings that it included fictional material. CBS executives who had been so glibly supportive of the program in October were in frantic backpedaling mode by early November, demanding last-minute changes and finally deciding to shift the program to parent company Viacom's pay-for-view channel Showtime, which thwarted any talk of an advertiser boycott but also meant that only a fraction of America would see the show, since the network was only purchased in 14 million homes, as opposed to the 108 million that received CBS.

It was left to the editorial page of the *New York Times* to understatedly point out that Reagan's "supporters credit him with forcing down the Iron Curtain, so it is odd that some of them have helped create the Soviet-style chill embedded in the idea that we, as a nation, will not allow critical portrayals of one of our own recent leaders." Indeed, while the Reagan defenders seized on a valid complaint over the AIDS dialogue, they themselves committed serial exaggerations in defending Reagan. His former press aide Marlin Fitzwater complained to the *Times* by asking, "Does it show he had the longest and strongest recovery in postwar history? That the economy, stimulated by the tax cuts, was creating something like 200,000 jobs a month, for years?" In fact, the 1980s economic expansion was not only shorter than those during the 1990s and 1960s but also less powerful by many measures. Nevertheless, Fitzwater's assertion was not corrected by the *Times*, and this untruth would become virtually gospel after Reagan's death.

At the same time, positive portrayals of the Gipper were flourishing in the early 2000s. The political upheavals of the Clinton and Bush eras and the growth of alternative media—talk radio, the cable networks and their increasing slant toward politics, political satire on late-night TV, and now the proliferation of Internet websites and blogs devoted to the same subjects—had also spiked interest in political books. There had already been a flurry of books in the late 1980s, culminating in Cannon's definitive 1990 White House years chronicle, that offered carefully balanced or even hard-hitting accounts, warts and all, of the policy wars of those years. Then, in the first two-thirds of the 1990s, there was little interest at all in Reagan, in keeping with the tenor of that time. But the political tomes that sold in the 2000s were those that threw ideological slabs of red meat to the farther right and farther left, and the Reagan legacy was ideal for that. The policy wonks were gone by 2001, replaced by the verbal equivalent of Operation Serenade from the people who advanced Reagan's long-remembered rhetoric, his highly ideological speechwriters.

Dinesh D'Souza set the template for these books in 1997, the same year that the Ronald Reagan Legacy Project was launched, with his *Ronald Reagan: How an Ordinary Man Became an Extraordinary Leader*. D'Souza was a contemporary and a bit of an ideological soulmate with Legacy Project founder Norquist. He had edited a right-wing student newspaper at Dartmouth in the early 1980s that notoriously outed gay students there, served as a lower-level domestic policy advisor for the last two years of the Reagan administration, and was surely eager to pay tribute to his ex-boss and perhaps to himself in the reflected rays of glory. He was also probably the first author to seek deep meaning in Reagan's very devoid-of-meaning everyday acts, insisting that when Reagan reached for jelly beans at a meeting, it didn't mean that the reportedly sweet-toothed Gipper was hungry but that "the participants were getting overly heated or technical."

But the passage of time, the Clinton sex scandals, and perhaps 9/11 and the Bush 43 ascendancy had soon rendered an account like D'Souza's—who for all his pomp was closer to the truth in capturing the contrast between Reagan's Everyman nature and what he achieved—as quaint, and way too understated. By 2001, Reagan was clearly the anti-Clinton, so much so that Peggy Noonan, author of the Pointe du Hoc speech and other emotional Reagan addresses, titled her hagiographic 2001 Reagan book *When Character Was King: A Story of Ronald Reagan*. Noonan also stresses a somewhat simpler view of her beloved ex-boss, focusing on his character and decency in dealing with those around him (not so much on his policies that affected so many millions more); yet even she is prone to exaggeration at times, writing of Reagan's 1980 campaign promises, "Done, done, done, done, done, done, and done. Every bit of it," even though those major promises included balancing the federal budget and shrinking the government.

But Noonan was just one whitecap in a tidal wave of Reagan hagiographies. Few were anything approaching a "fair and balanced" biography, while an increasing number of these books sought to seize on what the author had discovered was Reagan's secret key to success: not just his "character" but his "principle (John Harmer); his "conviction" (Peter Schweizer); his "wit, wisdom and eternal optimism" (son Michael Reagan, to whom his father once said at his graduation ceremony, "My name is Ronald Reagan, what's yours?"); his "spiritual values" (Paul Kengor); and his "strong and quiet faith" (Mary Beth Brown). Speechwriter Peter Robinson called his hagiograph quite simply *How Ronald Reagan Changed My Life,* although given the role that the words that Robinson penned for his boss at the Brandenburg Gate has defined the Reagan legacy, it could have just as easily been the other way around. Many of the books sold well, feeding on a conservative nostalgia for Reagan that only grew as Bush's poll numbers declined; they were backed by the growing number of well-funded right wing think tanks, a kind of Reago-Legacy complex.

The fact that so many of these books were written by speechwriters presented something of a conundrum for the Reagan legacy machine, however; his greatness was increasingly defined by his words and not by his policies, but if those words were the work of others like Peggy Noonan and Peter Robinson, then what exactly was it about the Great Communicator that was really so great, beyond his ability to deliver a line like "there you go again" with perfect timing and just the right cock of the head? There took on a new urgency in proving that the words flowed from something truly great within the soul of Ronald Reagan, that his own ideals and thought were the real force of his success and not his actor's skill in connecting with an audience. Thus it was a bonanza of sorts when Reagan backers in the early 2000s gained access to a treasure trove of documents that were written by the ex-president in his own hand, including his radio commentaries from the mid to late 1970s, his many letters, and even the diary he kept as president. The revelation that Reagan was a prolific writer did provide the desired jolt to the Gipper's reputation, and the blame for that may arguably lie with liberals who had gone way too far in portraying Reagan as an "amiable dunce" (a phrase with over seven thousand Google hits in 2008). The reaction among many liberals to the release of the documents seemed along the lines of "Wow, Reagan actually wrote things!"

In reality, the Reagan writings show that he was a man who was indeed very interested in the power and use of existing ideas, even if not in developing new ones, and they show how his consistency in verbally embracing a few bedrock principles, including his belief that freedom would trump totalitarianism and that less government is better, gave him a rare focus. That points to a unique type of intelligence that did indeed help to remake American politics, but does not support the stretch of a notion that converts him into a kind of public intellectual. One of the best reviews of works like *Reagan, In His Own Hand: The Writings of Ronald Reagan That Reveal His Revolutionary Vision for America* was by former Bill Clinton speechwriter Jeff Shesol, who praised Reagan but said his real skill was in adapting ideas to connect with voters. He concludes: "His brilliance—as Garry Wills observed nearly two decades ago in *Reagan's America*—was in his presentation of evidence and his near-perfect pitch. He understood America's hopes and fears—and played to both. Which makes him less a great intellect than, well, a great communicator."

But there was one more thing about Reagan's literary legacy makers, and it points in a dramatic way to how the reputation of a 1980s president had become so linked to politics in the 2000s. Ronald Reagan was now a man of God. Not that Reagan was ever someone completely divorced from religion, given the role of his devout mom Nelle and her Disciples of Christ in his upbringing, which led Reagan to the sect's Eureka College. But in many ways he was a personally secular president who rarely attended church while in office, perhaps influenced by Nancy Reagan, who is said to be not religious but who also became obsessed with astrology while in the White House, a heresy to many hard-core Christians. Clearly, Reagan understood the civic importance of religion, most famously when he mourned the *Challenger* astronauts who died in 1986 as men and women who "waved goodbye and slipped the surly bonds of earth to touch the face of God." More importantly, he found new ways to bring the religious right into GOP politics even as he walked a tightrope on key movement issues like abortion.

But now several books were seeking to cast Ronald Reagan as something more, as a force who derived the very essence of his power from God—tomes such as Paul Kengor's *God and Ronald Reagan: A Spiritual Life.* Yet here Christianity seems to come forth as mainly an instrument in Reagan's anticommunism tool box. An Associated Press review of the

Kengor book notes that Reagan "clearly had a sincere, sturdy and nonde-nominational faith in Jesus. But it's not evident what that meant in particular and we learn little about Reagan's Christian involvements as a mature adult." There may not have been so much to learn, but that did not stop George W. Bush from delivering a eulogy at Reagan's funeral that sounded at times as if his remarks had been prepared for Pope John Paul II's passing the following year.

Bush 43, in eulogizing Reagan, spoke heavily in religious terms, telling mourners that Reagan believed "we should strive to know and do the will of God." Bush also spoke of the calm that his predecessor had shown in revealing his disease: "Where is that courage learned? It is the faith of a boy who read the Bible with his mom. It is the faith of a man lying in an operating room who prayed for the one who shot him before he prayed for himself. It is the faith of a man with a fearful illness who waited on the Lord to call him home." Bush spoke at length of Reagan in purely religious terms, an odd tribute to a man whose greatest triumphs were truly in his secular idea that a world of free markets and free people would defeat communism. Some of Bush's strange choice of words no doubt lay in the nature of his own beliefs in the manifest destiny of the office of president, the view that he occasionally shared with others that America and Bush personally had a divine mission to fight evil, which no longer revealed itself as an empire but in a shadowy world of "evildoers." Bruce Bartlett, the former Reagan domestic policy advisor who became a critic of Bush's policies, told Ron Suskind for a *New York Times Magazine* article just a few months after Reagan's death that "just in the past few months, I think a light has gone off for people who've spent time up close to Bush: that this instinct he's always talking about is this sort of weird, Messianic idea of what he thinks God has told him to do." But never far away was also the politics of it all—not just the nitty gritty of Rove's drive to get 4 million evangelicals to the polls in 2004, but the more cosmic notion of God interwoven with country, of American good versus an evil enemy, and a line of succession that starts with Reagan the father and leads straight through to Bush 43, the adoptive son.

A president died on June 5, 2004, but it was his myth that ascended. *"Today history is what we say it is."* . . . The Reagan funeral marked the end, however, of an era that the Gipper and his PR-team-within-a-government had launched in the 1980s, an era when the nation's leaders could totally manage the news and the public perception that flowed from that. That's not how it seemed during Bush's first term, when all the president's men were able to control the story line and shift the discussion away from fighting the 9/11 terrorists and onto waging a war against a sovereign state that had absolutely nothing to do with the September 11 attacks, a feat almost as incredible as the seamless switch from war with Eurasia to war with Eastasia in Orwell's *1984*. The basic infrastructure had changed. While Reagan's message squad was fixated with prepackaging a headline, picture, and story to the nightly news of three networks, the Bush administration now had a pipeline that allowed it to bypass the traditional media and communicate directly with the conservative base. Scott McClellan, who served as press secretary during the middle of Bush's two terms but became a critic after leaving, said that the White House sent its nightly talking points directly to the popular right-wing evening commentators on Fox News Channel.

Ron Suskind, a journalist with a knack for getting inside the Bush administration, reported a jarring conversation that he had with a senior official during Bush's first term, in which the aide described journalists like Suskind as hailing from "what we call the reality-based community," fixated on empirical investigations of fact. The official explained the perspective from the White House: "That's not the way the world really works anymore. We're an empire now, and when we act, we create our own reality. And while you're studying that reality—judiciously, as you will—we'll act again, creating other new realities, which you can study too, and that's how things will sort out. We're history's actors . . . and you, all of you, will be left to just study what we do."

It was as if the Reagan mythmakers and the Bush image builders were working different sides of the same street for similar causes, one striving to rewrite the past while the other squad was fighting to control the present. But in the end, controlling the past is easier. Facts can truly be stubborn things, and difficult to contain when so many are coming at you all at once in real time. Ironically, it took Mother Nature to finally puncture the God-driven hubris of the Bush administration. On August 29, 2005, Hurricane Katrina slammed into the Gulf Coast near New Orleans, and within a day the high waters had inundated the Crescent City's fragile and neglected levee system. As the crisis in New Orleans escalated and the media questioned the absence of government aid—federal but also state and local—Bush was photographed at a naval base in Southern California strumming a gift guitar, then traveled to Arizona, where he shared a birthday cake with the man who would later attempt to replace him, Senator John McCain, then finally flew over the flood zone at high altitude on Air Force One, reinforcing the image that he was out of touch with the situation. It looked as if the criticism of Reagan-era official Leslie Janka—that "this was a PR outfit that became President"—had finally reached its sad climax. Katrina had cried out for a leader at the helm. Nearly 1,500 people died in New Orleans alone, most from the flooding after the levees collapsed.

The weakened state of those levees, managed by the U.S. Army Corps of Engineers, and the ineptness of the response efforts cast a harsh light on the nation's priorities under Bush. In the years leading up to Hurricane Katrina, for example, local officials had begged Washington for the money needed to raise several levees and strengthen flood control along Lake Pontchartrain, only to see the flow of cash reduced to a trickle as both cash and military manpower were diverted to the war in Iraq. "It appears that the money has been moved in the president's budget to handle homeland security and the war in Iraq, and I suppose that's the price we pay," a top local official said some fifteen months before Katrina struck. It's doubtful the financial aid could have salvaged the city's aging levees quickly enough if it had arrived, but the storm highlighted the conundrum of the Bush administration: thanks to Iraq as well as a few pet projects, federal spending was out of control yet not directed to where it was needed most here at home. As the TV pictures showed New Orleans mired under deep, dirty floodwaters, some angry critics dredged up an earlier quote from an advocate of Bush's rigid tax policies who said his mission in life was to shrink government "down to the size where we can drown it in a bathtub." The speaker was Grover Norquist, the founder of the Ronald Reagan Legacy Project.

Katrina was a turning point in public opinion about Bush, but it wasn't the only thing that was going badly during his second term. The situation in Iraq deteriorated into a religious civil war between Sunnis and Shiites, with American troops caught in the crossfire. The drive to deregulate the financial sector, a trend that accelerated under Reagan and continued into the 2000s with the encouragement of both Republicans and Democrats and their big business, big bucks donors, led to the widespread selling and then complicated trading of risky mortgage security packages, which then caused a credit crunch and an epidemic of foreclosures when the bubble in the housing market began to burst around 2007. The leaders of a Republican Party that once heralded the end of big government spent billions of dollars to rescue a private brokerage house, Bear Stearns, as well as the quasi-private Fannie Mae and Freddie Mac mortgage financiers. Meanwhile, the band of now middle-aged Reagan revolutionaries who had descended on Washington was part of a new permanent government inside the Beltway. That permanent government included Grover Norquist.

In 2006, press accounts revealed that Norquist had worked closely for a number of years with a lobbyist and GOP insider named Jack Abramoff, who eventually pleaded guilty to conspiracy to corrupt public officials, mail fraud, and tax evasion. (Norquist himself was never charged with any wrongdoing.) It was shown that Norquist, whose ties to Abramoff through the College Republicans even predated the Reagan years, worked with the lobbyist through Americans for Tax Reform in coordinating the use of donations from Indian tribes with casino gambling issues pending in Washington and elsewhere, and that Norquist and Abramoff were at the White House together when one of the influence-seeking tribal leaders got to meet with Bush. But even as the probes continued throughout Bush's second term, Norquist's influence within Republican circles did not diminish. In fact, it flourished as the party looked desperately for a successor to Bush, whose approval rating touched the lowest levels of any modern president.

And now that Reagan had passed away, the myth of the fortieth president only loomed larger over the process for electing the forty-fourth. You would think that claiming the Reagan mantle and then running the federal debt to record levels while directing an increasingly unpopular war and watching the nation's economic foundation heave would have tarnished the Gipper's legacy beyond repair. Instead, a new variation on the plot line emerged: that Bush 43 had become a failed president not because he had modeled his administration so carefully after Reagan, but because he had done it all wrong. In 2004, in the weeks when Reagan was nearly canonized in the media after his passing, Bush had been seen as heir to the legacy, so he must have been an imposter, and the new Republican president will be the one to actually restore the character and the glory of the Reagan White House. Since Dwight Eisenhower left the Oval Office in 1961, every GOP president besides Reagan had ended his presidency in defeat (Ford, Bush 41), disgrace (Nixon), or despair (Bush 43). The myth of Ronald Reagan, now enhanced every time a suburban parkway was renamed or a bronze statue was erected somewhere in red America, offered salvation.

As a crowded field of would-be Republican successors to Bush emerged, every man staked out a different claim to the Reagan inheritance—each claim full of holes. Former New York mayor Rudy Giuliani centered his campaign on the public's initial high approval of his response to 9/11; his vow of tough retribution to terrorists and would-be terrorists in the Middle East was, as we've seen, very much the opposite of how Reagan dealt with the Middle East. Former Arkansas governor Mike Huckabee was a Baptist minister and wild-card candidate who his allies in the Christian right believed would finally fulfill the promises that Reagan had made to fundamentalists in 1980, but other segments of the conservative base were wary of his big spending and seeming compassion on immigration. Former senator Fred Thompson of Tennessee had the most unique claim on the legacy, as he had gone from politics to acting and back to politics, but strangely he had none of the Reagan charisma. Former Massachusetts governor Mitt Romney, a good-looking and well-spoken family man, offered voters the most Reagan-like façade, but critics charged it was exactly that, that the scion of a well-known political family had veered far to the left to win elections in the liberal-leaning Bay State and was inventing a new persona on the spot. Romney replied by comparing his own reversal against abortion, and his moves further to the right in general, to the political evolution of the Gipper himself in the 1950s and 1960s. Then there was the case of McCain.

The former Vietnam POW had clearly zigzagged his way through the minefields of American politics in the 1980s, the 1990s, and the 2000s, a habit that made him a straight-talking maverick to his admirers (which seemed to include much of the Washington press corps) but an inconsistent flip-flopper to his critics. In 2000, as the Clinton years wound down, McCain gambled that voters wanted a candidate with a battle-tested character but with centrist or even center-left views, and so he played up his stands on liberal issues like campaign finance reform while suggesting his pro-life views weren't really so rigid. The Arizona senator badly underestimated the power with which the Reagan-era right-wing establishment would successfully seek to crush such talk in the GOP primaries. And so McCain reinvented himself yet again after his 2000 defeat, embracing George W. Bush (literally, in one famous photo), tacking to the right on most issues, and playing up his ties to Reagan even more than the first time around.

Unlike his main rivals, McCain did have a relationship with Reagan, but it was a complicated one. McCain and his first wife, Carol, had become friendly with the lame duck California governor and with Nancy after McCain's release from North Vietnamese captivity in 1973, but divorce was a complication. McCain left Carol for the much younger beer heiress Cindy Hensley just as the Reagans were ascending to the White House, and Nancy Reagan hired Carol for her staff in the White House. Politically, McCain wasn't exactly the "foot soldier" in the Reagan revolution that he would later claim to be; he arrived as a freshman member of the House in January 1983, when Reagan's popularity as president was at low ebb and the major accomplishment of the first term, the slashing of marginal income tax rates, had already taken place. The unpredictable McCain criticized his president on a number of issues—on deploying troops in Lebanon, as we've already seen, but also on job losses and the Republican administration's treatment of women and minorities. In one span McCain, elected to the Senate in 1986 after two terms in the House, opposed Reagan's positions on key legislation more than one-third of the time. Such independence might have been heralded by the 2000 McCain, but it was long forgotten in the unveiling of the 2008 model. TV commercials again showed the younger naval officer with the Gipper and other spots attacked Romney for more openly criticizing Reagan during the 1980s and 1990s.

The new ads were clearly effective with rank-and-file voters. McCain, whose candidacy appeared on the blink of extinction in the fall of 2007, in part because of his paltry financial support from the GOP activist base, racked up primary wins in key early states from New Hampshire to Florida. Still, McCain had clearly learned from 2000 that early voter support could be easily overwhelmed by the Republican elite, especially with its close connection to radio talkers like Rush Limbaugh and Sean Hannity who could whip up the hard-core conservatives. Ironically, McCain's political fortunes within the Republican Party started to turn around at about the same time he started playing footsie with his former enemy, Grover Norquist.

At one point early in the contest, it appeared that Norquist would actively fight to prevent McCain's nomination, just as he had done in 2000. When the race kicked off in 2007, Norquist's Americans for Tax Reform group was calling Republican voters in New Hampshire, urging that McCain and Thompson sign the group's no-tax pledge. When Norquist, as he later told *News-week,* ran into McCain on Capitol Hill, he brought up the Alternative Minimum Tax (AMT), a tax on affluent Americans that was enacted in 1970 and, ironically, was expanded by Reagan in 1986 when he signed that year's tax reform package, the very bill that Norquist's group was created to lobby for. But that was then; in 2007, Norquist wanted the AMT abolished. "You're not going to be able to," McCain said, as recounted by Norquist, but the two men exchanged memos on the subject and began a running dialogue. Norquist now said that McCain's position in 2001 against the Bush tax cut clearly had been motivated by lingering political resentments over the 2000 campaign, but "I'm not interested in long discussions about where they [referring to McCain] were five years ago. The Roman Catholic Church wants converts."

In fact, McCain was busily adopting Norquist's tax policies, one of the central tenets of the Reagan myth, with a religious zeal. The new GOP front-runner not only renounced his vote on the 2001 tax bill as a mistake but also promised on video to veto any tax increase sent to him by Congress. He didn't actually sign Norquist's no-tax pledge, but in a sense he went one better by proposing a new round of tax reductions that actually went further than anything Bush had supported—not only proposing to make the Bush tax cuts, slated to expire in 2010, permanent, but offering new breaks to big business and to the wealthy. McCain proposed slashing the corporate tax rate from 35 percent to 25 percent and accelerating write-offs for new equipment. Abolishing the AMT, a step that McCain had described as impossible just months earlier, was now a cornerstone of his policy, along with other changes that would lower the marginal rates paid by the rich but not affect the payroll tax burden on the middle class. The nonpartisan Tax Policy Center said McCain's plan, including extending the Bush tax cuts, would deprive the federal treasury of some $4 trillion from 2009 through the end of fiscal 2018. Some former allies were stunned at the new McCain. "He's tailoring [the tax cuts] to a Republican base," said former Republican senator Lincoln Chafee of Rhode Island, who had joined McCain in opposing the 2001 tax cut. "That requires a pretty much 180-degree turn on his part." But McCain added one more Reaganesque touch to his fiscal policies: he also promised a balanced federal budget by 2013.

McCain had truly swallowed the Reagan myth whole, accepting the economic policies that were a proven failure under two presidents while missing the lesson of Reagan's dramatic successes in dealing one-on-one with the Soviets. McCain instead wholeheartedly joined in denouncing his Democratic rival Senator Barack Obama after Obama declared that America should not be afraid to talk to its enemies. The self-proclaimed Reagan foot soldier even told a questioner at a town hall meeting that American troops might stay in Iraq for as long as a hundred years, a suggestion that would have been laughed out of the Reagan White House. And so it seemed possible in 2008 that American voters might really have a clear choice, between a candidate who wanted to return the nation to an idealized and even partly fictionalized version of the 1980s, and one who would bring the country into the new millennium with policies that were not nostalgia-based.

But as the general election loomed, it appeared that the Democrat Obama would not really be giving the electorate that second option, either. As noted earlier, he stunned many people—particularly his growing legion of hard-core supporters on the left—when he seemed to embrace the Gipper in his January 2008 talk to the *Reno Gazette-Journal* editorial board, saying that he wanted a Reagan-like approach in the sense that "We want clarity, we want optimism, we want a return to that sense of dynamism and entrepreneurship that had been missing." Facing criticism from his rivals in a close Democratic primary race, Obama and his aides quickly insisted they were talking about Reagan's skill in connecting with the public and not his actual policies. But the deeper meaning of Obama's interest in Reagan and the Reagan myth remained ambiguous as the fall election drew closer. In June, Obama met behind closed doors with evangelical leaders and later reported: "I opened up the meeting by quoting Ronald Reagan which was saying, I know you can't endorse me, but I endorse you." The Democratic standard-bearer did seem to understand the ways in which the Reagan legacy on foreign policy has been distorted, telling a Pennsylvania audience that "the truth is that my foreign policy is actually a return to the traditional, bipartisan, realistic foreign policy of George Bush's father, John F. Kennedy, of in some ways Ronald Reagan." But on economics he also seemed to absorb the notion that was cast in stone when Reagan trounced Mondale in 1984, that a candidate cannot win without promising more and more tax cuts. Although his tax proposals were aimed at helping the middle class and would increase levies on the wealthy, Obama's plan also raised serious issues about where he would get the money to pay for it; the same Tax Policy Center that blasted McCain's proposal noted that Obama's plan was nearly as expensive, costing an estimated $3 trillion over ten years.

But the biggest way in which the Reagan myth loomed over the 2008 race and now the future we all face today is this: that in a time of growing perils, from rising energy costs and diminishing supplies, from the dramatic threat posed by climate change, from a debt of nearly $10 trillion heavily owned by foreigners not always friendly to the United States, with aging baby boomers about to stress the Social Security and Medicare programs, with American prestige in retreat around the globe, there is no problem that cannot be solved with a mix of optimism and painless policy choices. The transparently false ideas that any economic malady can be cured with more irreversible tax cuts, and that foreign policy is simply a game of rock, paper, scissors in which rock always wins, are the core values of Reagan's distorted legacy, and in 2008 neither the Democrat or the Republican wanted to truly test those tenets of conventional wisdom, fearing that by challenging the legend of the Gipper he'd be handing the keys to the Oval Office to the other guy.

A new president took the oath of office on January 20, 2009, but the Reagan myth remained in power.

CHAPTER TEN

EXORCISING GIPPER'S GHOST

I t's always sunny at the Ronald Reagan Presidential Library & Museum in Simi Valley—or at least it seemed that way to a lifelong East Coaster who visited the imposing hilltop edifice in the desert-dry heat of an August morning, ninety-six days before the 2008 election. On this particular morning in America, the soft whistle of mountain winds was interrupted every minute or two by the hum of minivans carrying families making pit stops on cross-country caravans, rental cars emerging from the LAX sprawl, even the occasional tour bus. Fittingly, there's really no way to reach the remote Reagan Library that doesn't involve the burning of a lot of fossil fuels. The last half mile or so of Presidential Drive climbs steeply past banners of the other forty-one men who served as president; coincidentally or not, the failed chief executives who bracketed Reagan and then finally the divisive Clinton and Bush 43 are clustered near the entrance to the Gipper's glimmering red-tile shrine. A couple of the families I met this day had spent the previous afternoon on the wild and wet Hollywood razzle-dazzle of the rides and studio tour at Universal Studios, and now they were working their way up to a different type of stagecraft, the more serious kind, the stagecraft that made world history.

This landmark was now ground zero for the Ronald Reagan myth, where the Great Communicator still speaks in an odd kind of way from the Great Beyond to a new generation of American families, hundreds every day, from moms and dads who were still watching *The Smurfs* during the years of Reagan's presidency to their offspring, born when the eighties lived only on VH1. Simply put, Ronald Reagan is about as real to this generation as George Gipp and Knute Rockne were to moviegoers in 1940, and his saga has been increasingly repackaged in that same kind of cleaned-up and reshuffled Hollywood biopic style, except now in living Sunbelt–Big Sky Technicolor. Seemingly every artifact of Reagan's ninety-three years on Earth has been arrayed in Simi Valley with the same story-telling skill that Operation Serenade brought to the funeral week that concluded here. Visitors are told that Ronald Reagan won the Cold War and brought respect back to the American presidency. Inside the giant hangar of the Air Force One pavilion, the outer walkway is divided down the middle by a replica of the Berlin Wall. On the west side of the mock wall are Reagan's freedom exhortations, while east of the wall are written the worst of "We will bury you"–style commie propaganda. That's just a facsimile, but outside on the grounds is the real deal, a towering 6,668-pound graffiti-covered monolith that was picked up in 1990 from some newfangled German capitalists selling pieces for $125,000 each; the purchaser was hamburger mogul Carl Karcher of Carl's Jr. restaurants fame. (Karcher died in 2008; some of his other contributions to the cause of freedom included bankrolling a failed 1978 California measure called Proposition 6, which would have fired all gays and lesbians working in public schools, and also major fund raising for John Schmitz, a far-right Orange County congressman by way of the John Birch Society.)

Karcher is just one of the big-name donors whose names and plaques are strewn around the library building and grounds like so many rocks and boulders left behind by a glacier; the first thing a visitor to the com-plex notices are the signs along the walkway proclaiming "The Freedom Path . . . Provided by the Generosity of Harold Simmons." (So it's true what they say, that freedom isn't free.) Simmons is a Texan who got rich as a corporate raider in the Reagan-led 1980s economy and is now a bil-lionaire whose company backed the legal defense fund of two Iran-Contra figures and later gave $3 million to Swift Boat Veterans for Truth, which targeted John Kerry, and then nearly $3 million to a group running ads linking Barack Obama to a once-violent 1960s radical. The donor plaques from mostly Republican bigwigs and a few Hollywood stars like Merv Griffin and Bob Hope assault the visitor, who is also asked at several spots along the way to make his or her own donation, on top of the twelve-dollar admission fee. It doesn't escape notice that there are several donor citations either for Rupert Murdoch or his "fair and balanced" News Corporation, which includes the Fox News Channel, where top-rated host Sean Hannity is prone to ask viewers "What would Reagan do?" The library's "Founders" also include four sovereign nations that prospered mightily during the Reagan years: Japan, Taiwan, Saudi Arabia, and Kuwait.

In all fairness, the twelve-dollar E-ticket to see all those personal artifacts—and of course a ton of video—is also an enjoyable two-hour romp for any modern American history buff, and you have to keep reminding yourself that the real Prospero-like wizardry here is not so much what they leave in, but what they leave out. It starts in the very first hallway, where father Jack Reagan is no longer a nomadic alcoholic (as even Reagan himself described vividly in his autobiography) but rather someone from whom the Gipper is quoted as learning "the value of hard work and ambition and maybe a little something about telling a story." His non-combat military career is romanticized. He joined the Army Reserves Cavalry in 1937, and said, "Ever since I'd been addicted to Saturday matinees, I had an affection for those scenes when a troop of cavalrymen in blue tunics and gold braid, flags raised and bugles blowing, raced across the prairie to rescue beleaguered pioneers." A few feet farther on the museum walk, now-politician Reagan is portrayed as riding to the rescue of low taxes and small government, even if a few facts get hacked off along the ride. His epic $1 billion California tax increase in 1967, the largest of its kind at that time, is praised because he also "stood firm on a tax break for homeowners." A statue of a massively obese Uncle Sam is attached to his 1980 quote that "I believe it is clear that our government is over-weight and overfed. Indeed, it is time for the government to go on a diet," and leads into his promise for what we now know was a short-lived federal hiring freeze after he took office the following year.

There's no note for visitors about Reagan accumulating more debt in real dollars than all the presidents who came before him combined, or about the fact that the federal payroll increased from 1981 to 1989. Amazingly, there is also no mention anywhere of the Iran-Contra affair, the scandal that almost toppled his presidency. (The executive director, Duke Blackwood, told an interviewer in 2007 that some Iran-Contra material was taken out during some renovations and that "at some point in time, we hope to bring it back. But again, that's the fluidity of a museum. You can't have the same thing, you know, for ten, fifteen, twenty years.") The few nods to "balance" are so obscure they surely sail right over the heads of most casual visitors. A wall at the rear corner of the first big room does show some editorial cartoons criticizing Reagan (in bed with an MX missile, for example) but no captions to explain them to tourists, including those not yet born at the time. You would be shocked, *shocked* to learn that a Reagan museum seems to place a higher value on imagery and on symbolism than on facts; while there's no room for Iran-Contra, there's plenty of space for sculptor Veryl Goodnight's *The Day the Wall Came Down*, which shows a stampede of wild western horses toppling . . . well, by this point you can probably guess what they were toppling.

"Today history is what we decide it is."

Since Reagan died in June 2004, visits to the library have soared. More than one million people passed through the front entrance over the next four years, passing the denim-clad bronze cowboy of Reagan in the *After the Ride* statue, originally created for the Cowboy Hall of Fame, but instead standing guard at the library entrance. Needless to say, most don't come for the politics, but for the celebrity factor or simply the "wow" factor of walking through Air Force One. As I listened to the chatter of the visitors, mostly seniors or families with school-aged children, it was the pop culture stuff that always got the most commentary, especially for an exhibit of the former first lady's White House–era dresses and the like, called "Nancy Reagan—a First Lady's Style." The din grew as the summer crowd filed past the fiery hues and frills of Yves Saint Laurent and Oscar de la Renta. "Oh man, that is classy!" I heard one elderly man exclaim as he was wheeled past.

The most interesting comments I heard were from parents with their young kids; many of the parents had been in grade school themselves during the 1980s, and their recollections of Ronald Reagan seem a bit like those you might have of a benevolent distant father who died when you were young. While their images of Reagan had been shaped first around those fuzzy memories, they were sharpened by pictures, the ones on TV, the man who won the Cold War and brought home that concrete slab of the wall. "He was an optimist about this country, and when he got to the Oval Office he was honored to be there—there was something about [the way] he presented himself," Michael Clouse of Amarillo, Texas, told me. He, his wife, Kelly, and his son, Michael, had flown into Burbank the day before, gone to Universal Studios, then got up early to drive to Simi Valley. Kelly admitted in a softer voice that she was just too young when Reagan was in the White House, but "I learned a lot when he passed away." Had she watched a lot of the TV coverage?

"I watched it all day," she said. "I learned about how great he was."

The Reagan Library is also a place for that, but in the twenty-first century it also seems to be a great place to escape the real world. It offers an expansive horizon and dry cooling breezes, and limitless views of sage-brush hills and the mist shrouding the Pacific, and little else. It is another "shining city on a hill," and so in a strange way it reminded me of 1984 and New York governor Mario Cuomo's famous retort to the president's beloved phrase:

> But the hard truth is that not everyone is sharing in this city's splendor and glory. A shining city is perhaps all the President sees from the portico of the White House and the veranda of his ranch, where everyone seems to be doing well. But there's another city; there's another part to the shining city; the part where some people can't pay their mortgages, and most young people can't afford one; where students can't afford the education they need, and middle-class parents watch the dreams they hold for their children evaporate.

Simi Valley, California, may not be exactly the kind of place that Cuomo had in mind, but it could be today. Mostly invisible from the mountaintop library, it is a sprawling, centerless, earth-toned exurb of more than one hundred thousand souls. And like Cuomo's other city, Simi Valley is now a place where not "everybody seems to be doing well." The culprits have largely been rising gas prices and falling home values. On my way out of town, I paid $4.15 per gallon of gas, a price that would have been considered an outrage a couple of years earlier but on this day was an improvement. Right behind the station was an abandoned Kmart store and parking lot that marred the Sunbelt vision of uninterrupted progress. Also marring that vision was Wall Street analyst Hugh Johnson on my car radio, who was declaring that "I don't see this economy turning around unless something dramatic happens . . . something dramatic would be a drop in the price of oil, a lowering of interest rates by the Federal Reserve, or an easing of the credit crunch."

The signs of a credit crunch were not as easy for a day tripper in Simi Valley to see, but they, too, were there. Other areas were hit harder by the mortgage foreclosure crisis and the bursting of the housing bubble, including Antelope Valley and the Inland Empire, just to the east, but it was clearly feeling the pain. The total value of the homes in Ventura County that went into foreclosure during 2007, according to a local newspaper, was $750 million; meanwhile, the median sales price of a home in the same region had plunged by at least 17 percent from 2005, when the figure was $630,000, to the end of 2007 when the median price was $525,000—and average prices fell further in 2008. As I drove up Madera Road, about three miles from the Reagan Library I came upon a large back office for Countrywide Financial—or what used to be Countrywide Financial, which wrote so many bad home loans it had just been bought out by Bank of America. Most expected sizable layoffs around the time I was there; I cruised through the parking lot, which was fairly full except for some reserved managers' spots that were conspicuously empty. Even the Gipper would have had a hard time making people feel a sense of optimism about this scenario.

It is here on the back lot of Simi Valley, past the glitz of the Reagan Library, where a visitor can find the true legacy of Ronald Reagan, and not the low-hanging Cold War fruit so often plucked by the chattering classes and even by academia. It is not the things that the fortieth president did so right (brokering nuclear arms deals, restoring the spirits of the American public) or the things that he did so wrong (racking up debt, and allowing Iran-Contra). The most powerful but ignored legacy of Ronald Reagan lies in the things he didn't do at all. Reagan, and his skilled PR people such as Mike Deaver and David Gergen, revolutionized the presidency because they understood how words and images could create a story line that could change people's mood and then change their minds in order to ultimately change policy. And successors like Grover Norquist learned something that wasn't even thought of in that first 1980s moment; that they were at the same time creating a treasure trove of celluloid headlines, pictures, and stories that could be used to help change history and maybe even change some minds a generation later, after the Gipper was gone.

But there are two subjects that even the Ronald Reagan myth machine is not able to change.

Math and science. Especially science.

Reagan's optimism about the American spirit and about the human soul may have been infinite, but the supply of fossil fuels that powered so much of the economy's expansion while he was president is not. And so now the biggest crises facing America, its new president, and the planet are scientific at their core: the limited future of oil-powered automobiles and of cheap, fossil-derived energy, and, deeply related to our century of fuel burning, the warming of the planet, which threatens to drive up sea levels and wipe out animal species and coastal communities. It may have taken until the 2000s for these two issues, global warming and energy independence, to move to the front burner of American politics, but these problems were well-known and growing in the 1980s, when Reagan could have done something about them.

But the president whose leadership skills were to become the stuff of oversized bronze statues did nothing. That was his nature. Solving these environmental crises would have required the political values that were so alien to the popular Reagan: calling for collective teamwork rather than individualistic heroism, valuing scientific fact over emotional narrative, placing long-term societal gain ahead of short-term business pain, and asking Americans, as another well-remembered president of the twentieth century had done, what they could do for their country and not just what they could do for themselves. And that wasn't the worst part. Reagan would have risked sounding too much like the man whose ineptitude had handed him the keys to the White House in the first place . . . Jimmy Carter.

We now know that Jimmy Carter was the world's worst messenger, but with an important message that could have spared Americans a great deal of pain, if only anyone had bothered to listen. Remember Carter's "malaise" speech, the moment that came to define his inability to lead, or inspire? In hindsight, the speech deserves an F for connecting with voters and for impact, but an A- for accuracy. Carter scolded America that night:

"In a nation that was proud of hard work, strong families, close-knit communities, and our faith in God, too many of us now tend to worship self-indulgence and consumption. Human identity is no longer defined by what one does but by what one owns." But while he was tough on the American people—bad politics, there—he was also deadly serious about the nation's energy problems, and the risk of importing so much oil after U.S. production had peaked (it had around 1970). He said, "Beginning at this moment, this nation will never use more foreign oil than we did in 1977—never. From now on, every new addition to our demand for energy will be met from our own production and our own conservation. The generation-long growth in our dependence on foreign oil will be stopped dead in its tracks right now."

He backed up his words with solid proposals to tackle what he called "the moral equivalent of war": spending money to research alternative forms of energy with the same zeal that America had researched deadly new weapons, with tax credits to encourage the use of solar and wind power, and with government help for mass transit and to enact higher fuel standards. Earlier, Carter had donned a cardigan sweater and recommended that Americans consider lowering the thermostat to fifty-five degrees at night—commonsense advice that is ridiculed to this very day on right-wing talk radio (and finding echoes in the recent 2008 campaign, when the GOP tried to laugh at Barack Obama for noting that Americans could save gas by maintaining correct tire pressure). Although there were some boondoggles and missteps along the way, Carter's push for energy conservation was on many levels a rousing success—perhaps even worthy of some Reagan-like Mount Rushmore chatter, if only the effort had continued. Average fuel efficiency for American cars ultimately doubled from 1974 into the late 1980s (which was when Reagan finally successfully rolled back the standards). Energy conservation surged into the early 1980s, and oil consumption dropped.

But for Ronald Reagan, to win in 1980 he would not only destroy the messenger but his message as well. Here is what he said in his one and only debate with Carter that year: "[Carter] has blamed the people for inflation, OPEC, he has blamed the Federal Reserve system, he has blamed the lack of productivity of the American people, he has then accused the people of living too well and that we must share in scarcity, we must sacrifice and get used to doing with less. We don't have inflation because the people are living too well. We have inflation because the government is living too well." Attacking Carter's energy policies was something that cut to the core of what Reagan was all about, and it became another testing ground for his idea that free people and free markets could overcome any problem.

His belief that there should be no limitations on human striving was surely heartfelt. As noted by John Patrick Diggins, a professor at the City College of New York, Reagan embraced the consumer-oriented, pleasure-seeking culture that seemed to thrive during the 1980s and 1990s: "the genius of Ronald Reagan was, like that of [writer and philosopher Ralph Waldo] Emerson, to persuade us that we please God by pleasing ourselves and that to believe in the self is to live within the divine soul." Reagan also believed this kind of individualism was justified by its relationship to heroism, the idea that one man can make a difference. This was a notion that came through on the day of his 1981 inauguration when he highlighted the bravery of an obscure World War I soldier named Martin Treptow, who died with a pledge written in his diary to fight "as if the issue of the whole struggle depended on me alone." (Reagan's remarks also received some notoriety for falsely implying that Treptow was buried in Arlington National Cemetery though Reagan knew otherwise; it was the first documented lie of his presidency.) His quest continued with the gallery of heroes that he invited to the State of the Union address every year. Perhaps it makes sense, in hindsight, that Reagan was nicknamed for a role in which he asked teammates to "win one for the Gipper"—and not for themselves. He told America that "we have every right to dream heroic dreams."

But solving America's overreliance on foreign oil didn't really cry out for heroism, just simple teamwork: everyday citizens working together to drive smaller cars or take the train to work, or even, dare I say, putting on a heavy sweater and turning down the thermostat, fighting the overseas oil cartel one barrel of crude at a time. There certainly was no hero at 1600 Pennsylvania Avenue, where Reagan not only didn't see the need for "the moral equivalent of war" on importing oil from these unstable regions abroad but also essentially waved the white flag.

In fact, Reagan even took down the solar panels that Carter had installed on the roof of the White House. In August 1986, there was some work done on the roof below the panels, and they were never put back. Said a Reagan spokesman at the time: "Putting them back up would be very unwise, based on cost." That may have been a small gesture with greatly ironic overtones, but there were many other big decisions on energy policy that look extremely unwise today, with the aid of hindsight. The damage that the Reagan administration did to solar energy programs in general was much more severe. For example, Carter had created a Solar Energy Research Institute, which received $124 million in federal funding in 1980, but Reagan slashed that by more than half in just two years, and by 1985 the GOP-led White House had also allowed tax credits for homeowners using solar power to elapse. Reagan made identical moves against research and tax breaks for windpower.

By his second term, Reagan got help for these maneuvers from plummeting world oil prices, and for the most part they would remain low for the next generation. Of course, the steep downward spike in oil prices in 1986 had been largely due to the failure of the global OPEC oil cartel to remain united—and a key reason for that had been reduced demand from America and the West, thanks to conservation. It was a story whose moral was completely lost on the Reagan White House. Not only did the administration set back alternative energy research in America, but it also helped bring gas guzzlers back onto the American highways. Beginning in 1986, the Reagan team worked successfully to roll back the corporate automotive fuel economy standards, or CAFE, the federal program that had doubled average mileage on U.S. built cars to 27.5 miles per gallon; that standard was relaxed to as low as 26 miles per gallon. Reagan's transportation secretary Jim Burnley later explained that "the whole CAFE scheme is in terms of public policy ridiculous, and has the practical effects of driving U.S. jobs abroad." The first rumblings of the SUV, or sport-utility vehicle, also came during the Reagan presidency. In addition to the fuel economy issues, the Reagan administration also turned a blind eye in 1986 to consumer safety complaints about SUVs, keeping within the president's broad mandate that the U.S. auto industry "simply needs the freedom to compete unhindered by whimsical bureaucratic changes in energy, environmental, and safety regulations."

At the same time, the Reagan White House was ignoring a number of new reports showing that burning of fossil fuels was creating so-called greenhouse gases that were in turn accelerating the warming of the planet. In 1983, two years after leaving the White House, Carter chose environmental issues as the subject for his sharpest attack on the Reagan presidency, stating that Reagan "has stood almost alone in our refusal to cooperate with international efforts" on the new research into climate change, as well as other problems. That same year, a U.S. Environmental Protection Agency report that said "substantial increases in global warming may occur sooner than most of us would like to believe" was rejected at the White House as alarmist, and Reagan would not increase funding for global warming research until the end of his second term.

It didn't have to be this way. Other Western nations that started on the same road to alternative energy at the same time as the Carter administration—and didn't veer off into a political ditch—have reaped enormous benefits, including the kind of economic gains that are supposed to be at the core of Reaganism. In 2008, *New York Times* columnist Thomas Friedman visited Denmark, which like the United States was hammered by the Arab oil embargoes of the 1970s but stayed with a program of high taxes on oil and carbon emissions and kept strict standards for energy efficiency in construction. Today Denmark is completely energy independent, with no exports from the Persian Gulf but 20 percent of its energy from windpower, compared to just 1 percent in the United States. Friedman noted that Denmark also became a leading global exporter of wind turbine technology, pumping up its economy with a kind of high-tech expertise largely lacking in America.

But here at home, the mere fact that prices at the corner gas station dropped while Reagan was in the White House—without anyone having to resort to those unmanly sweaters and chilly thermostat settings—is proof that the Gipper's approach to energy issues worked and Carter's plan had been clearly un-American. When a newspaper columnist in my own home state of Pennsylvania praised Carter's once-discredited energy program and criticized Reagan's dismantling of it, a local resident wrote a letter to the *Allentown Morning Call* that said, "Each had a chance as president. Under President Carter there were shortages, gas lines, black marketing and stagflation. President Reagan ended gas lines, lowered the price of oil, and revived the economy."

Really?! The president of the United States has the power to end gas lines and lower the price of oil? Someone should have made that information known to Bush 43, who frequently told audiences in 2008 as the price soared past four dollars a gallon that he wished he had a "magic wand" to lower prices at the pump. Ronald Reagan didn't have a magic wand, either, but he and those who continue to invoke his name have something that's even better: magical thinking. The "American Prospero" came to Washington with a simple message of optimism, and when the price of oil collapsed (thanks to the energy conservation he was working to undermine), when inflation finally pulled back (the result of monetary policies started by his predecessor, and the passage of time), and finally when the Berlin Wall collapsed (after forty years of the American policy of containment), the audience didn't really want to know the secrets of how the magician did it.

The Ronald Reagan myth didn't die when the Gipper passed away in June 2004, it only grew stronger as it helped George W. Bush win reelection and then loomed over both parties in the 2008 race. Now, more than two decades after Reagan's last day in the Oval Office, his distorted legacy continues to haunt our future. It happens every time an American leader chooses to ignore the messy realities of science, it happens every time a new tax cut is proposed in a time of war and rising debts, and it increasingly happens in the arena of foreign policy.

Indeed, the Reagan myths surrounding international relations and military action are the most vexing, because, as we have seen, the twenty-first-century misunderstanding of Reagan's actual foreign policy is the most serious abuse of his legacy. Our leaders today seem to think there is no crisis around the globe that can't be confronted with a form of "Mr. Gorbachev, tear down this wall" bravado, even when that bluster is counterproductive, as it so often is. That was especially true in August 2008 when military action erupted between the independent nation of Georgia, once a Soviet republic but now an emerging democracy, and Russia. Not surprisingly, the sight of Russian tanks on the move created a kind of warped Cold War nostalgia for Reagan that helped to obscure more than a decade of inept management of U.S.-Russian relations and the fact that the issues bear scant resemblance to the 1980s.

"At one time, there was a president named Ronald Reagan who spoke very strongly about America's advocacy for democracy and freedom," Senator John McCain said in taking the toughest possible rhetorical line toward the Russians and their troop movements, even though there was much less of a safety net for avoiding escalation now than there had been in Reagan's day. Among Republicans locked in a difficult election season, there was almost glee over the Reagan echoes of the dangerous conflict; one right-wing supporter wrote in an online article that "the bear is still in the woods," referring to the political ad that Reagan ran on U.S.-Soviet relations in his 1984 campaign. Within days, Barack Obama had drifted rightward to a position similar to McCain's. Meanwhile, few writers mentioned Reagan's subsequent and successful efforts to strengthen relations with Moscow through dialogue.

Georgia, and an increasingly bellicose Russia, are just one of the global hot spots facing the new administration. From the oil-rich nations of the Persian Gulf, including a hostile Iranian government, to the growing instability of Pakistan, to the surging economic power of China and India, the United States was finding few solutions beyond threatening the use of its big military stick, and increasingly leaders were relying on Hollywood tough-guy dialogue instead of thoughtful diplomacy.

This is why the Reagan myth still matters so much today. The issues that dominate the American political landscape rotate in and out. Some still remain from the 1980s, such as the federal debt and how to distribute the tax burden, while others, such as the Cold War and the right-wing rebels in Central America, are increasingly the stuff of museums like the Reagan Library. But the political debates that Reagan won in 1980 and beyond—that the notion that sacrifice is to be ridiculed, and that Americans can conquer any problem simply through our can-do spirit with a lack of governmental interference, that the fading emotions at Pointe du Hoc matter more than the rising science of the greenhouse effect—still permeate our lives, even as they leave a stench of unregulated mortgage hustles, runaway fuel prices, and a "preemptive war" fought on top of the world's second-largest oil reserve. The odor permeated the Bush 43 White House, with its idea that America can ceaselessly cut taxes for the wealthy even when it's waging a war on two fronts, and when the only contribution asked of everyday citizens is to travel and go to the mall and spend more money. And sadly, the Reagan myth even infiltrated the 2008 fall presidential campaign, as Obama and McCain competed not over who would reduce the federal debt but over who would still cut taxes further, and as they punted on difficult choices on the energy-crisis front, telling Americans the simple answer was to "drill here and drill now."

In fact, the idea of an Orwellian political mythology as a force in American life seems to be growing. It has taken more than a decade, but some liberal activists and thinkers have just recently begun to take Reagan's distorted legacy more seriously, now that it has been allowed to take deep roots. At the left-leaning Institute for America's Future, president Robert Borosage said an informal working group began holding discussions in 2008 on how to best counteract the Reagan myth. "I don't think that politicians will take on this mission, because they want as many votes as they can get," says Borosage, voicing his frustration on a Reagan-inspired narrative that made it difficult for progressives to fight back on issues ranging from defense spending to tax policy. "So we ought to make the argument for them."

The flip side of this coin is the bizarre and often humorous campaign by a band of progressives to make a permanent impression for America of George W. Bush's presidential legacy—a deeply negative impression. The group Americans United for Change even dispatched a bus across the country before the 2008 elections with museum-like exhibits highlighting Bush's worst moments on issues ranging from Iraq to the environment. In San Francisco, voters were to cast ballots in November 2008 on a more permanent monument to our most unpopular American president: the city's largest wastewater facility would be renamed the George W. Bush Sewage Plant.

Funny stuff, but the reeking smell from that large oceanfront facility won't replace the bitter taste of Reaganism, as long as the ideas we now attribute, fairly or not, to the Gipper are treated instead as golden pearls. The only way to slay a myth is with those stubborn things—facts. Unfortunately one of the little-publicized moves of the Bush 43 administration was an executive order, issued just seven weeks after the terrorist attacks of 2001, when the national body politic was focused on other things, that gave ex-presidents and even their heirs the power to block the release of documents that were supposed to become public twelve years after that president left office (the post-Watergate reform was called the Presidential Records Act). The Bush order came shortly before the Reagan-era records were to become public under the act, and activists who are suing over the order say thousands of pages of 1980s White House records remain secret. In fact, Reagan's name was attached to a 2002 order, even though he'd been out of the public eye with Alzheimer's for eight years, asking to block the release of eleven specific documents including several from the Iran-Contra scandal. Hopefully, a new spirit of openness and reform—an American glasnost, if you will—is taking root with the new president and Congress that will lead to a reversal of this antidemocratic policy on openness in American government.

Stephen Knott, the founder of the Reagan Oral History Project, who now teaches at the Naval War College, said in an interview for this book that he was disappointed with what he claimed was tepid support the Reagan Library offered for his efforts. "The Reagan Library Foundation was more determined to build a hangar for the old Air Force One than they were in supporting the oral history project," Knott said, adding: "There were elements of Hollywood superficiality in certain aspects of Reagan's presidency and these aspects are apparent at his library." However, the biggest obstacle to a more honest reappraisal of the Reagan presidency is even more complicated, and that is a new, more reality-based approach to our modern history from the American news media. Arguably, the book you are reading right now is a tiny step in that direction, but for the U.S. citizenry to get a better read on what really happened—or didn't happen—inside the White House from 1981 through 1989, there must be a lot of help from the major news outlets. That is especially true of the news departments at the large cable and network TV broadcasters, who have the ability to take back the writing of "headline, picture, story" from ideological spin doctors.

A more realistic portrayal of Ronald Reagan and what really happened during his presidency, and its impact on the years that followed, would benefit all Americans, including the ideologues on the right who now cloak themselves in the shroud of a mythical Saint Reagan, and the ideologues on the left who will never see Reagan as anything more than the "amiable dunce" who said that "pollution comes from trees," and who thus have a hard time examining the things about Reagan that worked, the things that got him reelected with a higher vote percentage than any American candidate who has come along since.

The primary reason Reagan succeeded is that he understood he was an actor on a new kind of stage and a communicator who knew how to connect with his audience, even when his audience grew to one as massive and as diverse as the American people itself. Schooled in the newfangled twentieth-century ways of Hollywood, Reagan strove when possible to avoid dissonant facts—stubborn things though they may be—in favor of a compelling narrative. He knew, both instinctively and from experience, that the way to reach Americans was to sometimes play upon their fears but mainly to appeal to their hopes, their dreams, and their ideals of a nation of unlimited possibilities. Reagan truly did believe in America, in his interpretation of its founding principles, and its people, most notably himself, which is why he was not afraid to meet face-to-face with his great rival, Mikhail Gorbachev of the Soviet Union. On July 17, 1980, in accepting the Republican nomination for president, he laid out the contrast between his views and the meandering, failed presidencies of the 1970s:

> They say that the United States has had its day in the sun; that our nation has passed its zenith. They expect you to tell your children that the American people no longer have the will to cope with their problems; that the future will be one of sacrifice and few opportunities. My fellow citizens, I utterly reject that view.

So did America, which has never really looked back from that turning point in our history. Reagan spoke directly to the expansive frontier spirit that still lurked within the American soul, and made it clear that no future politician would succeed without the ability to draw on that reservoir.

Ronald Reagan had a God-given gift for connecting with the American people, but he abused it.

He abused his skill as a Great Communicator on issues of substance, for example preaching the gospel of less government even as the middle class in reality faced a worsening tax bite, but he also abused his power with the broader signals that he sent to the nation, that it was possible to have everything without making sacrifices or hard choices, with the implications that were voiced in that era on the movie screen by Gordon Gekko, that "greed, for lack of a better word, is good."

Andrew Bacevich, a retired army colonel and conservative social critic who soured on the Bush administration, wrote of the aftermath of that sea change in public attitudes in his 2008 book *The Limits of Power: The End of American Exceptionalism:*

> If one were to choose a single word to characterize [what it means to be a twenty-first-century American], it would have to be *more*. For the majority of contemporary Americans, the essence of life, liberty, and the pursuit of happiness centers on a relentless personal quest to acquire, to consume, to indulge, and to shed whatever constraints might interfere with those endeavors.

It was Ronald Reagan and his allies who fanned those flames of indulgence. And it was the keepers of the Reagan myth who whipped them even higher into the dark night of magical thinking in which inconvenient truths—from the ever-growing IOU on the federal debt to the grim forecasts of those maligned scientific "doom-and-gloomers"—are left to a future generation to deal with. In fact, when Reagan declared that 1970s leaders wanted you to "tell your children that the American people no longer have the will to cope with their problems," what actually happened in the 1980s and since has been even worse. We *demonstrated* to our children a lack of will for coping with problems, through our own inactions.

It hasn't always been that way. Just a generation earlier, an American president who was roughly a contemporary of Ronald Reagan laid out a different template for American progress. John F. Kennedy exhorted citizens to work voluntarily toward a greater nation: "ask not what your country can do for you; ask what you can do for your country." More specifically, JFK also confronted a problem of science, albeit a much more politically loaded one, in the issue of space exploration. The Soviets were seen as well ahead of the Americans when he took office in 1961, but Kennedy challenged the nation to send a man to the moon (and, of course, return him safely) by the end of the 1960s. The moon walk was an achievement accomplished by and for Americans, ending with Neil Armstrong and Buzz Aldrin on a stage set by thousands of bold and problem-solving citizens working behind the scenes. The moon mission was not achieved through daydreaming and the free market but by a sense of national purpose, powered by strong leadership, and huge public investments.

Of course, the world has changed since the 1960s. The Reagan speechwriter and now biographer Peggy Noonan, of all people, told the *Atlantic* in 2008 that Kennedy and the advisors who came with him carried "a faith they could be practical, pragmatic, worldly, that with these attributes they could manage what came over history's transom." That was before Reagan and his PR specialists created the roots of what today has become known as "the permanent campaign," the nonstop use of drama, imagery, and repetition to politicize everything—to rally the American people to support a cause and an agenda. In the twenty-first century, a smart and pragmatic approach to the crises the world throws your way is no longer considered enough to be a successful president. You must, instead, declare victory ("mission accomplished") without actually having achieved anything.

As much as it has been rightly criticized over the years, the permanent campaign as envisioned by Reagan, Deaver, Baker, Gergen et al. was perfected and refined by Democrat Bill Clinton and then by Republican George W. Bush for the only reason that anything survives for so long: it works. Indeed, the problem with the permanent campaign in American politics is not so much with the technique but with the short-sighted or self-serving policies that these unrelenting PR practices are used to sell.

The new occupant of the Oval Office—and indeed, the American electorate itself—can learn quite a bit from the presidency of Ronald Reagan, so long as it is not the warped version now peddled by a band of right-wing ideologues.

Indeed, our new president can accomplish a great deal by making the same appeal that Reagan did to Americans' innate sense of optimism and progress, with the same mastery of the art of communication, but with one huge difference. This time around, the rhetoric and the permanent campaign could be matched to policies that are actually supported by a majority of the American people: expanding health care and educational opportunities to all citizens, declaring war not on a faraway oil patch but permanently attacking the problem of U.S. energy dependence, building up our national defenses against *climate change*, and our only "crusade" being to pay off the federal debt.

Ronald Reagan said, "The American people, the most generous on earth, who created the highest standard of living, are not going to accept the notion that we can only make a better world for others by moving backwards ourselves." Now, imagine a new president for a new era, who uttered those words in announcing a new plan to eliminate the importation of foreign oil in ten years, with the same spirit of national unity and scientific adventurism that accompanied the similar one-decade vow to place a man on a moon. Picture a president rallying the can-do spirit of Americans around this problem, with programs not centered on what Reagan tarred as "the sharing of scarcity" but based on an explosion of intellectual wealth, with advanced forms of windpower and solar power and with cars that run on alternative sources and an electric mass transit system that is the envy of the world.

Ronald Reagan said, "We need rebirth of the American tradition of leadership at every level of government and in private life as well." Now, imagine a new president for a new era, who used the bully pulpit of the Oval Office to show that America can become a global leader, and not a petulant and reluctant follower, in the fight to reduce and eliminate the man-made causes of global warming, by urging all citizens, beginning with our schoolchildren, to understand the science of climate change and to feel that they hold a critical stake in solving the crisis. Picture a president who is able to portray any lifestyle changes that are associated with a livable planet not so much as a form of sacrifice—since, whether you like it or not, that word has been successfully banned from our political discourse—but as the strong and resolute answer to a challenge to America's courage and fortitude as a nation.

Ronald Reagan said, "Freedom is never more than one generation away from extinction. We didn't pass it on to our children in the bloodstream. It must be fought for, protected, and handed on for them to do the same, or one day we will spend our sunset years telling our children what it was once like in the United States when men were free." Now, imagine a new president for a new era, who uses the raw power of those words to roll back the worsening record of abusing the U.S. Constitution that arose with Watergate and Iran-Contra and flourished in the years of Dick Cheney and George W. Bush, undoing our proud traditions of freedom with torture, unwarranted spying, illegal renditions, and an assault on the right of habeas corpus. Picture a president who promised to renew our vows of liberty at home instead of pushing a warped and coercive version of democracy abroad.

Ronald Reagan said, "You and I, as individuals, can, by borrowing, live beyond our means, but for only a limited period of time. Why, then, should we think that collectively, as a nation, we're not bound by that same limitation? We must act today in order to preserve tomorrow." Now, imagine a new president for a new era, who takes those words from the Gipper's 1981 inauguration to heart and to the American people, to build support for the difficult choices that will remove this massive debt burden from our children's generation and others to follow.

Ronald Reagan said, "The defense policy of the United States is based on a simple premise: The United States does not start fights. We will never be an aggressor." Imagine a new president for a new era who says the exact same thing—and this time really means it.

When I visited Simi Valley, my last stop was the high burial ground where Reagan is laid to rest. There is a hazy void between his sun-soaked resting place and the complicated world that begins at the Pacific Ocean's edge. It is there that one finds the epitaph for this American man of legend: "I know in my heart that man is good. That what is right will always eventually triumph. And there is purpose and worth to each and every life."

The message of optimism that Ronald Reagan brought to the Oval Office in 1981 is the same one that he left this earth with twenty-three years later. But the stubborn fact is that right will never triumph unless we Americans, and our innate goodness, are brave and strong enough to confront the truth, that moving forward as a nation involves placing faith in science as well as in spirituality, and that finding our true purpose may involve difficult choices and even some struggle along the way. It has been a straight line, unfortunately, from the public's eager embrace of Reagan's optimism to the magical thinking and cynical manipulations of our current politics by the self-proclaimed keepers of the Reagan myth.

Someday, the Oval Office will be home to a president who is not only a Great Communicator but also a visionary leader, who will appeal to this nation's spirit but with an agenda grounded in reality and with a common sense of mission, propelling citizens in the direction we want to go, toward a society that is prosperous but also fair, with opportunity once again for all Americans. Reagan was right when he said that Americans don't want to look to the government to solve every problem, but neither do we want to live in a world where problems such as limited resources, pollution, and complex international relations are so easily ignored or laughed away for future generations. This new president, who will connect with America's better angels to truly improve our nation itself and not just the national mood, may already be in the White House, or we may have to wait another generation. But when that man or woman finally comes, then—and only then—will it be time for the geologists to go and investigate whether Mount Rushmore has room for one more.

NOTES

CHAPTER ONE

1 "Who controls the past": George Orwell, *1984: A Novel* (New York: Signet Classic, 1990), 35.

1 The block letters were stenciled: http://en.wikipedia.org/wiki/VC-137C_SAM_27000, drawn from Von Hardesty, *Air Force One: The Aircraft That Shaped the Modern Presidency* (San Diego: Tehabi, 2003).

2 The debate producer was: Anna Bakalis, " 'My crazy idea' for debate," *Ventura County Star,* Jan. 30, 2008, http://www.venturacountystar.com/news/2008/jan/30/my-crazy-idea-for-debate/.

3 On this Wednesday: Associated Press, "5 US Soldiers Killed in Northern Iraq," Jan. 28, 2008, http://abcnews.go.com/WN/wireStory?id=4200183.

3 a heated exchange: Philip Shenon, "Mukasey Offers View on Waterboarding," *New York Times,* Jan. 30, 2008, http://www.nytimes.com/2008/01/30/washington/30justice.html.

3 That afternoon, the Wall Street rating agency: Associated Press, "S&P Mulls $500 Billion in Mortgage Downgrades," Jan. 30, 2008, http://capitalmarketsnews.blogspot.com/2008/01/s-mulls-500b-in-mortgage-downgrades.html.

3 UBS AG, posted a quarterly loss: Elena Logutenkova and Elizabeth Hester, "UBS Reports Record Loss After $14 Billion Write-down," *Bloomberg News Service,* Jan. 30, 2008, http://www.bloomberg.com/apps/news?pid=20601087&sid=abmkbN0PseIc&refer=home.

3 nearly three thousand miles to the east: Bucknell University News Service, "Jim Cramer challenges 'laissez faire' government," Jan. 30, 2008, http://www.bucknell.edu/x40027.xml.

4 CNN's moderator, Anderson Cooper: "Transcript of GOP debate at Reagan Library," CNN.com, http://www.cnn.com/2008/POLITICS/01/30/GOPdebate.transcript/.

6 Ironically, that was a sharp: Carrie Dann, "The Gipper Steals the Show,"

MSNBC.com, May 3, 2007, http://firstread.msnbc.msn.com/archive/2007/05/03/181839.aspx.

6 Asked about Iran's reported: "California Republican Debate Transcript," May 3, 2007, http://www.msnbc.msn.com/id/18478985/.

7 One historian wrote: Kyle Longley et al. *Deconstructing Reagan: Conservative Mythology and America's Fortieth President* (Armonk, N.Y.: M. E. Sharpe, 2007), xxii.

7 In the winter blitzkrieg: Ariel Alexovich, "McCain Ad: A 'True Conservative,'" *New York Times* Caucus blog, Feb. 1, 2008, http://thecaucus.blogs.nytimes.com/2008/02/01/mccain-ad-a-true-conservative/.

7 which made a claim: Howard Kurtz, "McCain Seeks Reagan Mantle," *Washington Post* Trail blog, Feb. 1, 2008, http://blog.washingtonpost.com/the-trail/2008/02/01/mccain_seeks_reagan_mantle.html.

7 What's more, McCain ran ads: Foon Rhee, "McCain ads hit Romney on fealty to Reagan," *Boston Globe* Political Intelligence blog, http://www.boston.com/news/politics/politicalintelligence/2008/02/mccain_ad_hits.html.

9 The first stops: "Welcome to Reagan School," http://www.pbvusd.k12.ca.us/Reagan/rhome.html.

9 one in the Valley town: Patty Mandrell, "Chowchilla's newest school officially dedicated," *Merced (Calif.) Sun-Star,* Sept. 4, 2007.

9 Be sure to stop: Jeff Horseman, "Reagan Official Meese to Speak," *Riverside (Calif.) Press-Enterprise,* March 16, 2008, B1.

9 Ronald Reagan Park in Diamond Bar: "List of honors named for Ronald Reagan," http://en.wikipedia.org/wiki/List_of_honors_named_for_Ronald_Reagan.

9 Another small shrine: Liz Neeley, "Community Center renamed," *San Diego Union-Review,* Aug. 27, 2004, B-3.

9 Of course, given Reagan's: "List of honors named for Ronald Reagan," http://en.wikipedia.org/wiki/List_of_honors_named_for_Ronald_Reagan.

9 Then there is the Ronald: Kenneth R. Weiss, "UCLA to Name Medical School After Ronald Reagan," *Los Angeles Times,* April 20, 2000, A-1.

10 It is getting harder: "List of honors named for Ronald Reagan," http://en.wikipedia.org/wiki/List_of_honors_named_for_Ronald_Reagan.

10 Increasingly, small newspapers: Kara Vaught, "City Council rejects development on Ronald W. Reagan," *Community Impact Newspaper*/Leander-Cedar Park, June 20, 2008.

10 This one appeared around: "Carjacking Victim Shot, Dumped on Ronald Reagan Highway," WLWT, Cincinnati, June 24, 2008, http://www.wlwt.com/news/16692822/detail.html.

10 Not far from the stretch: Francis X. Clines, "Reagan Contends Jackson's Missions May Violate Law," *New York Times,* July 5, 1984, A-1.

11 Actually, Reagan could have: "School named after Reagan opens this fall," United Press International, March 14, 1984.

11 Ten years later: John W. Gonzalez, "Reagan High honors namesake with service," *Houston Chronicle,* June 12, 2004, A-37.

11 In New Hampshire: Warren Hastings, "Mount Clay to Become Mount Reagan," *Manchester Union-Leader,* May 30, 2003, A-1.

11 Even some Democratic-voting: Elizabeth Public Schools, "School #30: Ronald Reagan Leadership Academy," http://www.elizabeth.k12.nj.us/newconstruction/index30.htm.

12 Less successful: James Bradley, "Pier Pressure," *Village Voice,* March 17, 1998, 27.

12 Other Reagan tributes seem: Jessica Brown, "Reagan Park Drawing Rave Reviews," *Cincinnati Enquirer,* Aug. 2, 2006, 1-B.

12 In the northwestern suburbs: John Patterson, "Start county anew? Breaking up is hard to do," *Daily Herald (Ill.),* April 27, 2008.

12 The Ronald Reagan Missile Defense Site: U.S. Air Force, "Missile Defense Site Named After Ronald Reagan," April 12, 2006, http://www.af.mil/news/story.asp?id=123018979.

12 It joins a larger: "List of honors named for Ronald Reagan," http://en.wikipedia.org/wiki/List_of_honors_named_for_Ronald_Reagan.

12 To some dreamers back: William Bunch, "People want Reagan's face on something," *Philadelphia Daily News,* June 11, 2004.

13 When lawmakers in Utah: Robert Gehrke, "Reagan Day Is Declared," *Salt Lake Tribune,* Feb. 8, 2008.

13 New Hampshire Republican: Jennifer Feals, "Exeter's Ioka Theatre presents 'Ronald Reagan—A Retrospective'," Seacoastonline.com, June 17, 2008, http://www.seacoastonline.com/apps/pbcs.dll/article?AID=/20080617/NEWS/806170352/-1/rss04/.

14 The Simi Valley location: Seth Mydans, "Elite Group to Dedicate Reagan Library," *New York Times,* Nov. 1, 1991, A-14.

15 federal spending grew 2.5 percent: William A. Niskanen, "Reaganomics," *Concise Encyclopedia of Economics,* http://www.econlib.org/library/Enc/Reaganomics.html.

16 an October 1989 interview: Josh Barbanel, "Reaganism Now Liability for Giuliani," *New York Times,* Oct. 11, 1989.

16 Romney, who offered: David Lightman, "Romney wasn't always such a Reagan fan," *Miami Herald,* Dec. 24, 2007.

16 And if McCain returned: "A Navy Veteran Warns of Excessive Pentagon Spending," *National Journal*, March 5, 1983, 501.

16 Two years later, he: Michael Kilian, "The War Hero is a Senator Now," *Chicago Tribune*, July 29, 1987, C-1.

19 "The Reagan Cult of Personality": Author telephone interview with Rick Perlstein, May 8, 2008.

21 "Reagan's devotion to certain": Author e-mail interview with Stephen Knott, May 13, 2008.

21 "Ronald Reagan changed the trajectory": Greg Sargent, "Obama: Reagan Changed Direction Of Country In Way Bill Clinton Didn't," Talking Points Memo Election Central, Jan. 16, 2008, http://tpmelectioncentral. talkingpointsmemo.com/2008/01/obama_reagan_changed_direction_of_ country_in_way_bill_clinton_didnt.php

21 John Edwards, the former: Julie Bosman, "Edwards Attacks Obama for View of Reagan," *New York Times*, Jan. 18, 2008.

CHAPTER TWO

23 "I got a tremendous": Rotesh Ratnesar, "20 Years After 'Tear Down This Wall,' " *Time*, June 11, 2007, http://www.time.com/time/world/arti cle/0,8599,1631828,00.html.

23 The *New York Times'* coverage: Gerald M. Boyd, "Raze Berlin Wall, Reagan Urges Soviet," *New York Times*, June 13, 1987.

24 One journalist who reviewed: Josh Ward, "Reagan's 'tear down this wall' speech turns 20 in thoroughly changed Berlin," Associated Press, June 12, 2007.

24 According to Richard Reeves: Richard Reeves, *President Reagan: The Tri-umph of Imagination* (New York: Simon & Schuster, 2005), 401.

24 The image of the towering: Lou Cannon, *President Reagan: The Role of a Lifetime* (New York: PublicAffairs, 2000), 695.

25 In 2007, for example: Larry King, "50 Years of Pop Culture," CNN, May 3, 2007, transcript.

25 Three years earlier, CBS's: *The Early Show*, CBS, Aug. 5, 2003, CBS News transcript.

25 Madeleine Albright, the secretary: Madeleine Albright, *Memo to President Elect: How We Can Restore America's Reputation and Leadership* (New York: Harper, 2008), 33.

25 In fact, when Reagan: Glenn Greenwald, "The Chamberlain/appease-ment cliché," Unclaimed Territory blog, Aug. 31, 2006, http://glenngreen wald.blogspot.com/2006/08/chamberlainappeasement-cliche_31.html.

26 Gorbachev himself told: Robert G. Kaiser, "Gorbachev: 'We all lost Cold War,' " *Washington Post*, June 11, 2004, A-1.

26 James Mann, author: James Mann, "Tear Down That Myth," *New York Times*, op-ed, June 10, 2007.

27 When reporters tried: Steven R. Weisman, "Reagan's Visit to Tidelands Irks Environmental Critics," *New York Times*, July 11, 1984, A-16.

27 just nineteen months after Reagan: Thomas Griffith, "The Bite Without the Sting," *Time*, Aug. 16, 1982.

27 "He's an actor": Mark Hertsgaard, *On Bended Knee: The Press and the Reagan Presidency* (New York: Farrar Straus Giroux, 1988), 46.

28 "The mythologizing of him": Author telephone interview with Mark Hertsgaard, June 9, 2008.

29 Presidential historian Robert Dallek: Robert Dallek, *Ronald Reagan: The Politics of Symbolism* (Cambridge, Mass.: Harvard University Press, 1999), 7.

29 Many Reagan biographies stress: Edmund Morris, *Dutch: A Memoir of Ronald Reagan* (New York: Random House, 1999).

29 "What he was able": Author telephone interview with Robert Dallek, April 24, 2008.

30 But Ronald Reagan was: Cannon, *President Reagan: The Role of a Lifetime*, 172.

30 former Reagan aide turned biographer: *Think Tank with Ben Wattenberg*, "What Is Reagan's Legacy?" Public Broadcasting System, June 10, 2004, transcript, http://www.pbs.org/think tank/transcript817.html.

31 The source of his sense of optimism: Haynes Johnson, *Sleepwalking Through History: America in the Reagan Years* (New York: Norton, 1991), 43.

31 "When you read Reagan's": Peggy Noonan, *When Character Was King: A Story of Ronald Reagan* (New York: Penguin, 2003).

32 family found him distant: Jonathan Alter, "Review: *Dutch: A Memoir of Ronald Reagan*," *Washington Monthly*, December 1999.

32 Gerald Ford: Lou Cannon, *Governor Reagan: His Rise to Power* (New York: PublicAffairs, 2005), 398.

32 "for the first time": *The American Experience*, "Ronald Reagan Speaks About Family," Public Broadcasting System, http://www.pbs.org/wgbh/amex/reagan/sfeature/tour_earlyyears.html.

33 As guild president, Reagan: "SAG President Ronald W. Reagan: Testimony to House Un-American Activities Committee," Oct. 23, 1947, http://www.cnn.com/SPECIALS/cold.war/episodes/06/documents/huac/reagan.html.

34 Reagan himself wrote in: Paul Kengor and Peter Schweizer, eds., *The Rea-*

gan Presidency: Assessing the Man and His Legacy (Lanham, Md.: Rowman & Littlefield, 2005), 28.

34 It was army officials: "First Motion Picture Unit," http://www .genordell.com/stores/lantern/FMPU.htm.

35 Cannon and other contemporary: Cannon, *President Reagan: The Role of a Lifetime,* 431.

35 One academic during the 1980s: Martin Tolchin, "How Reagan Always Gets the Best Lines," *New York Times,* Sept. 9, 1985, B-9.

36 "free world is in mortal": "Text of Wilson's Defense Plea to the People Through the Press of the Nation," *New York Times,* April 27, 1951, 14.

37 As noted by Thomas W. Evans: Thomas W. Evans, "The GE Years: What Made Reagan Reagan," History News Network, Jan. 8, 2007, http://hnn .us/articles/32681.html.

37 By then, Reagan: Johnson, *Sleepwalking Through History,* 69–70.

38 "A Time for Choosing": Ronald Reagan speech, "A Time for Choosing," Oct. 27, 1964, http://www.reaganlibrary.com/reagan/speeches/rendezvous.asp.

39 At large campaign rallies: Rick Perlstein, *Nixonland: The Rise of a President and the Fracturing of America* (New York: Scribner, 2008), 90.

39 On January 2, 1967: Sean Wilentz, "The Legacy of 1967: A Leading Historian Assesses the Year That Split America in Two," *Rolling Stone,* July 12, 2007, http://www.rollingstone.com/politics/story/15255443/the_ legacy_of_1967_a_leading_historian_assesses_the_year_that_split_amer ica_in_two.

40 Lou Cannon, who covered: Author telephone interview with Lou Cannon, May 29, 2008.

41 The mid to late 1970s: Kiron K. Skinner, et al., eds., *Reagan, In His Own Hand: The Writings of Ronald Reagan That Reveal His Revolutionary Vision for America* (New York: Simon & Schuster, 2001), 396, 12.

42 Carter went before the nation: Jimmy Carter, "The 'Crisis of Confidence' Speech, July 15, 1979, http://www.pbs.org/wgbh/amex/carter/film more/ps_crisis.html.

42 The contrast in styles: Scott Dikkers, *Our Dumb Century: The Onion Presents 100 Years of Headlines from America's Finest News Source* (Philadelphia: Running Press, 2004), http://www.opendemocracy.net/globalization-climate_ change_debate/article_900.jsp.

43 "we could pave": Cannon, *President Reagan: The Role of a Lifetime,* 163.

43 But as biographer Lou Cannon: Cannon, *Governor Reagan: His Rise to Power,* 505.

43 Carter showed up: "Debate Transcript," Commission on Presidential Debates, Oct. 27, 1980, http://www.debates.org/pages/trans80b.html.

CHAPTER THREE

47 "It's a zero-sum": "Wall Street 1987 Movie Quotes," http://www.movie quotes.com/repository.cgi?pg=3&tt=82791.

48 "And this is only": Maureen Santini, "Reagan signs tax, spending cuts into law," Associated Press, Aug. 13, 1981.

48 "marked an end": Bruce Bartlett, "Remember Reagan's Tax Cuts," *Human Events*, Aug. 14, 2006, http://findarticles.com/p/articles/mi_qa3827/is_200608/ai_n17182708.

49 America's unemployment rate reached: Gil Troy, *Morning in America: How Ronald Reagan Invented the 1980s* (Princeton, N.J.: Princeton University Press, 2005), 113.

49 Here's what Thomas B. Edsall: Thomas B. Edsall, "Reagan Wins May Be Far-Reaching; Tax and Budget Cuts Could Transform Nation's Political Balance," *Washington Post*, Aug. 13, 1981, A-2.

50 A desperate Rudy Giuliani: "Giuliani wants to cut corporate, capital gains taxes," Reuters, Jan. 10, 2008.

50 "There was a big inflation problem": Author telephone interview with Paul Krugman, April 23, 2008.

51 Reagan told the nation: "Transcript of Reagan's Address on the State of the Nation's Economy," *New York Times*, Feb. 6, 1981, A-12.

52 The number of millionaires: Paul Krugman, "Paul Krugman on the Great Wealth Transfer," *Rolling Stone*, Nov. 20, 2006, http://www.rollingstone.com/politics/story/12699486/paul_krugman_on_the_great_wealth_transfer/print.

52 Just six months after: Anthony Lewis, "At Home Abroad: The Cost of Reagan," *New York Times*, Sept. 27, 1989, A-27.

53 Including Reagan's old benefactor: *New York Times* business brief, Nov. 7, 1974, 78.

53 By October 1980: "Carter Criticizes Federal Reserve Board," Associated Press, Oct. 2, 1982.

53 "High tax rates": Robert G. Kaiser, "Reagan's Politically Potent Promise—An Income Tax Cut," *Washington Post*, June 16, 1980, A-3.

54 group of economic rebels: Haynes Johnson, *Sleepwalking Through History: America in the Reagan Years* (New York: Norton, 1991), 105–8.

54 Reagan, according to Lou Cannon's: Lou Cannon, *President Reagan: The Role of a Lifetime* (New York: PublicAffairs, 2000), 737.

55 The new president's path: Richard Reeves, *President Reagan: The Triumph of Imagination* (New York: Simon & Schuster, 2005), 12.

55 The president's message was: "We Can No Longer Procrastinate and Hope Things Get Better," *Washington Post*, Feb. 19, 1981, A-12.

55 And Americans responded: Reeves, *President Reagan: The Triumph of Imagination*, 20.

56 The Democratic Speaker: Reeves, *President Reagan: The Triumph of Imagination*, 57.

56 Reagan clinched the deal: Martin Schram, "Reagan the Tax Lobbyist: An Artist at Work," *Washington Post*, Aug. 13, 1981, A-3.

56 When the tax bill: Schram, "Reagan the Tax Lobbyist."

56 Darman told Stockman: Michael Duffy, "Man in the Muddle; Dick Darman helped create the budget mess, but he can't find a way to solve it," *Time*, Oct. 15, 1990, 40.

57 But there was a lot: Kyle Longley et al. *Deconstructing Reagan: Conservative Mythology and America's Fortieth President* (Armonk, N.Y.: M. E. Sharpe, 2007), 45.

57 As the Associated Press: Sally Jacobsen, "The Tax Cut and You: Oil Taxes," Associated Press, Aug. 14, 1981.

57 Supply-side boosters: Frank W. Slusser, "Stocks go nowhere in dull August week," United Press International, Aug. 14, 1981.

57 the federal deficit rose: Stephen Koepp, "In the Shadows of the Twin Towers; How America's budget and trade deficits grew to daunting heights," *Time*, Nov. 2, 1987, 46.

57 Experts like Michael A. Meeropol: Michael A. Meeropol, "A Tale of Two Tax Cuts; What recent history teaches about recessions and economic policy," Economic Policy Institute, http://www.epi.org/content.cfm/issuebriefs_ib157.

58 "In fact, no peacetime": Paul Krugman, "The Great Taxer," *New York Times*, June 4, 2004.

58 "It's been dishonestly portrayed": ABC News Transcripts, *World News Tonight*, Aug. 10, 1982.

58 The measure, Joshua Green: Joshua Green, "Reagan's Liberal Legacy: What the New Literature on the Gipper Won't Tell You," *Washington Monthly*, Jan./Feb. 2003.

58 Bruce Bartlett, the leading: Bruce Bartlett, "A Taxing Experience: The stars are aligning for a tax increase," *National Review Online*, Oct. 29, 2003, http://www.nationalreview.com/nrof_bartlett/bartlett200310290853.asp.

59 Stockman wrote: Reeves, *President Reagan: The Triumph of Imagination*, 92.

59 By 1982, even the conservative: Howell Raines, "Executives Bid Reagan Cut Deficit," *New York Times*, March 13, 1982, 31.

59 "The rest of the story": Author telephone interview with Lou Cannon, May 29, 2008.

60 When Reagan took office: Krugman, "The Great Taxer."

61 In fact, the federal government: Michael Kinsley, "Reagan's Record," *Slate*, Feb. 9, 2001, http://www.slate.com/id/100474/.

61 "The major failure": Peter T. Kilbourn, "Where the Reagan Revolution Went Awry," *New York Times*, Nov. 8, 1987.

62 Howard Baker, who blurted: Cannon, *President Reagan: The Role of a Lifetime*, 231.

63 Stockman, of all people: Bernard Sherman, "Reaganomics: Why Ronald Reagan's 1981 Tax Cut Did Not Cause the 1983 Recovery or Boost Tax Revenues," http://www.bsherman.org/rushmore.html.

63 "As for Reagan being": Michael J. Mandel, "Reagan's Economic Legacy," *BusinessWeek Online*, June 21, 2004, http://www.businessweek.com/magazine/content/04_25/b3888032_mz011.htm.

64 "A largely unregulated financial": Harold Meyerson, "Bailing Out the Reaganites," *Washington Post*, April 2, 2008, A-19.

65 "Portentous change": John Aloysius Farrell, "The Electronic Election," *Boston Globe*, Nov. 13, 1988, 1.

65 "In less than a decade": Dale Russakoff, "Brawn Forged Into Brain; Muscles of Steel Atrophied, Pittsburgh Turns to Services," *Washington Post*, April 12, 1987, A-1.

65 Those huge budget deficits: CBS News, *60 Minutes*, "Bush Sought 'Way' to Invade Iraq," June 11, 2004, http://www.cbsnews.com/stories/2004/01/09/60minutes/main592330.shtml.

65 By 2008, the amount: Michael R. Sesit, "A wealth of funds in hiding," Bloomberg News, April 9, 2007.

66 Economist John W. Sloan: Longley et al. *Deconstructing Reagan*, 56.

66 As Paul Krugman and other: Paul Krugman, "Introducing This Blog," Conscience of a Liberal, Sept. 19, 2007, http://krugman.blogs.nytimes.com/2007/09/18/introducing-this-blog/.

67 The percentage of individual citizens: "The Poverty Figures," *Washington Post*, Sept. 1, 1988, A-22.

67 The pay for corporate CEOs: "Just Capitalism; Not all attacks on business are crazy. Here is the sane version," *Washington Post*, Dec. 22, 2006.

67 William Safire, the conservative: William Safire, "Essay; Ode to Greed," *New York Times*, Jan. 5, 1986, 19.

68 "The public seemed fascinated": Bill Barol, "The Eighties Are Over," *Newsweek*, Jan. 4, 1988, 40.

68 "There's a great deal": Cannon, *President Reagan: The Role of a Lifetime,* 231.
68 urging America at the depth: "Transcript of the President's State of the Union Address to the Nation," *New York Times,* Jan. 27, 1982, 16.

CHAPTER FOUR

71 "[Reagan] said that killing": Lou Cannon, "U.S. Seeks to Cool Hopes For Hostages' Early Release; Outside Mediators Restricted," *Washington Post,* June 22, 1985, A-1.
71 "We never intended the film": Jay Cocks, "The Nightmare Comes Home; ABC's movie *The Day After* stirs a storm of nuclear debate," *Time,* Oct. 24, 1983, 84.
72 "the fact that the telecast": Tom Shales, " 'The Day After' Approaches; ABC's Movie on Nuclear War Runs Into Early Fallout," *Washington Post,* Oct. 11, 1983, C-11.
72 *Time* had featured a Pershing: Strobe Talbott, "Playing Nuclear Poker," *Time,* Jan. 31, 1983, http://www.time.com/time/magazine/article/0,9171,951904,00.html.
73 "What this movie does": Shales, " 'The Day After' Approaches."
73 Eagle Forum's Phyllis Schlafly: Fred Rothernberg, "Demonstrations, Counseling Planned Around 'The Day After,' " Associated Press, Nov. 20, 1983.
73 "We have set ourselves": Harry F. Walters et al., "TV's Nuclear Nightmare," *Newsweek,* Nov. 21, 1983, 66.
74 "Well, Jim, *The Sound of Music*": Lou Cannon, *President Reagan: The Role of a Lifetime* (New York: PublicAffairs, 2000), 37.
74 "If things get hotter": Lawrence S. Whitter, "What Activists Can Learn from the Nuclear Freeze Movement," History News Network, Aug. 18, 2003, http://hnn.us/articles/1636.html.
74 "It is powerfully done": Daniel McCarthy, "Revising Reagan: Was the 40th president a peace-loving moderate?," *Reason,* June 2007, http://www.reason.com/news/show/119735.html.
74 On January 16, 1984: "Transcript of Reagan's Speech on American-Soviet Relations," *New York Times,* Jan. 17, 1984, A-8.
75 Reagan sent a remarkable: Joe Niccum, "Fallout from 'The Day After,' " *Lawrence World-Journal,* Nov. 19, 2003, http://www.lawrence.com/news/2003/nov/19/fallout_from/.
76 Reagan, in fact, promised: Cannon, *President Reagan: The Role of a Lifetime,* 290.
76 On July 7, 1985: Lou Cannon, "What Happened to Reagan the Gun-

slinger? Now His Problem Is Convincing Skeptics He Isn't a Pussycat," *Washington Post,* July 7, 1985, B-1.

78 "One enormous reason all": Helen Dewar, "Dole Counterattacks on Senate Floor; Defending Bush, Minority Leader Lashes Out at Mitchell's Remarks," *Washington Post,* Nov. 16, 1989, A-8.

78 A poll published in *USA Today*: "Respondents Say Gorbachev Most Responsible for Wall's Demise," Associated Press, Nov. 13, 1989.

78 former Reagan aide Pat Buchanan: Pat Buchanan, Address to the Republican National Convention, Aug. 17, 1992, American Rhetoric Online Speech Bank, http://www.americanrhetoric.com/speeches/patrickbuchanan 1992rnc.htm.

78 At a Republican presidential: *Hardball,* MSNBC transcript, Sept. 6, 2007.

79 as *Newsday*'s Marie Cocco: Marie Cocco, "A President's Long Shadow: Reagan and his mythology," *Newsday,* June 6, 2004, A-57.

79 Historian Robert Dallek: Robert Dallek, "Dallek: Historians Will Regard Ford as 'Distinctly Minor President,' " Council on Foreign Relations, Jan. 3, 2007, http://www.cfr.org/publication/12336/dallek.html.

80 In 1982, he spoke: "Text of Reagan's Address to Parliament on Promoting Democracy," *New York Times,* June 9, 1982, A-16.

80 Although Reagan had criticized: Cannon, *President Reagan: The Role of a Lifetime,* 670.

81 As historian Michael Schaller: Kyle Longley et al., *Deconstructing Reagan: Conservative Mythology and America's Fortieth President* (Armonk, N.Y.: M. E. Sharpe, 2007), 12.

81 budget director David Stockman: William Greider, "The Education of David Stockman," *Atlantic,* December 1981, http://www.theatlantic .com/doc/198112/david-stockman.

82 "The Soviet Union never": Jeffrey W. Knopf, "Did Reagan Win the Cold War?," *Strategic Insights,* August 2004.

82 Reagan had dreamed: Peter Kramer, "STAR WARS; influence of motion picture on Ronald Reagan," *History Today,* March 1, 1999, 41.

83 Richard Ned Lebow: Richard Ned Lebow and Janice Gross Stein, "Reagan and the Russians," *Atlantic,* February 1994, http://www.theatlantic.com/ politics/foreign/reagrus.htm.

83 "The more American": George Parry, "Ronald Reagan's Last Secret," *Consortium News,* Nov. 25, 1999, http://www.consortiumnews.com/1999/ 112599a.html.

84 "since at least the time": Morris, *Dutch.*

84 "The country was being stifled": Robert G. Kaiser, "Gorbachev: 'We All Lost the Cold War,' " *Washington Post,* June 11, 2004, A-1.

84 The ex-president: Jonathan D. Salant, "Nixon on Reagan: Not 'pleasant to be around,'" Associated Press, Dec. 10, 2003.

84 Anatoly Dobrynin: Doyle McManus, "Ronald Wilson Reagan, 1911–2004: A Cold War Hawk Who Set the Stage for Peace," *Los Angeles Times*, June 6, 2004, A-1.

85 As he recovered: Richard Reeves, *President Reagan: The Triumph of Imagination* (New York: Simon & Schuster, 2005), 53.

85 a tough-talking Reagan: "Text of Reagan's Address to Parliament on Promoting Democracy," *New York Times*, June 9, 1982, A-16.

87 Robert Parry: Robert Parry, "Reagan and the Salvadoran Baby Skulls," *Consortium News*, Jan. 30, 1987, http://www.consortiumnews.com/2007/012907.html.

88 Cannon said Reagan told: Cannon, *President Reagan: The Role of a Lifetime*, 291.

88 In 1988, the president: Kiron K. Skinner et al., eds., *Reagan: A Life in Letters* (New York: Simon & Schuster, 2003), 487.

88 such as the bellicose Patrick J. Buchanan: Lou Cannon, "What Happened to Reagan the Gunslinger? Now His Problem Is Convincing Skeptics He Isn't a Pussycat," *Washington Post*, July 7, 1985, B-1.

89 The overwhelming use of American: Nicholas Wapshott, *Ronald Reagan and Margaret Thatcher* (New York: Sentinel, 2007), 202.

90 Just after the military: Barry Sussman, "Grenada Move Earns Reagan Broad Political Gains, Poll Shows," *Washington Post*, Nov. 9, 1983, A-3.

90 In fact, Reagan wrote: Ronald W. Reagan, "Memoirs: 'An American Life' Part 2," *Time*, Nov. 12, 1990, 66.

91 "I do not see any obtainable": "Lebanon Cease-Fire Agreed, National Reconciliation Talks Set; U.S. Congress OKs Troop Stay," *Facts on File World News Digest*, Sept. 30, 1983.

91 The official U.S. response: Farouk Nassar, Associated Press, Oct. 26, 1983.

CHAPTER FIVE

93 In early July of that: David Hoffman, "Confidence in Reagan on Deficit Declines; Poll Finds Greater Trust in Congressional Democrats to Handle Red-Ink Problem," *Washington Post*, July 2, 1987, A-12.

94 Reagan's personal popularity: Jack Nelson, "Shadow of Earlier Self: Age, Scandal Take Toll on Reagan, Aides Say," *Los Angeles Times*, July 13, 1987, 1.

94 "companies were closing": David Broder, "The People Saw It Coming," *Washington Post*, Oct. 25, 1987, C-7.

94 "all the glitter is gone": Lou Cannon, "Why the Band Has Stopped Playing for Ronald Reagan," *Washington Post*, Dec. 21, 1986, D-1.

95 By October 1987, *Time:* Walter Isaacson, "After The Fall," *Time*, Nov. 2, 1987, http://www.time.com/time/magazine/article/0,9171,965864,00.html.

95 "The Reagan era is over": George de Lama, "A President's Shrinking Stature—Aides Scramble to Stop Erosion of Reagan Magic," *Chicago Tribune*, Feb. 15, 1987, C-1.

95 Newt Gingrich, still: Marci McDonald, "A State of Disgrace," *Maclean's*, March 9, 1987, 18.

95 "often seems distracted": G. Barker, "The Decline of a President," *Sydney Morning Herald*, July 16, 1987.

95 Current aides and old friends: Nelson, "Shadow of Earlier Self," 1.

95 "Is the president suffering": Richard Restak, "Reagan and the Age Issue," *Washington Post*, Jan. 18, 1987, C-1.

96 Overseas journalists: Alex Brummer, "Reagan Unwilling to Learn," *Guardian*, Aug. 9, 1987, 9.

96 A *Newsweek* poll: Larry Martz et al., "Reagan's Failure," *Newsweek*, March 9, 1987, 16.

97 Social programs like nonmilitary: Sara Fritz, "Senate Frees MX Funds, 55 to 45; President's Lobbying Credited; Missile Faces Another Vote Today," *Los Angeles Times*, March 20, 1985, 1.

97 cuts that were crippling: Barry Siegel, "No Brain Study Grant, Cuts Wound Biomedical Researchers," *Los Angeles Times*, March 20, 1985, 1.

97 That was driven home: Howard Mintz and Mary Anne Ostrom, " 'A Great American Life': 40th President Rode Boundless Optimism," *San Jose Mercury News*, June 6, 2004, 1A.

98 Over the eight years: Alex M. Gallup, Frank Newport, and the Gallup Organization, *The Gallup Organization: Public Opinion* (Lanham, Md., Rowman & Littlefield, 2006), 231.

98 Nor was it true: *World News Tonight*, ABC News Transcript, June 6, 2004.

101 Reagan's emotional speech: Mark Hertsgaard, *On Bended Knee: The Reagan Presidency and the Press* (New York: Farrar Straus Giroux, 1988), http://www.thirdworldtraveler.com/Ronald_ReaganOn_Bended_Knee.html.

101 misting up as he said: Ronald Reagan, "The Boys of Pointe du Hoc," June 6, 1984, http://www.realclearpolitics.com/articles/2007/06/the_boys_of_pointe_du_hoc_1.html.

101   San Franciscan named Hal Riney: Elisabeth Bumiller, "Reagan's Ad Aces; the Tuesday Team, Making America Feel Good About Itself," *Washington Post*, Oct. 18, 1984, D1.

101   "If you're going to sell": Lou Cannon, "Reagan & Co.; Reagan Appeals to Aspirations Not Captured by Image Makers," *Washington Post*, June 4, 1984, A-2.

102   "luscious photography": Bumiller, "Reagan's Ad Aces," D1.

102   The team's media director: Peter Goldman et al., "Making of a landslide; An American eagle soaring higher," *Newsweek*, Election Extra, November 1984, 87.

102   a dozen years later Deaver: James Bennett, "For the president, the Olympics will be an enviable stage," *New York Times*, July 19, 1996, A-14.

103   ABC had paid $10 million: John Aloysius Farrell, "The Electronic Election," *Boston Globe*, Nov. 13, 1988, 1.

103   "is a Prospero": Lance Morrow, "Yankee Doodle Magic: What makes Reagan so remarkably popular a president?," *Time*, July 7, 1986, 12.

103   That meant a White House: Hertsgaard, *On Bended Knee*.

104   Two academics: Thomas Ferguson and Joel Rogers, "The Myth of the American Turn to the Right," *Atlantic*, May 1986.

106   "RR totally lost": Timothy Noah, "Saint Ronald, Part 2," *Slate*, Nov. 6, 2003, http://www.slate.com/id/2090898/.

108   It would be the latter: Lou Cannon, *President Reagan: The Role of a Lifetime* (New York: PublicAffairs, 2000), 655.

109   "I hoped that there": Pete Yost, "Former House Speaker Regrets Haste of Iran-Contra Probe," Associated Press, Oct. 26, 1993.

109   "At an early caucus": Seymour M. Hersh, "The Iran-Contra Committees: Did They Protect Reagan?," *New York Times*, April 29, 1990, Section 6, 46.

109   Reagan's own pollster: Steven R. Weisman, "Can the Magic Prevail," *New York Times*, April 29, 1984, Section 6, 39.

110   Even so, Reagan benefited: Steven V. Roberts, "Reagan's Final Rating is Best of Any President Since '40s," *New York Times*, Jan. 18, 1989, A-1.

110   He did sign the 1983 law: Kyle Longley et al., *Deconstructing Reagan: Conservative Mythology and America's Fortieth President* (Armonk, N.Y.: M. E. Sharpe, 2007), 85.

110   in 1988 the National Center: Warren E. Leary, "Blacks' Lifespan Fall for 2nd Consecutive Year," *New York Times*, Dec. 20, 1988, C-14.

111   "Our government's response": Robert Scheer, "Early Indifferences to AIDS Is Blamed for Its Spread," *Los Angeles Times*, Nov. 29, 1986, 1.

111   the Hollywood-nurtured Reagan: Lou Cannon, *Governor Reagan: His Rise to Power* (New York: PublicAffairs, 2005), 242.

111   A few years later: "Reagan Regarded AIDS 'Like It Was Measles,' Former Doctor Says," Associated Press, Sept. 1, 1989.

112   "are always going to be people": Steven V. Roberts, "Reagan on Homelessness: Many Chose to Live in the Streets," *New York Times*, Dec. 23, 1988.

112   Even Reagan's daughter: David Lazurus, "Downside of Reagan Legacy," *San Francisco Chronicle*, June 9, 2004, http://www.sfgate.com/cgi-bin/article.cgi?f=/c/a/2004/06/09/BUGBI72U8Q1.DTL.

112   Ironically, it was Reagan: Bernard Weinraub, " 'A National Crusade': In Drug War, Congress Has the Big Guns," *New York Times*, March 15, 1987.

112   Near the end: "Reagan's Drug Bust," *New York Times*, Nov. 13, 1987, A-13.

113   one of the administration's last: Michael Weisskopf, "Reagan Aide Blocks Greenhouse Rule; Agencies Would Have Had to Weigh Plans' Effects on Global Warming," *Washington Post*, Jan. 11, 1989, A-4.

113   "Mr. Reagan argued": Roberts, "Reagan's Final Rating," A-1.

114   homeschooling advocate Michael Farris: Clyde Wilcox, *Onward Christian Soldiers* (Boulder, Colo.: Westview Press, 2000), 89.

115   "Already the flack": Howard Kurtz, "Ronald Reagan, In His Own Words; Portrait Emerges in Diary Excerpts," *Washington Post*, May 2, 2007, A-1.

115   In July 1987, for example: "President Signs McKinney Bill on Board to Aid Homeless," Associated Press, July 23, 1987.

116   "Significantly, Mr. Reagan": David K. Shipler, "Reagan's Search for New Year's Resolutions," *New York Times*, Jan. 3, 1988, Section 4, 3.

116   As some—most notably: Joshua Green, "Reagan's Liberal Legacy: What the New Literature on the Gipper Won't Tell You," *Washington Monthly*, January/February 2003.

116   In October 1987: David S. Broder, "Things Are Moving The GOP's Way," *Washington Post*, Sept. 30, 1987, A-19.

CHAPTER SIX

120   To many voters, he: "Bush Wanted to 'Kick the Hell' Out of Doonesbury Cartoonist," Associated Press, Oct. 15, 1987.

120   Norquist, inspired: Susanna McBee, "Sept. 7 Shaping Up as a Series of Prop. 13 Lookalike Contests," *Washington Post*, Sept. 10, 1978, A-3.

120 Norquist had some enthusiastic: Bob Woodward, "Origin of the Tax Pledge; In '88, Bush Camp Was Split on 'Read My Lips' Vow," *Washington Post,* Oct. 4, 1992, A-1.

121 When Bush announced: Paul Taylor, "President Sidesteps Flap Over Robertson Remark; Candidate to Address Issue at Unity Meeting," *Washington Post,* Oct. 19, 1987, A-3.

121 "People brought this up": Woodward, "Origin of the Tax Pledge," A-1.

125 On July 21, 1988: Michael Dukakis, Democratic National Convention Acceptance Speech, July 21, 1988, http://www.4president.org/speeches/mikedukakis1988acceptance.htm.

125 Nancy Reagan reportedly turned: Marianne Means, "Bush Won't Bow at the Reagan Altar," *Contra Costa (Calif.) Times,* Feb. 27, 2000, F9.

125 Panels of focus groups: Haynes Johnson, *Sleepwalking Through History: America in the Reagan Years* (New York: Norton, 1991), 395.

126 cruelly aided by Reagan: William M. Welch, "Reagan Remark Focuses Attention on Candidates' Medical Records," Associated Press, Aug. 3, 1988.

126 "So I leave as": Helen Thomas, "Reagan previews his final budget," United Press International, Jan. 7, 1989.

126 Finally, on January 11: "Transcript of Reagan's Farewell Address to the American People," *New York Times,* Jan. 12, 1989, B8.

127 Minutes after Bush took: Lou Cannon, *President Reagan: The Role of a Lifetime* (New York: PublicAffairs, 2000), 13.

127 The SAM 27000 flew: Dale Russakoff, "Brawn Forged Into Brain; Muscles of Steel Atrophied, Pittsburgh Turns to Services," *Washington Post,* April 12, 1987, A-1.

127 The Reagans' opulent jet: Donald L. Barlett and James B. Steele, *America: What Went Wrong* (Riverside, N.J.: Andrews McMeel, 1992), 32.

128 As the jet neared: Leslie Berkman, "Loss of Job in Orange County Often Devastating," *Los Angeles Times,* Jan. 15, 1989, Section 4, 1.

128 Bush was forced: Dave Skidmore, "Bush Unveils S&L Bailout Plan," Associated Press, Feb. 6, 1989.

129 raising the government's interest: John D. McClain, "Ballooning Federal Deficit Headed Toward Yearly Record," Associated Press, Sept. 13, 1991.

129 For much of 1990: Douglas Jehl and James Risen, "Reagan Legacy of Deficits Seen Curbing Bush Action," *Los Angeles Times,* Nov. 8, 1991, A-1.

130 Richard Darman: Woodward, "Origin of the Tax Pledge," A-1.

130 His aides had badly misread: Robert Dvorchak, "For Lip Readers, Bush's Turnabout Flops—Even in Peoria," Associated Press, June 27, 1990.

131 The recession of 1990–91: James Risen, "History May Judge Reaganomics Very Harshly," *Los Angeles Times*, Nov. 8, 1992, Part D, 1.

131 The despair of the American: Barlett and Steele, *America: What Went Wrong*, 13.

133 In August 1991: Anne Gowan, "Reaganites raise glasses to good old days of tax cut," *Washington Times*, Aug. 15, 1991, E-1.

133 "George Bush has defined": Patrick Buchanan, "Bush 'A Big Government Man All the Way,' " *Seattle Post-Intelligencer*, Oct. 3, 1990, A9.

133 Perot went on TV shows: *Larry King Live*, CNN transcript, Feb. 20, 1992.

134 In New York, the number: David Kocieniewski, "Murder Rate Fell 30% in the First 9 Months of '95," *New York Times*, Oct. 28, 1995, Section 1, 25.

134 "I am not a gloom-and-doom": David E. Rosenbaum, "Bush Says Recession Is Possible," *New York Times*, Nov. 16, 1990, D-1.

135 For many, the archetypal: Andrew Rosenthal, "Bush Encounters the Supermarket, Amazed," *New York Times*, Feb. 5, 1992, A1.

135 In March 1990: John Robinson, "Ortega fares poorly in poll of US voters," *Boston Globe*, March 1, 1990, 10.

135 That same month, viewers: Thomas N. DeFrank, "A diminished Ron, a refurbished Jimmy: The perils of former presidents," *Newsweek*, April 2, 1990, 3.

135 Nancy Reagan's autobiography: Walter V. Robinson, "Reagan's legacy loses luster during his year in retirement," *Boston Globe*, Feb. 12, 1990, 1.

137 In March 1992: Martin Walker, "Economy Haunts Bush," *Manchester Guardian Weekly*, March 15, 1992, 1.

137 In June 1992: "N.Y. Federal Reserve Bank Blasts Reaganomics," Japanese Economic Newswire, June 12, 1992.

137 "Only about 14 percent": Robert B. Reich, "Is Deficit Spending Evil? Not Always; But Reagan and Bush saddled our kids with paying for our expenses instead of their future," *Newsday*, July 23, 1992, 93.

138 He told a rally: Ed Moreno, "Reagan Stirs Up Republican Support Going Into Election," Associated Press, Oct. 30, 1992.

139 Ultimately, the Democrat reduced: Michael Kinsley, "Reagan's Record," *Slate*, Feb. 9, 2001, http://www.slate.com/id/100474/.

139 Representative David Obey: Alan Fram, "Clinton Plan Reverses Reaganomics But Leaves Deficits Untamed," Associated Press, Aug. 6, 1993.

139 The lower deficit created: Jonathan Weisman, "Good luck was put to good use; Debate rages over Clinton's role in boosting the economy," *USA Today*, Jan. 12, 2001, 6A.

139 In fact, the week after: Nancy Gibbs et al., "The Low Road to Revolution;

Why Clinton's slim victory with a watered-down budget could still be the start of something big," *Time*, Aug. 16, 1993, 20.

CHAPTER SEVEN

141 Reagan hadn't completely vanished: "Reagan hits 'false' statements by Oliver North," United Press International, March 17, 1994.

141 That August, a reporter: John McCaslin, "Inside the Beltway," *Washington Times*, Aug. 22, 1994, A5.

142 "He was having": Michael R. Gordon, "In Poignant Public Letter, Reagan Reveals That He Has Alzheimer's," *New York Times*, Nov. 6, 1994, Section 1, 1.

142 Clinton, with the best ear: "Clinton pauses at rally to pay homage to ailing Reagan," Agence France-Presse, Nov. 6, 1994.

143 With Reagan guaranteed kind: Tom Rhodes, "Historians vote Clinton less than average leader," *Times of London*, Dec. 15, 1996.

143 But just two months later: Nancy Benac, "Reagan, Bush, Clinton seen as so-so in pantheon of presidents," Associated Press, Feb. 7, 1997.

143 The two studies so close: Alvin S. Felzenberg, "There You Go Again: Liberal Historians and the *New York Times* Deny Ronald Reagan His Due," *Policy Review*, March/April 1997, http://findarticles.com/p/articles/mi_qa3647/is_199703/ai_n8753652.

144 Exit polls: Rick Henderson, "Class Consciousness; The House Republican freshmen: always aggressive, sometimes obnoxious, hardly monolithic," *Reason*, January 1996, http://www.reason.com/news/show/29807.html.

144 Exit polls from 1994: A. B. Stoddard, "Twelve years later, myths about the Contract persist," *Hill*, April 5, 2006.

145 "There needs to be": Robert Whereatt, "Budget stalemate frustrates some in rural Minnesota," *Minneapolis Star-Tribune*, Nov. 19, 1995, 1A.

145 The economy was continuing: Jerry Heaster, "Voters are too comfy to listen," *Kansas City Star*, Oct. 18, 1996, A1.

145 The interest rate: Jack Torry, "Issues: The Economy," *Pittsburgh Post-Gazette*, Oct. 20, 1996, A-6.

145 When the Republican nominee: Mortimer B. Zuckerman, "Dole's Simple(minded) Idea," *Daily News* (New York), Aug. 7, 1996, A-3.

146 Lest there be any: Thomas B. Edsall, "GOP's Line of Succession Leads to Dole; 'I'm Willing to Be Another Ronald Reagan,' Front-Runner Tells RNC," *Washington Post*, July 16, 1995, A-6.

146 "There's just no enthusiasm": Donald Lambro, "Conservatives at the end of rope?," *Washington Times,* Aug. 1, 1996, A16.

146 Progress in the inner cities: Sylvia Nasar, "Legacy of the '90s Boom: More Jobs for Black Men," *New York Times,* Dec. 13, 1998.

147 By January 1998: "Thirty-year Treasury note, used to set mortgage rates, sinks to 5.73% from 5.82%," Associated Press, Jan. 6, 1998.

147 the numbers were staggering: Richard Benedetto, "President Made Impact in Key Areas," *USA Today,* Jan. 11, 2001, A9.

147 Voters noticed: "Gallup Polls Shows Clinton Enjoying a Second Honeymoon," *Bulletin's Frontrunner,* April 22, 1997.

148 E. J. Dionne: E. J. Dionne, Jr., "One Big Mess, In Search of a Big Idea," *Washington Post,* July 27, 1997, C01.

148 Even the most radical: Lloyd Grove, "A Grand Old Party With Nothing to Celebrate," *Washington Post,* Jan. 20, 1997, C01.

149 House Speaker Gingrich: *Evans and Novak Show,* CNN transcript, Dec. 30, 1995.

149 The first Reagan salvos: Grover G. Norquist et al., "Reagan Betrayed: Are Conservatives Fumbling His Legacy?," *Policy Review,* July/August 1997, http://findarticles.com/p/articles/mi_qa3647/is_199707/ai_n8779102.

151 The Reagan Legacy Project: Bob Barr, "Ronald Reagan National Airport," congressional press release, Oct. 23, 1997.

152 The announcement didn't even: Mike Allen, "Ronald Reagan Airport? Republican Governors Back Proposal to Rename National," *Washington Post,* Nov. 23, 1997, A1.

152 "The guy ended": Susan Baer, "Tributes to Reagan are in the running; For some, the more his name and legacy live on, the better," *Baltimore Sun,* Dec. 2, 1997, 1A.

152 Like most political junkies: Thomas B. Edsall, "Right in the Middle of the Revolution; Activist Rises to Influence in Conservative Movement," *Washington Post,* Sept. 4, 1995, A1.

153 By 1997, Norquist: Tucker Carlson, "What I Sold at the Revolution," *New Republic,* June 9, 1997, 15.

154 A decade later: Lance Williams and Carla Marinucci, "Key GOP lobbyist had no visa, work permit," *San Francisco Chronicle,* Feb. 21, 2008, A1.

154 "Someone 30 to 40 years": Michael Mechanic, "A fitting memorial," *Mother Jones,* March/April 2001, 24.

154 The initial media coverage: Stephen M. Silverman, "Reagan's Sweet Legacy," *People,* Sept. 17, 1997, http://www.people.com/people/article/0,,621702,00.html.

155 As young Kamburowski said: David Lightman, "The Reagan Name Game," *Hartford Courant,* Dec. 27, 1997, A1.

155 What most modern Americans: Christopher A. Thomas, *The Lincoln Memorial & American Life* (Princeton, N.J.: Princeton University Press, 2002), xxvii.

155 Barry Schwartz: Barry Schwartz, *Abraham Lincoln and the Forge of National Memory* (Chicago: University of Chicago Press, 2000).

156 The glorification of Lincoln: Melvyn Stokes, "Civil War Nostalgia," UCL History Department Alumnus Association, 2002, http://www.uclhistory .co.uk/ArchiveLincolnMyth2002.htm.

157 Republican activist Jack Pitney: Dick Polman, "Reagan as mantra," *Philadelphia Inquirer,* March 8, 1998, E3.

158 even as polls showed: Dan Balz, "Public Still Giving Probe the Cold Shoulder, Polls Show; While Personal Approval of Clinton Is High, Image Has Suffered a 'Character Gap'," *Washington Post,* Aug. 16, 1998, A25.

158 In February 1999, Norquist: "Reagan Legacy Project Announces Board of Advisors, Forms State Advisory Committees in 5 States," U.S. Newswire, Feb. 4, 1999.

158 One of its members: Douglas Turner, "Nicholson Says Latest Charge Against Clinton Is 'Credible,' " *Buffalo News,* Feb. 27, 1999, A7.

158 Another Reagan Legacy: Phyllis Schlafly, "How did the turtle get on the fence post," Copley News Service, Dec. 2. 1997.

159 Governor Keating: Chris Casteel, "Governors Push Agenda; Impeachment Shouldn't Stall Process, Keating Says," *Daily Oklahoman,* Dec. 5, 1998, 6.

159 The pumping up of Reagan: Geraldine Baum, "Defining, Deifying of Reagan," *Los Angeles Times,* April 3, 1998, Part 1, 1.

159 In Washington: Ayesha Morris, "Ron Over," *Washington City Paper,* Nov. 30–Dec. 6, 2001.

160 The most ironic tribute: Mary Voboril, "Freed by Design/The Architect Behind Two Washington Monuments," *Newsday,* July 6, 1998, B03.

160 There was one man: "No to a Reagan Tribute," *New York Times,* March 9, 2001.

160 Coverdell, the Senate sponsor: Maureen Groppe, "U.S. lawmaker puts in his 10 cents' worth; Indiana's Souder wants to replace image of Franklin Roosevelt on the dime with Reagan's," *Indianapolis Star,* Nov. 26, 2003, 1B.

160 There were other big: "USS *Ronald Reagan* Christened in Newport News, Virginia," CNN, March 4, 2001.

161 Norquist and his Americans: Robert Novak, "Disgraced Consultant Back; Clinton Pushed on Tax Cuts," *Augusta (Ga.) Chronicle*, April 26, 1997, A4.

161 Norquist told friends: Paul West, "Bush takes the lead without leaving home; His low-profile strategy has Republicans flying to Texas for lunch," *Baltimore Sun*, March 7, 1999, 1A.

162 As chronicled by Jonathan Chait: Jonathan Chait, *The Big Con: The True Story of How Washington Got Hoodwinked and Hijacked by Crackpot Economics* (Boston: Houghton Mifflin, 2007), 94.

162 He told National Public Radio: *Talk of the Nation*, NPR transcripts, Oct. 7, 1999.

162 On June 8, 1999: David E. Rosenbaum, "If Elected, Bush Says, He'll Oppose Tax Increase," *New York Times*, June 10, 1999, A-24.

162 "Why believe the son?": Ralph Z. Hallow, "With Bush's no-tax-increase vow, entire Republican field on board," *Washington Times*, June 10, 1999, A4.

CHAPTER EIGHT

163 The *Wall Street Journal* reported: Richard K. Neumann, Jr., "Conflicts of interest in *Bush v. Gore:* Did some justices vote illegally?," *Georgetown Journal of Legal Ethics*, Spring 2003, http://findarticles.com/p/articles/mi_qa3975/is_200304/ai_n9221306.

164 "We think we have": "Reagan shadow hovers over GOP: Republican candidates quick to use popular president's legacy to bolster campaigns," *Detroit News*, Jan. 6, 2000.

165 Joining in the scrum: "McCain campaign spars with anti-tax group," Associated Press, Jan. 6, 2000.

165 Bush, for his part: *The World Today*, CNN transcript, Dec. 1, 1999.

165 The proposal caused key: Glen Johnson, "Bush gains Dole's backing, criticizes McCain on taxes," Associated Press, Dec. 4, 1999.

165 In early 1999: Richard L. Berke, "The President's Trial: The Poll; Damaged by Trial, Senate's Standing Sinks in New Poll," *New York Times*, Feb. 3, 1999, A1.

165 In January 2000: William M. Welch, "Tax cut apathy puzzles Republicans," *USA Today*, Jan. 19, 2000, 11A.

167 An unnamed Republican strategist: Bill Keller, "The Radical Presidency of George W. Bush: Reagan's Son," *New York Times Magazine*, Jan. 26, 2003, 26.

167 The two candidates struck: Boyd Tonkin, "A Week in Books: A surreal stand-off between Gush and Bore," *Independent*, Nov. 18, 2000, http://www.independent.co.uk/arts-entertainment/books/features/a-week-in-books--a-surreal-standoff-between-gush-and-bore-683234.html.

170 Bill Keller: Keller, "The Radical Presidency of George W. Bush," 26.

171 Indeed, Bush made a few: Sheryl Gay Stolberg, "Bush and Kennedy Nurture Common Ground on Legislative Goals," *New York Times*, July 4, 2007.

171 And Greenspan had made: Alice Ann Love, "Fed Chairman Cautions Against Cutting Taxes Now," Associated Press, July 28, 1999.

171 All of Washington: "Greenspan Testimony to Senate Budget Committee," CNN/FN, Jan. 25, 2001.

172 Democrats were flabbergasted: Robert Dodge, "Greenspan surprises by backing tax cuts; Fed chairman suggests 2nd rate reduction," *Dallas Morning News*, Jan. 26, 2001, 1A.

172 A 2002 in-depth analysis: Citizens for Tax Justice, "Year-by-Year Analysis of the Bush Tax Cuts Shows Growing Tilt to the Very Rich," June 12, 2002, http://www.ctj.org/html/gwb0602.htm.

173 "Obviously, we've got budget": "Remarks by the President at Taft for Governor Luncheon," May 10, 2002, http://www.whitehouse.gov/news/releases/2002/05/20020510-3.html.

173 In January 2002: Glenn Kessler, "Dueling Parties Pick and Choose Data as the Surplus Disappears," *Washington Post*, Jan 13, 2002, A4.

173 In fact, Bush's second: Dana Milbank and Jim Vandehei, "Bush's Retreat Eased Bill's Advance," *Washington Post*, May 23, 2003, A5.

174 Jim Nussle of Iowa: David E. Rosenbaum, "Favoring Tax Cuts and Tolerating Deficits," *New York Times*, June 10, 2004, A22.

174 Norquist, who insisted: Judy Keen and Laurence McQuillan, "Bush's drive for tax cuts fueled by his principles," *USA Today*, May 19, 2003, 10A.

174 Meanwhile, the value: Edmund L. Andrews, "U.S. Affects a Strong Silence on Its Weak Currency," *New York Times*, Oct. 10, 2007, C1.

174 Because of Bush's large: Dave Chandler, "Dollar Madness," Earthside.com, April 11, 2007.

175 By 2008, foreigners owned: "Rep. Jose Serrano Hearing on 2008 Treasury Department Budget," Political Transcript Wire, March 30, 2007.

176 "The richest country": John Boudreau, "Nobel economist worries about recession," *San Jose Mercury News*, Nov. 16, 2007.

177 While George H. W. Bush was: "Excerpts from Pentagon's Plan: 'Prevent

the Re-Emergence of a New Rival,' " *New York Times*, March 8, 1992, Section 1, 14.

177 In spring 1997: William Bunch, "Invading Iraq Not a New Idea for Bush Clique," *Philadelphia Daily News*, Jan. 30, 2003, 3.

177 In a 2000 white paper: *Nightline*, "The Plan," ABC News Transcripts, March 5, 2003.

178 But behind the scenes: Bunch, "Invading Iraq Not a New Idea for Bush Clique," 3.

179 Delaware Democrat Joe Biden: Matthew Lee, " 'Axis of evil' label not a prelude to US invasion: Powell," Agence France-Presse, Feb. 5, 2002.

179 The short answer was, yes: Julian Borger, "Inside story: 'How I created the axis of evil,' " *Guardian*, Jan. 28, 2003, 6.

179 A couple of weeks later: Anne E. Kornblut, "In Seoul, Bush Tries to Assuage Those Wary of His Intent on North Korea," *Boston Globe*, Feb. 20, 2002.

179 What the world didn't know: Gareth Porter, "Burnt Offering," *American Prospect*, May 21, 2006, http://www.prospect.org./cs/articles?article Id=11539.

179 In 2008, in a speech: "President Bush Addresses Members of Knesset," White House transcript, May 15, 2008, http://www.whitehouse.gov/ news/releases/2008/05/20080515-1.html.

180 "Our commitment": "President Bush Discusses Freedom in Iraq and the Middle East," White House transcript, Nov. 6, 2003, as viewed online at http://www.whitehouse.gov/news/releases/2003/11/20031106-2.html.

181 In December 1983: James Ridgeway, "You Got Him? Get Out!," *Village Voice*, Dec. 23, 2003, 26.

181 *New York Times* reported: Patrick E. Tyler, "Officers Say U.S. Aided Iraq in War Despite Use of Gas," *New York Times*, Aug. 18, 2002, Section 1, 1.

181 One bizarre example: Craig Unger, "The War They Wanted, the Lies They Needed," *Vanity Fair*, July 2006, 92.

182 Bruce Bartlett: Bruce Bartlett, "Good Reasons to Leave Iraq," NewYork-Times.com's The Right Stuff, Jan. 16, 2007, http://bartlett.blogs.nytimes .com/2007/01/16/good-reasons-to-leave-iraq/.

182 Lou Cannon and his son: Lou Cannon and Carl M. Cannon, *Reagan's Disciple: George W. Bush's Troubled Quest for a Presidential Legacy* (New York: PublicAffairs, 2008), 207.

182 Meanwhile, Lawrence Korb: Lawrence Korb, "Reagan and the Draft," *Washington Times*, May 16, 2008, http://washingtontimes.com/news/ 2008/may/16/reagan-and-the-draft/.

183 Lou Cannon has pondered: Author telephone interview with Lou Cannon, June 1, 2008.

183 He knew nothing: *60 Minutes*, "The Reagans; Nancy Reagan talks about her life with former President Ronald Reagan and how life has changed since his diagnosis of Alzheimer's," CBS News Transcript, June 4, 2003.

CHAPTER NINE

185 The phone call: Ken Rodriguez, "History-making Latino set to retire from U.S. Secret Service," *San Antonio Express-News*, June 22, 2008, http:// sachapter.blogspot.com/2008/06/news-article-of-hapcoa-member-tony .html.

185 "At the last moment": "Reagans shared one last moment," CNN.com, June 7, 2004.

186 In fact, the event: Jacob M. Schlesinger, "Operation Serenade: Laying Groundwork For Reagan's Funeral," *Wall Street Journal*, June 10, 2004.

186 His widow, Jackie: *ABC World News Tonight*, ABC News Transcripts, June 12, 2004.

187 Reagan's death and funeral: Schlesinger, "Operation Serenade."

187 Ahearn, the *Washington Post* reported: Mike Allen, "Reagan Veterans Bring Back the '80s; Ex-Officials Are Embraced by Washington," *Washington Post*, June 11, 2004, A31.

188 "Each gesture was minutely": Richard Goldstein, "Das Rongold," *Village Voice*, June 8, 2004, http://www.villagevoice.com/2004-06-08/news/ das-rongold/.

188 "I was worried": *CNN Reliable Sources*, "Did Press Go Overboard in Paying Tribute to Ronald Reagan?," CNN Transcript, June 13, 2004.

188 One unnamed TV executive: Jim Hoagland, "Keep Reagan's Record in Balance," *Washington Post*, June 10, 2004, A19.

189 Fox did invite: Frank Rich, "What O.J. Passed to the Gipper," *New York Times*, June 20, 2004.

189 Thomas Kunkel: Thomas Kunkel, "Fade-Out," *American Journalism Review*, August/September 2004, http://www.ajr.org/Article.asp?id=3710.

189 Perhaps it was a function: Rich, "What O.J. Passed to the Gipper."

189 Even reporters who waded: *CNN Reliable Sources*, "Did Press Go Overboard in Paying Tribute to Ronald Reagan?"

189 Leave it to a reporter: Julian Borger, "Ronald Reagan: Reagan Was His Lifelong Hero," *Guardian*, June 11, 2004, 3.

190 For the long week: Elisabeth Bumiller, "Trying on Reagan's Mantle, But It Doesn't Exactly Fit," *New York Times,* June 14, 2005, A5.

193 The first major piece: Jim Rutenberg, "Grumbling Trickles Down From Reagan Biopic; Some See Peril to Presidential Legacy From TV Movie Coming Next Month," *New York Times,* Oct. 21, 2003, Section E, 1.

194 Some noted that Reagan: Sidney Blumenthal, "Old Times There Are Not Forgotten," Salon.com, Nov. 8, 2003, http://dir.salon.com/story/ opinion/feature/2003/11/08/apologies/.

194 It didn't help that: Rutenberg, "Grumbling Trickles Down."

194 Brent Bozell: Bernard Weinraub, "CBS Is Re-Considering Mini-Series on Reagan," *New York Times,* Nov. 4, 2003, E1.

194 An obscure Republican political: Michael Janofsky, "The Man Who Would Save Reagan From a TV History," *New York Times,* Nov. 6, 2003, A10.

194 What's more, even the chairman: Will Lester, "GOP Chairman Blasts Miniseries on Reagans," Associated Press, Nov. 1, 2003.

195 His former press aide: Rutenberg, "Grumbling Trickles Down."

196 Dinesh D'Souza: Richard L. Berke, "Remembering the Gipper," *New York Times,* Nov. 23, 1997, Section 7, 11.

196 By 2001, Reagan: Joshua Green, "Reagan's Liberal Legacy: What the New Literature on the Gipper Won't Tell You," *Washington Monthly,* January/ February 2003.

198 One of the best reviews: Jeff Shesol, "The Legacy Project," *New York Times,* May 22, 2005, Section 7, 35.

198 most famously when he: "They Slipped the Surly Bonds of Earth to Touch the Face of God," *Time,* Feb. 10, 1986, http://www.time.com/time/ reports/space/disaster1.html.

198 Yet here Christianity seems: Richard N. Ostling, "A political scientist plumbs Ronald Reagan's sometimes mysterious religion," Associated Press, March 15, 2004.

199 Bush 43, in eulogizing: Dana Milbank, "Words of Praise From Father and Son; Bushes Saw in Reagan the Traits That Have Defined Them," *Washington Post,* June 12, 2004, A01.

199 Bruce Bartlett, the former: Ron Suskind, "Without a Doubt," *New York Times Magazine,* Oct. 17, 2004, 44.

200 Scott McClellan, who served: "McClellan: Fox News Commentators Use The 'Talking Points' That The White House Sends Them," Think Progress, July 26, 2008, http://thinkprogress.org/2008/07/26/mcclellan-fox -talking-points/.

200 Ron Suskind, a journalist: Suskind, "Without a Doubt."

201 In the years leading: Will Bunch, "When the levee breaks," Attytood/
     Philadelphia Daily News, Sept. 1, 2005.

201 As the TV pictures: Johann Hari, "The Floods Have Exposed a Washed-
     Up President and His Bankrupt Philosophy," *Independent*, Sept. 6, 2005.

202 It was shown that Norquist: John Cassidy, "The Ring Leader: How Gro-
     ver Norquist Keeps the Conservative Movement Together," *New Yorker*,
     Aug. 1, 2005, 42.

205 When the race kicked off: Matthew Mosk and John Solomon, "N.H. Is
     Already Flooded With Attack Ads; Atmosphere More Charged Than in
     Iowa," *Washington Post*, Jan. 4, 2008, A10.

205 When Norquist: Seth Colter Walls, "For McCain, the 'Right' Friends,"
     Newsweek, Feb. 11, 2008, http://www.newsweek.com/id/109843.

206 The nonpartisan Tax Policy Center: Justin Jouvenal, "John McCain's radi-
     cal tax plan," Salon.com, July 9, 2008, http://www.salon.com/news/
     feature/2008/07/09/mccain_taxes/.

207 In June, Obama met: Sarah Posner, "Obama to Evangelical Leaders: 'I
     Endorse You,' " *American Prospect*, June 18, 2008, http://www.prospect
     .org/csnc/blogs/tapped_archive?month=06&year=2008&base_name=
     how_far_will_obama_go_to_get_t.

207 The Democratic standard-bearer: Alain Robert-Jean, "Obama tries to
     wrest Clinton's blue-collar base in Pennsylvania," Agence France-Presse,
     March 29, 2008.

207 Obama's plan also raised: Robertson Williams and Howard Gleckman,
     "An Updated Analysis of the 2008 Presidential Candidates' Tax Plans,"
     Tax Policy Center, Sept. 15, 2008, http://www.taxpolicycenter.org/publi
     cations/url.cfm?ID=411750.

CHAPTER TEN

210 Karcher died in 2008: Eric Mainic, "Carl Karcher, 90; entrepreneur turned
     hot dog stand into a fast-food empire," *Los Angeles Times*, Jan. 12, 2008,
     http://www.latimes.com/news/obituaries/la-me-karcher12jan12,1,3348
     299.story.

210 Simmons is a Texan: Dan Moran, "Billionaire Harold Simmons funded ad
     linking Obama, ex-Weatherman Ayers," *Los Angeles Times*, Aug. 23, 2008,
     http://www.latimes.com/news/politics/la-na-simmons23-2008aug23,0,
     2360525.story.

211 The executive director, Duke Blackwood: *Life and Times*, KCET Radio, July
     12, 2007, http://www.kcet.org/lifeandtimes/archives/200707/20070712
     .php.

213 "But the hard truth": Mario Cuomo, Keynote Address to the Democratic National Convention, July 16, 1984, http://www.americanrhetoric.com/speeches/mariocuomo1984dnc.htm.

214 The total value: Scott Hadley, "Declining values, defaults, foreclosures catch many local residents by surprise," *Ventura County Star,* Feb. 17, 2008, http://www.venturacountystar.com/news/2008/feb/17/a-crisis-hits-home/.

215 Remember Carter's "malaise" speech: Jimmy Carter, "The 'Crisis of Confidence' Speech," July 15, 1979, http://www.pbs.org/wgbh/amex/carter/filmmore/ps_crisis.html.

216 Average fuel efficiency: Union of Concerned Scientists, "Fuel Economy Basics," http://www.ucsusa.org/clean_vehicles/solutions/cleaner_cars_pickups_and_suvs/fuel-economy-basics.html.

216 Here is what he said: "Debate Transcript," Commission on Presidential Debates, Oct. 27, 1980, http://www.debates.org/pages/trans80b.html.

217 Reagan embraced the consumer-oriented: Daniel McCarthy, "Revising Ronald Reagan: Was the 40th president a peace-loving moderate?," *Reason Online,* June 2007, http://www.reason.com/news/show/119735.html.

217 This was a notion: Lou Cannon, *President Reagan: The Role of a Lifetime* (New York: PublicAffairs, 2000), 75–77.

217 In fact, Reagan even: "White House Will Not Replace Solar Water-Heating System," Associated Press, Aug. 24, 1986.

218 For example, Carter had: Arthur Allen, "Prodigal Sun," *Mother Jones,* March/April 2000, http://www.motherjones.com/news/feature/2000/03/solar.html.

218 Beginning in 1986: John Cushman, Jr., "Tougher Fuel Economy Rules Planned, in Shift From Reagan," *New York Times,* April 15, 1989.

218 The first rumblings of the SUV: "The Hidden History of the SUV," PBS, Feb. 21, 2002, http://www.pbs.org/wgbh/pages/frontline/shows/rollover/etc/script.html.

219 In 1983, two years after: Philip Shabecoff, "Reagan Environment Policy Sharply Attacked by Carter," *New York Times,* June 3, 1983, Section A, 18.

219 That same year, a U.S.: Spencer Weart, "The Discovery of Global Warming," American Institute of Physics, July 2007, http://www.aip.org/history/climate/Govt.htm.

219 columnist Thomas Friedman: Thomas L. Friedman, "Flush With Energy," *New York Times,* Aug. 9, 2008.

219 When a newspaper columnist: R. Bruce Matthews, "Reagan, not Carter, had better energy policies," *Allentown (Pa.) Morning Call,* July 14, 2008, A10.

220 "At one time": Dan Eggen and Robert Barnes, "McCain's Focus on Geor-

gia Raises Question of Propriety; After Chiding Obama, He Dwells on Crisis as a President Might," *Washington Post,* Aug. 15, 2008, A16.

222 At the left-leaning Institute: Author telephone interview with Robert Borosage, May 12, 2008.

222 Americans United for Change: Michael Abramowitz, "Critics Take the Lead in Defining Bush's Legacy," *Washington Post,* Feb. 4, 2008, A19.

222 Unfortunately one of the little-publicized: Deb Riechmann, "Bush extends restrictions on release of presidential records," Associated Press, Nov. 1, 2001.

223 In fact, Reagan's name: Todd J. Gillman, "SMU pressed to fight Bush's secrecy," *Dallas Morning News,* Feb. 5, 2007.

223 Stephen Knott, the founder: Author e-mail interview with Stephen Knott, May 13, 2008.

224 "They say that": Ronald Reagan, 1980 Republican National Convention Acceptance Speech, July 17, 1980, http://www.americanrhetoric.com/speeches/ronaldreagan1980rnc.htm.

225 "If one were to choose": Quoted in Rod Dreher, "A Nation Unprepared," *Dallas Morning News,* Aug. 17, 2008, 6P.

226 The Reagan speechwriter: James Fallows, "Rhetorical Questions," *Atlantic,* September 2008, http://www.theatlantic.com/doc/200809/fallows-debates.

227 "The American people": Ronald Reagan, 1980 Republican National Convention Acceptance Speech, July 17, 1980, http://www.americanrhetoric.com/speeches/ronaldreagan1980rnc.htm.

228 "You and I, as individuals": Ronald Reagan, First Inaugural Address, Jan. 20, 1981, http://www.reaganlibrary.com/reagan/speeches/first.asp.

ACKNOWLEDGMENTS

November 4, 1980, was a memorable night for me, even if it wasn't the one I expected. I was a college senior, proud owner of the only TV set in my dorm (a hideous 9-inch black-and-white contraption), and a young political junkie. My poli sci buddy Dave Torrence (we were both majors) came by with a sixpack of beer (well, maybe it was more) to watch what was supposed to be a political nail-biter, a neck-and-neck election night battle between President Jimmy Carter and a conservative sixty-nine-year-old upstart, Ronald Reagan. Instead, we'd barely cracked the first cold one when Walter Cronkite & Co. were declaring Reagan the landslide winner. It was the first time I was surprised by the Gipper, but not the last.

Less than a year later, I was a rookie journalist off for Washington . . . not the Beltway but little Washington, Pennsylvania, in a fading coal-and-steel region that had been buffered and battered by the economic upheaval of the 1970s and early 1980s. I never covered Ronald Reagan, but for the next seven years I had something even better, a front row seat for Ronald Reagan's America. I spent half that time in Birmingham, Alabama, watching the rise of massive megachurches, the incubator for a right-wing revolution; writing about a backwoods camp that trained mercenaries to fight in Central America and about the diaspora of Alabama steelworkers; and seeing the Reverend Jesse Jackson sign up thousands of new voters who felt abandoned by their government. Long Island, where I spent Reagan's second term, reflected the other side of those years. An upper-middle-class bedroom community was doing pretty well, although the stunning revelations of the Iran-Contra scandal on the newsroom TV set were a frequent distraction. Since then, I've watched this divisive Ronald Reagan become the gold standard for modern American presidents, with entire elections centering on who can best take the political handoff from the Gipper. By this time I shouldn't be surprised by Ronald Reagan, or the Reagan myth. Yet I still am. The result is this book.

It would not have happened without help from many, many people, including a number of very smart folks who took some time as I was embarking on this project to talk to me or share their thoughts about Reagan's legacy. This list includes Rick Perlstein, Paul Krugman, Mark Hertsgaard, Robert Dallek, Robert Borosage, Stephen Knott, Kyle Longley, Douglas Kmiec, and especially Lou Cannon, whose five books on the fortieth president—especially *President Reagan: The Role of a Lifetime*—remain the definitive even-handed works on Reagan.

My bosses at the *Philadelphia Daily News*—Michael Days, Pat McLoone, Gar Joseph, and Wendy Warren—gave me a lot of leeway to work on this project, which I greatly appreciate, and I am equally grateful for all the much-needed encouragement I received from all my friends at this spunky urban tabloid that simply refuses to die. Through the *Daily News*'s support of my blog Attytood, I've been able to develop an amazing network of reformers and rabble-rousers who've given me some encouragement and—with my constant nagging—have occasionally highlighted my work. This list sadly doesn't come close to including everybody, but among those people are Vance Lehmkuhl, Fred Mann, John Amato, Duncan Black, Suzie Madrak, Jay Rosen, Karl Martino, Josh Marshall, Jane Hamsher, Jeff Jarvis, Greg Mitchell, Keith Olbermann, Richard Blair, Joe Conason, Todd Gitlin, Monika Bauerlein, Michael Tomasky, Mark Karlin, Eric Boehlert, Rem Reider, Jennifer Nix, John Byrne, Dan Rubin, and Dan McQuade. Special thanks for their support and all the people who've backed or joined the community on Attytood these last four years.

One blogger and writer who deserves special mention and my deep gratitude is Cliff Schecter, the author of *The Real McCain*. It was Cliff who, though not even knowing me that well, offered a ton of help and advice that turned around a minor midcareer crisis and, albeit inadvertently, started the chain of events that led to this book.

Cliff introduced me to my agent, Will Lippincott of Lippincott Massie McQuilkin, who to my constant amazement has treated a once-published (long ago) author as if he were John Grisham or something, from the moment of our very first phone call. Will's dedication and the enormous time and effort he put into both shaping this project and helping me through the process has been nothing short of remarkable. I am incredibly grateful for all his work and the help from his crew, including Rachel Vogel.

And it was Will who brought this project to Martin Beiser at Free Press, who has been not only the kind of editor every writer dreams of— passionately committed to the project with a uniquely laid-back yet forward-moving style—but also a new friend to commiserate with about the foibles of our Philadelphia Phillies. I greatly appreciate his support and that of everyone else at Free Press who touched this, including Kirsa Rein.

Finally, I want to thank my family for their remarkable patience with this project (and with me!), especially my dad, Bryan Bunch, who is a nightly sounding board and source of encouragement; my wife, Kathy Boccella, who got behind this thing even though I think she thought it was crazy at first; and my wonderful children, who stayed off the computer long enough to let me dedicate this book to them.

INDEX

ABOUT THE AUTHOR

Will Bunch is senior writer for the *Philadelphia Daily News* and author of its popular blog Attytood.com. He has also worked at *Newsday/New York Newsday*, where he was a key member of the team that won the Pulitzer Prize in 1992 for spot news reporting. He has written for such national publications as *The New York Times Magazine*, *American Prospect*, and *Mother Jones*, among others. Will is the author of one previous book, *Jukebox America*. He lives in the Philadelphia suburbs with his family.